THE MODERNIST EXOSKELETON

Edinburgh Critical Studies in Modernist Culture
Series Editors: Tim Armstrong and Rebecca Beasley

Available

Modernism and Magic: Experiments with Spiritualism, Theosophy and the Occult
Leigh Wilson

Sonic Modernity: Representing Sound in Literature, Culture and the Arts
Sam Halliday

Modernism and the Frankfurt School
Tyrus Miller

Lesbian Modernism: Censorship, Sexuality and Genre Fiction
Elizabeth English

Modern Print Artefacts: Textual Materiality and Literary Value in British Print Culture, 1890–1930s
Patrick Collier

Cheap Modernism: Expanding Markets, Publishers' Series and the Avant-Garde
Lise Jaillant

Portable Modernisms: The Art of Travelling Light
Emily Ridge

Hieroglyphic Modernisms: Writing and New Media in the Twentieth Century
Jesse Schotter

Modernism, Fiction and Mathematics
Nina Engelhardt

Modernist Life Histories: Biological Theory and the Experimental Bildungsroman
Daniel Aureliano Newman

Modernism, Space and the City: Outsiders and Affect in Paris, Vienna, Berlin, and London
Andrew Thacker

Modernism Edited: Marianne Moore and the Dial *Magazine*
Victoria Bazin

Modernism and Time Machines
Charles Tung

Primordial Modernism: Animals, Ideas, transition (1927–1938)
Cathryn Setz

Modernism and Still Life: Artists, Writers, Dancers
Claudia Tobin

The Modernist Exoskeleton: Insects, War, Literary Form
Rachel Murray

Forthcoming

Slow Modernism
Laura Salisbury

Modernism and the Idea of Everyday Life
Leena Kore-Schröder

Novel Sensations: Modernist Fiction and the Problem of Qualia
Jon Day

Hotel Modernity: Literary Encounters with Corporate Space
Robbie Moore

Modernism and Religion: Poetry and the Rise of Mysticism
Jamie Callison

Abstraction in Modernism and Modernity: Human and Inhuman
Jeff Wallace

www.edinburghuniversitypress.com/series/ecsmc

THE MODERNIST EXOSKELETON

Insects, War, Literary Form

Rachel Murray

EDINBURGH
University Press

Edinburgh University Press is one of the leading university presses in the UK. We publish academic books and journals in our selected subject areas across the humanities and social sciences, combining cutting-edge scholarship with high editorial and production values to produce academic works of lasting importance. For more information visit our website: edinburghuniversitypress.com

© Rachel Murray, 2020, 2022

Edinburgh University Press Ltd
The Tun – Holyrood Road, 12(2f) Jackson's Entry, Edinburgh EH8 8PJ

First published in hardback by Edinburgh University Press 2020

Typeset in 10/12.5 Adobe Sabon by
IDSUK (DataConnection) Ltd

A CIP record for this book is available from the British Library

ISBN 978 1 4744 5819 1 (hardback)
ISBN 978 1 4744 5820 7 (paperback)
ISBN 978 1 4744 5821 4 (webready PDF)
ISBN 978 1 4744 5822 1 (epub)

The right of Rachel Murray to be identified as the author of this work has been asserted in accordance with the Copyright, Designs and Patents Act 1988, and the Copyright and Related Rights Regulations 2003 (SI No. 2498).

CONTENTS

List of Figures — vi
Acknowledgements — viii
Series Editors' Preface — xi
Abbreviations — xii

Introduction — 1
1 Shell Bursts: Wyndham Lewis — 24
2 Formication: D. H. Lawrence — 61
3 Cocoon States: H.D. — 95
4 Larval Forms: Samuel Beckett — 129
Conclusion: 'Things that won't quite formulate' — 166

Bibliography — 176
Index — 200

FIGURES

I.1	'Die "Chlorreiche" Germania' [The 'Chlorine-Rich' Germania]. *De Groene Amsterdammer*, 9 May 1915, 11.	6
I.2	Film stills from *The Acrobatic Fly*, 1910. British Film Institute.	10
1.1	Murex shell (*Murex pecten*). Photograph by Didier Descouens, 2009. Reproduced under Creative Commons License CC-BY SA 4.0.	25
1.2	Whelk shell (*Nucella lapillus*). Photograph by H. Zell, 2014. Reproduced under Creative Commons License CC-BY SA 3.0.	25
1.3	HMS *Underwing* with dazzle camouflage pattern, *c.*1918. Photograph by Oscar Parkes (undated). Image No. SP 142, Imperial War Museums Collection. Reproduced under Creative Commons License CC0 1.0 Universal.	32
1.4	Tiger moth (*Arctia caja*). Photograph by Martin Landry, 18 July 2013. Reproduced by permission of Martin Landry.	32
1.5	Wyndham Lewis, 'Mr Wyndham Lewis as a Tyro', *c.*1920–1. © Wyndham Lewis Memorial Trust/Bridgeman Images, 2019.	51
1.6	Wyndham Lewis, 'Self-Portrait', 1932. © Wyndham Lewis Memorial Trust/Bridgeman Images, 2019.	51
3.1	Film stills from *Skilled Insect Artisans*, 1922. British Film Institute.	100

FIGURES

4.1	Beckett in his garden at Ussy (undated). Samuel Beckett MS-122, Rauner Special Collections Library, Dartmouth College. Reproduced by permission of Dartmouth College.	150
4.2	Beckett digging holes at Ussy (undated). Pamela Mitchell Collection MS 5060, University of Reading Special Collections. Reproduced by permission of University of Reading.	150
4.3	Saint-Lô, June 1944. German Federal Archive, Image No. 146-1984-043-03.	152
4.4	Double plate illustration depicting embryos of a fish, salamander, turtle, chick, pig, cow, rabbit and human, at 'very early', 'somewhat later' and 'still later' stages. From Ernst Haeckel's *Anthropogenie*, 1874. Reproduced under Creative Commons License CC0 1.0 Universal.	160

ACKNOWLEDGEMENTS

This exoskeleton was not formed by me alone: I am very grateful to those who have contributed to its development over the years. My thanks, first and foremost, to Ralph Pite, who guided me through much of the writing process, encouraged me to be adventurous in my thinking, and taught me a great deal about what it means to be receptive. I would also like to thank Kirsty Martin for her skill and sensitivity as a close reader during the formative years of the project, and Laura Salisbury, whose incisive feedback helped to sharpen my thinking at a crucial stage.

My sincere thanks to Andrew Blades, Danny Karlin, Gareth Mills, Derek Ryan, and Oliver Tearle, for reading and responding to various drafts and sections of this book; to David Trotter for asking searching questions that tested my argument in important ways, and to Steven Connor whose generous insights improved this book considerably. Camilla Bostock, Penny Cartwright, Rowena Kennedy Epstein, Alex Goody, Douglas Mao, Laura Marcus, John McTague, Natalie Pollard, Nathan Waddell, Martin Willis and Michael Whitworth all made helpful suggestions along the way for which I am very grateful. A special thanks to my series editors, Tim Armstrong and Rebecca Beasley, for their brilliant advice and suggestions for improvement, and to my anonymous readers for their valuable recommendations. I would also like to thank Jackie Jones and Ersev Ersoy at Edinburgh University Press for their diligence and patience throughout the editing process, as well as my copy editor Peter Williams for his attention to detail.

ACKNOWLEDGEMENTS

I am grateful to the Wyndham Lewis Memorial Trust for granting me permission to use two self-portraits by Lewis; Reading University Special Collections and Rauner Special Collections at Dartmouth College for permission to reproduce two photographs of Samuel Beckett; Bart Wursten for granting me permission to use his photograph 'Picasso Bug (*Sphaerocoris annulus*)' as the cover image; Martin Landry for allowing me to use his photograph of a tiger moth; and the Authors League Fund and St Bride's Church, as joint literary executors of the Estate of Djuna Barnes, for granting me permission to quote from Barnes's 'Rite of Spring'. 'The Walls Do Not Fall' by H.D., from *Collected Poems, 1912–1944*, copyright © 1982 by The Estate of Hilda Doolittle, and *Helen in Egypt*, copyright © 1961 by Norman Holmes Pearson are reprinted here by permission of New Directions Publishing Corp. My thanks also to James Hirst for locating material from the Wyndham Lewis Collection at Cornell University Library on my behalf. An early version of Chapter 4 won the British Society for Literature and Science Early Career Essay Prize in 2016 and was published in the *Journal of Literature and Science*. The editors have kindly allowed me to reproduce parts of the article here. Every effort has been made to trace all other copyright holders but if any have been inadvertently overlooked the publisher will be pleased to make the necessary arrangements at the first opportunity.

I would like to thank the Arts and Humanities Research Council for funding the research on which this monograph is based, the Universities of Bristol and Exeter for providing institutional support, and Chantelle Payne and Rose Jones at the South, West and Wales Doctoral Training Partnership for their administrative assistance. Loughborough University awarded me a research fellowship that enabled me to complete this book, and the School of the Arts, English and Drama provided additional funding that allowed me to secure image permissions. A number of colleagues in the School of Arts, including Nick Freeman, Eleanor Morgan, Sarah Parker, Claire Warden and Nigel Wood, made helpful suggestions while I was finishing this book – my thanks to them.

This book began its life at Bristol University, where I benefited enormously from the supportive research community there. I would like to thank, in particular, Marianna Dudley, Stephen James, Michael Malay, Merle Patchett, Vicky Smith and Jane Wright for their exemplary kindness and intellectual sustenance. Bristol's postgraduate community has also been an invaluable support to me over the years, especially Jen Baker, Louise Benson James, Amy King, Alessandra Monorchio and Leonie Thomas. I would not have reached this point without my wonderful early mentors at Cambridge and Sussex – Louise Joy, David Clifford, Rod Mengham and Sara Crangle – who started me on this journey.

A big thank you to the friends and family members who have put up with and in some cases actively encouraged my insect fervour: Anna Glendenning,

ACKNOWLEDGEMENTS

Martin Lloyd, Mark O'Connor, Alice Roberts, Jackie Summers, the Taylor family, the Thackers and the York gang. My mother and father, and my lovely siblings, Sam, Katy and Rose, deserve my greatest thanks for always being there for me and for providing much needed distraction, laughter and advice. And finally, to Jack, for his eternal optimism, love and support, especially during the hard bits – this book is for you.

SERIES EDITORS' PREFACE

This series of monographs on selected topics in modernism is designed to reflect and extend the range of new work in modernist studies. The studies in the series aim for a breadth of scope and for an expanded sense of the canon of modernism, rather than focusing on individual authors. Literary texts will be considered in terms of contexts including recent cultural histories (modernism and magic; sonic modernity; media studies) and topics of theoretical interest (the everyday; postmodernism; the Frankfurt School); but the series will also re-consider more familiar routes into modernism (modernism and gender; sexuality; politics). The works published will be attentive to the various cultural, intellectual and historical contexts of British, American and European modernisms, and to interdisciplinary possibilities within modernism, including performance and the visual and plastic arts.

Tim Armstrong and Rebecca Beasley

ABBREVIATIONS

Wyndham Lewis

B	'Bestre'
BB	*Blasting and Bombardiering*
C	*The Childermass*
CD	*The Caliph's Design*
CSM	'Cantleman's Spring Mate'
MWA	*Men Without Art*
RL	*The Revenge for Love*
SB	*Snooty Baronet*
T	*Tarr: The 1918 Version*

D. H. Lawrence

AR	*Aaron's Rod*
K	*Kangaroo*
L	*The Fox, The Captain's Doll, The Ladybird*
LCL	*Lady Chatterley's Lover*
R	*The Rainbow*
RDP	*Reflections on the Death of a Porcupine*
STH	*Study of Thomas Hardy*
TP	*D. H. Lawrence: The Poems*, Vol. 1
WIL	*Women in Love*

H.D.

A	*Asphodel*
BL	*Bid Me to Live: A Madrigal*
H	*Her*
MM	'The Mask and the Movietone'
P	*Palimpsest*
TF	*Tribute to Freud*
WDNF	*The Walls Do Not Fall*

Samuel Beckett

CDW	*Samuel Beckett: The Complete Dramatic Works*
CSP	*Samuel Beckett: The Complete Short Prose, 1929–1989*
HI	*How It Is*
M	*Murphy*
PTD	*Proust and Three Dialogues*
TN	*Three Novels: Molloy, Malone Dies, The Unnamable*

INTRODUCTION

Art is like the dauntless, plastic force that builds up stubborn, amorphous substance cell by cell, into the frail geometry of a shell.
Hope Mirrlees, *Madeleine: One of Love's Jansenists*, 1919

It's only insects, but it makes you think.
Čapek Brothers, *The Insect Play*, 1922

Shortly after the outbreak of the Second World War, Virginia Woolf recorded the following observation in her reading notebook: 'The point of view of any individual is bound to be not a birds eye view but an insects eye view [*sic*], the view of an insect too on a green blade, which oscillates violently with local gusts of wind.'[1] Woolf's curious analogy hints at a fundamental shift in perspective, in which the subject's point of view is aligned not with the sweeping aerial vantage point of a bird in flight, but with a helpless bug clinging on to some frail support. A panoptic model of vision is here replaced by a state of optical precariousness, as the avian elevation descends to a position scarcely above ground level. That the author had recent world events in mind when she made these remarks is hinted at by the rest of the entry, which consists of her reading notes from Sigmund Freud's *Group Psychology and the Analysis of the Ego* (1921) and includes references to the herd instinct, Hitlerism and the relation of women 'to war and society'.[2] Faced with a new outbreak of military aggression, Woolf saw in Freud's writing an image of the modern subject as an imperilled organism caught up in the violent oscillations of history, politics and mass society – whose frame of vision trembles with the intensity of these turbulent 'gusts'.

Like many of her fellow modernists, Woolf turned to the insect world in order to express the plight of the modern subject. In 1922, Ezra Pound warned that in his 'entanglement in machines, in utility, man rounds the circle almost into insect life'. T. S. Eliot would echo these sentiments in a 1926 lecture, declaring that it was the task of modern poets to rescue society from its descent into 'a highly perfected race of insects'.[3] For writers and thinkers during this period, insects provided an image of the transformation of human society by socio-political, technological and economic forces, lending a kind of definition to the dehumanising effects of industrial capitalism on the individual. This way of understanding insects extends to modernist criticism: Hal Foster, for instance, asserts that the 'becoming-insect of the body' in modernist art is closely linked to the 'becoming-machine of man', while Holly Henry posits that 'military aggression, in many modernist writers' assessment, had reduced industrialised European societies to little more than an insect existence'.[4] Such readings, however, tend to overlook the rich complexity of insects in modernist writing. Without denying the 'entanglement' of the insect body with the conditions of urban modernity and industrial warfare, this book proposes that there is another way of reading insects in the modernist text – one in which bugs are able to function as more than mere metaphors for the mechanical degradation of human life.

Woolf's tremulous bug may have something more to tell us about the modern subject's self-image than initially meets the eye. In an essay written a few years earlier, 'Walter Sickert: A Conversation' (1934), which consists of a dinner party discussion of 'the change wrought upon our senses by modern conditions', Woolf writes of 'those insects said still to be found in the primeval forests of South America, in whom the eye is so developed that they are all-eye'. While visiting a recent exhibition of Sickert's paintings, one guest notes, 'I became completely and solely an insect':

> Colours went spirally through my body lighting a flare as if a rocket fell through the night and lit up greens and browns, grass and trees, and there in the grass a white bird. Colour warmed, thrilled, chafed, burnt, soothed, fed and finally exhausted me.[5]

To be human, the essay suggests, is to be deprived of the capacity for sensory perception, whereas by 'revert[ing] to the insect stage of our long life', before 'the eye shrivelled', it becomes possible to experience an enhanced, albeit short-lived, perspective on one's surroundings, in which the self is capable of 'drinking, eating, indeed becoming colour'. Art is presented as the catalyst for this metamorphosis, with Woolf emphasising that it is only upon 'entering a picture gallery', when the subject is safe from 'the perils of the street' that this sensory apparatus may be restored.[6] In this state of heightened perception, non-human life takes centre stage, with the speaker noticing 'grass and trees, and there in the grass a white bird'. To see the world with an 'insect's eye view, we might then conclude, is to overcome the myopia induced by 'modern conditions' and to develop a vision of life beyond the human frame.

As a key theorist and practitioner of the modernist novel, as well as an author whose enthusiasm for entomology has been well documented, Woolf provides a useful starting point for this study of modernism's aesthetic interest in invertebrates.[7] Paying close attention to the work of Wyndham Lewis, D. H. Lawrence, Hilda Doolittle (H.D.) and Samuel Beckett, this book identifies a sustained preoccupation with insects in modernist writing that is not only bound up with widespread concerns regarding the effects of modernisation on the human sensorium, but which is also closely linked to writers' efforts to make sense of these altered conditions. What Pericles Lewis refers to as modernism's 'culture of experiment', which sought to break away from traditional 'narrative techniques and generic conventions' in search of 'new methods of representation appropriate to life in an urban, industrial, mass-oriented age', I argue, owes a significant debt to popular studies of entomology which proliferated in the early decades of the twentieth century.[8] After examining the conjunction of historical factors that gave rise to this interest, I propose that the figure of the exoskeleton (or outer shell) can shed new light on modernism's linguistic and formal innovations, its engagement with key psychological and socio-political concerns, as well as its questioning of the limits of the human.

The Age of Insects

Since antiquity, writers have turned to the insect world to represent instances when the boundaries of the human subject appear compromised in some way. In Homer's description of the approaching Myrmidon troops 'streaming out like wasps ... with a tireless clamour arising' in *The Iliad*, the chaotic energy of this mass of male bodies begins to resemble that of a hymenopteran swarm. Subjects that deviate from dominant conceptions of humanness can also appear bug-like to the onlooker. When Victor Frankenstein comes face to face with his monstrous creation, he cries 'Begone, vile insect!', while in Conrad's *Heart of Darkness* (1899), Marlow describes how the Congolese natives 'black and naked, moved about like ants'.[9] Here and elsewhere, insect imagery is used to signal moments where the human form appears disfigured in the eyes of the observer – whether literally, as is suggested by Shelley's *Frankenstein* (1818), or, in the case of Conrad's protagonist, by the dehumanising effects of imperialism.

There is, however, an important distinction to be made between discerning entomological traits in others and in recognising one's own bug-like qualities. In a wide-ranging survey of the insect metaphor in literature, Cristopher

Hollingsworth observes that while these life forms traditionally tend to signify a mode of otherness that arises from the perspective of an individual 'surveying a group from a sovereign position', in early-twentieth-century writing, the image of the self as insect – a figure exemplified by Gregor Samsa – emerges with surprising frequency.[10] To liken oneself to an insect would seem to suggest that this position of sovereignty had become unavailable, and that it was now no longer possible to extricate oneself from the hordes of modern society and obtain a privileged vantage point (a bird's eye view) over one's surroundings. In tacit recognition of this, Marina Warner presents Kafka's tale as something of a watershed moment in literary representations of bodily transformation, arguing that in contrast to earlier works, in which 'the subjects achieve final personality in this new form', Samsa's metamorphosis 'does not express self-knowledge but destroys the possibility of self-recognition'.[11]

Initially at least, Samsa's perspective does appear to conform to this view: lying helplessly on his back, all he 'managed to see' was his belly 'sectioned off by little crescent-shaped ridges into segments and his 'numerous legs, pathetically frail . . . wav[ing] feebly before his eyes'. These fragmentary glimpses of his segmented body present a vision of the self in pieces, unable to take on a coherent outline. Over time, however, Samsa begins to develop a new sense of self:

> He was particularly given to hanging off the ceiling; it felt very different from lying on the floor; he could breathe more easily; a gentle thrumming vibration went through his body; and in the almost blissful distraction Gregor felt up there, it could even happen that to his own surprise he let himself go, and smacked down on the floor. Of course his physical mastery of his body was of a different order from what it had been previously, and so now he didn't hurt himself, even after a fall from a considerable height.[12]

In his altered state, Samsa is able to perceive himself as well as the world around him with a new clarity: from this elevated vantage point, he becomes aware of the true feelings of his family members, finding himself able to 'see through everything more acutely'. Like Woolf's insect-like gallery-goer, Samsa is eventually 'exhausted' by this state of being, reduced over the course of the narrative to a 'flat and desiccated' husk.[13] But during moments such as this he is also suspended – quite literally – from the pressures of his former existence, with his weighty exoskeleton exhibiting a paradoxical lightness. Enveloped in an entomological casing, Kafka's protagonist appears sturdier ('now he didn't hurt himself') and yet also more sensitive ('a gentle thrumming vibration went through his body'). Until his shell is purposefully damaged by his father, it is able to function both as a shock absorber and an amplifying membrane, protecting him from harm while also enabling him to tune into his surroundings in new ways. Consequently, while Samsa's plight is suggestive of the powerlessness of the modern subject amid an increasingly dehumanising social reality, this book is interested in how modernist writing seeks to adapt to these circumstances, transforming a sharp fall in status into a new order of creative mastery.

Kafka's *Die Verwandlung* [*The Metamorphosis*] emerged at a key moment in history: although the text was written before the outbreak of the First World War, by the time it was published in 1915, millions of young men across Europe were being pressed into the service of the first fully industrialised conflict. On the battlefield the human figure underwent a radical transformation as soldiers were strapped into bug-like gas masks and disguised beneath camouflage uniforms; they crawled through the mud in armoured tanks and lived in holes in the ground. Many were disfigured by artillery shells, which tore through flesh and ripped off limbs. Between 1914 and 1918, twenty million men were severely wounded and a large proportion were left with permanent disabilities.[14] Confronted with bodies that had been drastically reshaped by military technologies, writers turned to life forms that bore little resemblance to the human form. Encountering a group of wounded servicemen at Waterloo Station, Woolf likened these disabled figures to 'dreadful looking spiders propelling themselves along the platform . . . legs trimmed off close to the body'.[15] From his observation post, Wyndham Lewis, who served as an artillery officer and war artist on the front line, spotted a group of his fellow soldiers 'become stuck like houseflies upon a section of flypaper, in a marshy patch' (*BB* 161). The long-range optics of the conflict resulted in a drastic reduction of the human scale, which was reflected in the serviceman's diminished self-image. As the war poet Siegfried Sassoon remarked in his diary in early 1917: 'The soldier is no longer a noble figure. He is merely a writhing insect among this ghastly folly of destruction.'[16] No longer was the status of the insect confined to certain others – now everyone appeared insectile, even to themselves.

Lugging his kitbag through the Sussex mud shortly after the war, Ford Madox Ford likened himself to an 'insect Sisyphus', a 'dung beetle . . . alternately climbing, then rolling backwards clinging on to his pellet of dung'.[17] Ford's sense of himself as repeatedly 'rolling backwards' evokes a kind of evolutionary atavism, as though his experiences of muddy combat had left him struggling to cling on to his human identity. The beetle's regressive movement is suggestive of the ongoing reverberations of Darwinian theory in early twentieth-century British society – what Robert Crawford characterises as an 'intellectual climate' in which 'humanity was linked continually to the life of lower organisms'.[18] Significantly, though, Ford's entomological analogy may also be linked to the physical conditions of the First World War, which served to further muddy the distinction between humans and insects. Lice, mosquitoes and flies proliferated in the trenches, quickly becoming one of the main sources of illness and death among soldiers. Faced with the rapid spread of typhus, malaria and trench fever (spread by lice), the War Office teamed up with entomologists to exterminate this enemy within.

These weren't just any entomologists. Established in the late nineteenth century, economic entomology treated insects as vectors of disease and competitors for the earth's resources, and during the war its proponents forged a close alliance with the chemical industry.[19] In a 1919 article for the *Scientific Monthly*, the economic entomologist L. O. Howard boasted that 'war conditions have intensified the work of the entomologists and have enabled them to make the importance of their researches felt almost as never before'. Howard lists some of their recent accomplishments, including 'the control of the body louse', and the deployment of 36,000 pounds of white arsenic against 'insect enemies'.[20] These remarks demonstrate the frequent overlap in the writing of this period between the rhetoric of warfare and the language of environmental control. As Edmund Russell notes, 'what set the twentieth century apart from earlier epochs was the *scale* on which people could annihilate human and natural enemies'.[21] Consequently, at the same time that British soldiers were undergoing regular fumigation to rid them of lice, they were also being gassed by the German army with chemicals that had previously been used as insecticides. One Dutch newspaper was quick to notice the uncanny resemblance between gas warfare and pest control (Figure I.1).

Figure I.1 'Die "Chlorreiche" Germania' [The 'Chlorine-Rich' Germania], *De Groene Amsterdammer*, 9 May 1915

Published in May 1915, this satirical illustration depicts the female embodiment of Germany (who is somewhat aptly called 'Germania') releasing a cloud of chemicals over a helpless group of soldiers. At first glance she appears to be delousing them, but on closer inspection she is exterminating them with chlorine.

Curiously, however, if modernist writers felt that humans had come to resemble what Hugh Kenner describes as 'exoskeletal beings – insects or crustaceans', it was to these life forms that they turned as a way of understanding their predicament.[22] Perhaps because people felt closer to insects than ever, during and after the First World War a craze for popular entomology developed. Britain's bug-mania had been building throughout the nineteenth century as part of a widespread interest in natural history, and many modernist writers, including Eliot and Woolf, participated in the Victorian hobby of insect collecting as children. In the early decades of the twentieth century, however, more popular studies of insect life were written and sold in Britain than ever before.[23] What Wyndham Lewis referred to in 1919 as an 'adulation for the universe of creatures, and especially for the world of insects' (*CD* 77), appears to have arisen in accordance with a growing emphasis in contemporary biology on the living organism as opposed to the dead specimen.[24] In addition to popular texts by the Belgian dramatist and entomologist Maurice Maeterlinck, the American zoologist W. M. Wheeler, as well as the Swiss myrmecologist Auguste Forel, the work of French entomologist Jean-Henri Fabre was central to this new trend. Described by Darwin as an 'inimitable observer', Fabre's approach to the study of insects contributed to a wider shift in the life sciences during the late nineteenth century from taxonomy, or the collection and classification of natural specimens, to ethology, which involved the study of living creatures in their natural habitats.[25] This shift in attitude is described in a 1915 article in *The New Statesman*, written by the aptly titled 'Lens', who characterises Fabre, along with Maeterlinck and Forel, as proponents of the 'new entomology'. Rather than simply 'invent[ing] names' for new species, and 'record[ing] their differences in death', these figures are 'concerned with the lives of insects' and their 'incalculable significance, vital and mortal, for all else that lives'.[26]

As well as dramatising the macabre mating rituals of mantises and the predatory instincts of parasitic wasps, Fabre sought to emphasise what G. V. Legros described in 1913 as the 'unsuspected talents' and 'original industries' of insects.[27] In one article, he likens the home-building skills of the leaf-cutting bee to 'the fulcrum for which Archimedes clamoured in order to lift the world with his system of levers'.[28] This example hints at the central axis on which Fabre's studies often turn: the suggestion that Archimedes can only 'clamour' for what the leaf-cutter achieves effortlessly is consistent with his efforts to elevate his lowly subject matter beyond the heights of human achievement.

Translated into English in the 1910s, Fabre's studies were read by a number of modernist writers and artists, including Vanessa Bell, William Empson, D. H. Lawrence, Wyndham Lewis, Katherine Mansfield, Ezra Pound, Marcel Proust, John Rodker, Rebecca West and Virginia Woolf, as well as Marianne Moore, who listed Fabre's ten-volume magnum opus, *Souvenirs entomologiques* [*Entomological Memories*] (1879–1900), in a list of 'great literary works'.[29] William Carlos Williams even wrote in his autobiography that 'Henri Fabre has been one of my gods', adding in somewhat ant-like terms that he 'induced in me a patient industry'.[30]

In two essays published in 1920 and 1921, Ezra Pound described the writing of Fabre, along with that of the anthropologist James Frazer, as 'essential to contemporary clear thinking', adding: 'As Voltaire was a needed light in the eighteenth century, so in our time Fabre and Frazer have been essentials in the mental furnishings of any contemporary mind qualified to write of ethics or philosophy.'[31] This may seem like a somewhat extravagant claim, but Fabre's studies did exert a significant influence over intellectual life during this period. Henri Bergson's *Creative Evolution* (1911), which is discussed in Chapter 4, proposes a model of instinct based on Fabre's entomological observations, while Remy de Gourmont's *Physique de l'amour* [*The Natural Philosophy of Love*] (1903), which Pound translated into English in 1922, draws on Fabre's studies of insect mating behaviour to develop a theory of human sexuality. Tim Armstrong has gathered evidence to suggest that the popular entomology of Fabre and others fed into contemporary biology, informing the work of geneticists and endocrinologists, while Caroline Hovanec has uncovered a sustained preoccupation with insect perception in the writing of popular scientific thinkers such as Julian Huxley and J. B. S. Haldane.[32] As we shall see in Chapters 2 and 3, the work of entomologists such as Fabre helped to shape the ideas of pioneering psychologists, including Wilfred Trotter's theory of crowd psychology and W. H. R. Rivers's account of shell shock.[33] Insects, it seems, played a surprisingly prominent role in Western society's self-understanding during this period, helping scientists and artists alike to think through some of the central concerns of the modern age.

The insect world was also a source of consolation to modernist writers during the war. Marianne Moore's poem 'To A Stiff-winged Grasshopper' (1915) begins by asserting:

> As I unfolded its wings,
>   In examining it for the first time,
>   I forgot the war[34]

Although the grasshopper is presented as entirely sealed off from the surrounding human conflict, enfolded in its own world, the poem's act of separation is really a bringing together – the speaker's claim to have forgotten the war serves to call it to mind. That the study of insects provided a new perspective on the conflict is further suggested by tantalisingly incomplete remarks made by Roger Fry to Woolf in 1918 after bumping into her on a London street. Woolf reports that before hurrying off to an appointment, Fry confessed to being 'somewhat relieved in his mind by reading Fabre' who 'makes him see that after all, our war, hideous though it is – but here we parted'.[35] Although Fry may have been 'relieved' by the realisation that humans were not alone in such acts of mindless barbarism, another possibility is that the inordinate fondness displayed by Fabre towards the lives of maggots and nut-weevils enabled him to look beyond war's 'hideous' devaluation of life.

As a testament to Fabre's extraordinary popularity, Fry may have encountered his studies in a number of venues, including the *Daily Mail* and *The Fortnightly Review*. He may also have read Fabre's most recent article in the literary magazine *The English Review*, which published his work from 1912 to 1922 alongside the work of modernist writers. In a piece published in the September 1917 issue entitled 'The Scavengers', Fabre turns his attention to the sacred beetle (also known as the dung beetle), one of nature's 'mastercraftsmen' renowned for its fertilisation of the soil. 'Out of the filth she creates the flower', he marvels, expressing a sense of wonder at the beetle's transformation of animal dung into a source of new life.[36] This anecdote, which finds its way into the writing of both Wyndham Lewis and D. H. Lawrence, offers an insight into what Fabre's insect studies helped Fry and his contemporaries to see – namely, that if the war had reduced humankind to helpless bugs crawling around in the dirt, then learning more about artisans of waste such as the sacred beetle offered a means of reconciling this destructive atmosphere with the possibility of artistic creation.[37] As we shall see, much of the writing examined by this study appears to be born out of processes of decay. From the dissolving caterpillars of H.D.'s war fiction to the wormlike mud-dwellers of Beckett's post-war prose, many of the texts under consideration explore the notion that the decomposition of existing forms may be the key to their renewal.

Fabre was not alone in emphasising the remarkable talents of insects, or in presenting them as artists in their own right. In 1914, the *National Geographic* published the first book of insect macrophotography by David and Marian Fairchild, who write in their introduction that these 'tiny monsters . . . have powers which neither man nor any other mammal ever dreamed of having'.[38] A few years earlier, an image based on the short film *The Balancing Bluebottle* (1908), directed by the pioneering nature documentary maker F. Percy Smith, featured on the frontpage of the *Daily Mirror* alongside the curious announcement: 'FLY NURSES A MINIATURE DOLL'.[39] The film features a magnified fly juggling with various items including a shell, a cork and a tiny dumbbell

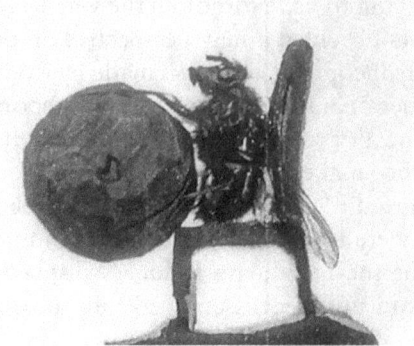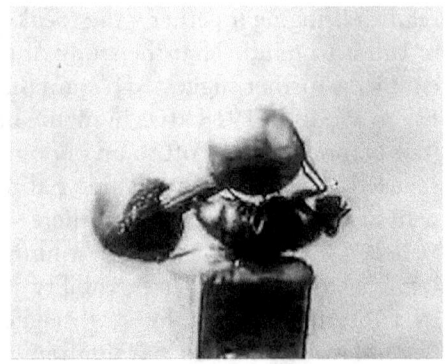

Figure I.2 Stills from *The Acrobatic Fly*, 1910

(Figure I.2), and the anthropomorphism of the paper's headline is suggestive of the emphasis, also seen in Fabre's writing, on the gentler instincts displayed by insects: observed closely, their behaviour could appear not only monstrous but also surprisingly tender.[40]

The development of natural history filmmaking was interrupted by the war, but between 1922 and 1933 more than 140 nature shorts directed by Smith and others were screened at British cinemas as part of an educational series entitled 'Secrets of Nature', with a significant proportion devoted solely to insects.[41] Like Fabre, Smith was eager to counteract the much maligned reputation of aphids, wasps and weevils: 'If I think anything is a pest', he once remarked, 'I make a film about it; then it becomes beautiful.'[42] A number of these films were screened by the London Film Society, which Woolf, along with artists and writers such as Roger Fry and H. G. Wells, is known to have attended.[43] In a 1927 essay, fellow cinema-goer H.D. wrote of her amusement at witnessing 'the exaggerated antics of enormous ants' and 'gargantuan night-moths' on the cinema screen (*MM* 118–19). One of the films to which H.D. may have been alluding, *Skilled Insect Artisans* (1922), is suggestive of the appeal of insects to modernist writers during this period: the depiction of insects as 'artisans', in particular, hints at their association with natural forms of creativity that remain untouched by modern industry.

If human beings had been scaled down to insects by scientific, technological and military-industrial forces, then the scaling up of insects – both on the cinema screen and in the wider cultural imagination – appears to have helped many to see that life is able to endure, and even flourish, at this level. In 1922, while broadcasting the 'first radio entomological lecture' from New York entitled 'Bugs and Antennae', the doyen of diptera E. P. Felt voiced a growing sense of admiration towards insects:

> This has been called the age of man. Is it not really the age of insects? ... Dare any man say that our latest advancement in applied science, namely the radio telephone, is more than a relatively crude modification of methods that have been used by insects for countless ages?[44]

Transmitted to the human ear through antennae – a term that initially denoted the sensory appendages of insects before being expanded at the turn of the twentieth century to refer to a radio's 'receiving system' – Felt's talk highlights the close proximity between modern forms of technology and the insect body.[45] Kenner identifies a similar conjunction in Pound's description of the artist as 'the antennae of the race', arguing that when the author made these remarks he was presumably thinking 'not only of the mantis but of Marconi'.[46] As an exercise in what would now be called public engagement ('May we suggest to radio enthusiasts a similar attitude towards gall midges'), Felt's talk assumes a new receptiveness on the part of its listeners to the possibility of learning from, as well as about, nature's original technicians.[47] This is not to say that this attitude was unique to this period in history – as is apparent from the well-known saying from Proverbs 6:6, 'Go to the ant, thou sluggard; consider her ways, and be wise' – human beings have sought to learn from insects for millennia. But in an era in which civilisation seemed to be advancing, as Eliot put it in 1934, 'progressively backwards', Felt's sense that the 'age of man' was really an 'age of insects' is suggestive not only of the resemblance between early twentieth-century society and the insect world, but also of a more surprising recognition of humankind's indebtedness to invertebrates.[48]

Forming the Exoskeleton

A further clue as to what the idea of the insect offered modernist writers may be found in its etymology: deriving from the Latin *insectum*, meaning notched or cut into, the word insect can be traced back to the Greek word *entomon*, meaning divided into sections.[49] Coined by Aristotle to describe the tripartite structure of the insect body, which he believed that once 'cut into pieces, can still live', the term describes a similar state of division to that which is often displayed by modernist writing.[50] Eric C. Brown could easily be describing a text by Lewis or H.D. when he notes that the etymology of the insect 'makes a convenient model for reading them as formulations of incoherence ... distortion, derangement, and fragmentation'.[51] Like modernism itself, moreover, which Latham and Rogers describe as a 'mobile, expansive, and ultimately unsettled concept', insects pose a problem of categorisation.[52] Creatures with too many legs such as arachnids and millipedes are excluded from the Linnaean classification of the term, as are the legless – earthworms, maggots, slugs and snails. In common parlance, an insect can be almost any small thing that creeps, flutters or crawls, and this study adopts the term in this broader, catch-all sense to accommodate the diverse array of critters that populate the modernist universe.

Mary Douglas, in her cultural study *Purity and Danger*, posits that insects' lack of clear definition imbues them with a strange potency: 'beetles and spiders who live in the cracks in the walls', she surmises, 'attract fears and dislikes' and the 'kind of powers attributed to them symbolise their ambiguous, inarticulate status'.[53] Insects seem to defy our best efforts to hold them in our sights and in our minds, slipping through the gaps in our thought structures. And yet at the same time, this order of life is often associated with taxonomic stability: when the entomologist Stein shows Marlow his mausoleum of beetles and butterflies in Conrad's *Lord Jim* (1900), he draws his attention to '[t]he beauty – but that is nothing – look at the accuracy, the harmony'.[54] For Conrad, the catching and naming of a specimen is linked to the notion, however futile, of being able to order the chaos of the surrounding world into something orderly and fixed. The appeal of insects to modernist writers, I want to suggest, presents something of a paradox: these little articulated bodies offered a way of articulating experiences that verge on unrepresentability, particularly during times of war, arming writers with a store of imagery with which to express the pressing concerns of the modern age. And yet insects also seem closely linked to writers' cultivation of states of semantic unruliness that challenge the prospect of readability.

In Samuel Beckett's *The Unnamable* (1958), the dissolution of the subject and its forms of expression is figured as a frenzied myrmecological motion: 'the words swarm and jostle like ants, hasty, indifferent, bringing nothing, taking nothing away, too light to leave a mark' (*TN* 326). Part of the appeal of insects to writers such as Beckett seems to lie in their ability to exceed and confound the meanings that we attribute to them, functioning as unstable signifiers that continually thwart our human designs. Modernist writers are also interested in the uncertain status of the insect in relation to the category of the formless, as well as that which is, like Eliot's Prufrock, 'formulated, sprawling on a pin', with much of the writing examined by this study shuttling (or rather scuttling) between states of fluid amorphousness and rigid formalism.[55] Readers have reflected on the ways in which modernist texts often appear to be struggling to reconcile these polarities of reification and disintegration, hermetic enclosure and radical self-division, at the level of form. Insects are able to embody these extremes. As Steven Connor puts it: 'Armour, the hardened carapace, retrieves what the thought of insects disperses, namely the possibility of putting something in its place. The other side of insect life, multiplicity, prohibits this armoured representability.'[56]

Insects can help us to think through the double-sidedness of modernist writing – its impulse to attribute form to the chaos of experience coupled with its resistance to anything resembling a definitive outline. They can also help to focalise modernism's anxious inquiry into the nature of form itself – its questioning of its basic tenets: What is a form? What can form do? And perhaps most importantly: What are its limits? Responding to the host of possible meanings contained within the word 'form' (which can denote, among other things, a body, a style, a frame or an ideal), Angela Leighton argues in insect-like terms that its 'multiform potential' as a signifier suggests in itself 'something of the very multi-dimensionality, the unsettled busyness, of the artwork'.[57] As well as being connected to writers' efforts to exploit the multivalent properties of language, its shifting patterns of sense, not to mention its obscurities and categorical slippages, insects can also help us to think through modernism's reflexive attention to its own form – its relentless pursuit of novelty, its constant struggle to adapt, unmake and remake itself anew. Much has been written about modernist writers' attempts to undermine the stable, realist architecture of the nineteenth-century novel, but I want to suggest that it is the resistance of modernist writing to its own aesthetic formulas that leads it to embark on what H.D. refers to as a process of 'hectic experimenting'.[58]

Through their various engagements with entomological life forms, Lewis, Lawrence, H.D. and Beckett discovered not only a world of formal possibilities, but also a welcome limitation, in the figure of the exoskeleton. This structure, which derives from the Latin *exo*, 'outer, external', provides a key to writers' sustained aesthetic interest in the insect body, surfacing as both a localised image and as an overarching feature of the writing under consideration. As we shall see in the chapters that follow, the exoskeleton, which is periodically shed, regrown and modified over the course of the insect life cycle, is closely bound up with writers' efforts to break away from what Lawrence describes as 'ossiferous' forms of narrative representation.[59] Lewis's surface modifications, Lawrence's aesthetic exuviations, H.D.'s pupal provisionality and Beckett's vermicular spasms all resemble a continual struggle to maintain the liveliness of the literary text in order to prevent it from hardening into a fixed and final form. As a conceptual articulation, the exoskeleton surfaces in accordance with writers' efforts to find a 'form that accommodates the mess', as Beckett puts it, providing a way of ordering and of giving a shape and significance to thoughts and sensations that test the limits of representability.[60]

Formed as it is around ideas of enshellment, this study might appear to run the risk of pressing its writers into too definitive a mould, in turn squeezing out some of the nuances and complexities that emerge from, and are indeed central to, modernism's entomological aesthetics. Yet through a series of close readings, I argue that the writing of Lewis, Lawrence, H.D. and Beckett strives to emulate the polymorphousness of the insect body – its ability to blend into its surroundings and adapt to danger, its swarming formations and distinct stages of growth. The exoskeleton, which is frequently outgrown, re-formed and at times discarded, can function agonistically in the modernist text, thwarting writers' efforts to push against the constraints of language and literary form. And yet crucially, this structure remains instrumental to writers' efforts to re-establish the boundaries of the text as a means of protecting the artwork from various forms of bombardment – sensory, military, ideological. For the purposes of this study, moreover, it provides a way of housing the swarm of associations generated by insects in the modernist text, which can threaten to multiply out of control. As Maurice Maeterlinck reveals in his introduction to *The Life of the Ant* (1930), working with insects is no easy task:

> One can get no hold upon one's subject . . . The material available is too rich, too vast: its ramifications are endless; we soon lose our way, and our interest is dispersed in all directions . . . We must therefore observe certain limits.[61]

The exoskeleton, then, can help to contain the vast richness of entomological material on offer in modernist writing, even as it threatens to multiply in all directions.

This study is by no means the first to identify an exoskeletal aesthetic at work in modernist writing. In a lecture on 'modernism's insect life', Steven Connor argues that '[a]ssaulted by shock, overload, complexity, and the threat of so-called female deliquescence, modernism appeared to borrow the idea of a defensive armour from insects'. Jessica Burstein attributes the modernist 'fantasy of the insect body' to a longing for invulnerability during the First World War, reasoning: 'Ants, wasps, and bees don't bruise.'[62] Though rich and insightful, these readings participate in a way of understanding of the modernism that this book seeks to revise. While the insect body is undoubtedly bound up with axioms of resistant hardness, exteriority and self-protection, modernist writers were also interested in the exoskeleton as a site of encounter between self and surroundings – one that enables the subject to interact with the world in new ways. Consistent throughout this study will be an emphasis on writers' efforts to develop forms of expression that are robust enough to survive the descent into industrial warfare and rapid modernisation but also adaptable to the relentless pace of social and technological change – solid, but also, to recall the opening epigraph by Hope Mirrlees, a 'dauntless, plastic force'.

The dominant understanding of the modernist text as a kind of resistant armour or shield against sensation can be traced back to the work of late nineteenth- and early twentieth-century theorists of modernity. In 'The Metropolis and Mental Life' (1903), Georg Simmel describes how the urban subject has been forced to evolve a 'protective organ for itself against the profound disruption with which the fluctuations and discontinuities of the external milieu threaten it'. Simmel's account recalls Max Nordau's account in *Degeneration* (1895) of the modern subject as an overtaxed organism struggling to conserve its vitality beneath a 'dead shell'. Max Weber's *The Protestant Ethic and the Spirit of Capitalism* (1904) adds another layer to this apparatus, characterising the 'shell as hard as steel' that encases the modern citizen, whose life is determined from birth by the 'technical and economic conditions of machine production'.[63] Together these examples indicate that this adaptive process is necessary but ultimately debilitating, with the exoskeleton functioning as a recurrent metaphor for the way that the modern psyche, faced with a relentless onslaught of sensation, has been forced to sacrifice an outer layer of vitality in order to maintain itself intact. As Susan Buck-Morss notes, in the latter half of the nineteenth century, the sensory system of the modern subject 'reverses its role. Its goal is to *numb* the organism, to deaden the senses, to repress memory', adding that 'the cognitive system of synaesthetics has become rather one of *an*aesthetics'.[64]

That the concept of the 'dead shell' emerges as an aesthetic principle in pre-war modernist writing has already been well documented. Tim Armstrong notes that a 'defence of the self' is central to the formal strategies of 'Men of 1914' such as Lewis, who sought to transform the artwork into a protective shield against the 'jellyish diffuseness' of modern life (*T* 313–14).[65] Like Lewis, Pound was influenced by T. E. Hulme's vision of 'dry hardness' in art, with the pair espousing an aesthetic of 'bareness and hardness' in their Vorticist manifesto, published in the first issue of *BLAST*. A year earlier, in 1913, Pound published his Imagist manifesto, outlining a poetics that is 'harder' and '"nearer the bone"' than previous forms of expression. That same year, H.D.'s first 'crystalline' Imagist poems appeared in print, as did D. H. Lawrence's novel *Sons and Lovers* – written in what the author described as a 'new . . . hard, violent style'.[66] Peter Nicholls details how the rhetoric of hardness espoused by modernist writers came to represent 'a constellation of "textural" features that favour definiteness of presentation', the 'Classical' as opposed to the 'Romantic' outlook, 'the external "shell" over the "muzziness" of unfettered introspection'.[67] Developed in opposition to the techniques associated with literary Impressionism and the stream of consciousness method, hard modernism sought to protect the artwork from various kinds of otherness that were perceived as a threat to artistic expression, including lowbrow culture and so-called feminine fluidity.

This vision of enshellment would appear to be one of exclusion – an attempt to hold the chaos of the outer world at bay. Significantly, however, the outbreak of war, and more specifically the phenomenon of shell shock, delivered a significant blow to this masculine ideal of hardness. Early on in his novel *Tarr* (1918), much of which was written 'during the first year of the War', Lewis's titular protagonist reflects that the 'whole of English training' is a 'system of *deadening feeling*', warning that once this 'armature' begins to break down, the self beneath 'is subject to shock, over-sensitiveness'.[68] Tarr concludes that it is time to 'discard this husk', noting that a 'superficial sensitiveness allows of a harder core' (*T* 42; original emphasis). This argument is a far cry from Tarr's more famous championing of an art of 'deadness' modelled on exoskeletal defences – the 'armoured hide, a turtle's shell' (*T* 299). Yet crucially, the somewhat contradictory stance adopted by the young art student, widely considered to be a mouthpiece of his author, is suggestive of the ways in which, following the outbreak of the war, modernist writers began to develop a more nuanced understanding of the modern subject's psychic defences, moving beyond the 'dead shell'. The impact of shell shock on modernist form has been well established: Paul Sheehan notes that 'more than just a modern pathology, or an event-specific neurosis, shell shock is . . . a platform on which modernism, modernity and shock can meet and interact'.[69] Yet, as is often the case in critical responses to modernism, this distillation of features – 'modernism, modernity and shock' – neglects to consider that the shell too is a platform on which these elements come into contact.

Tarr's emphasis on the 'superficial sensitiveness' of the subject's defences bears a marked resemblance to Freud's post-war account of the stimulus shield. Written after he had examined several sufferers of shell shock, *Beyond the Pleasure Principle* (1920) argues that the individual psyche is equipped with a 'protective shield' against 'the enormous energies at work in the external world'. Like Simmel and others, Freud conceives of the modern mind as a sensitive substance encased within a hard outer shell, but rather than merely offering 'protection against stimuli', this psychic integument is equipped with a layer that 'serves as an organ for receiving stimuli'. This 'receptive cortical layer', Freud notes, takes '*samples* of the external world' in a manner akin to 'feelers which are all the time making tentative advances towards the external world and then drawing back from it'.[70] Implicit in this image is the notion that in order to protect itself from harm, the psyche must remain in touch with, as well as protected from, the disruptive forces at work in its surroundings – advancing and drawing back from the 'enormous energies' of the outer world like a set of quivering antennae.

Freud's innovation of the stimulus shield in the aftermath of the war may be likened to a process of innervation, with the author attributing a new nerve-force to this insentient armour. By comparing this psychic structure to the 'feelers' of invertebrates, Freud's essay exhibits a tendency shared by modernist writing, whereby the insect body helps to define a new mode of sensory awareness. Woolf evokes a similar idea when she writes that people 'secrete an envelope which connects them & protects them from others'.[71] Together these exoskeletal observations suggest that the efforts of writers and intellectuals to develop new ways of conceptualising the human psyche were informed, directly or indirectly, by a concurrent fascination with insect life. They also serve to complicate traditional accounts of modernism's 'strategies of inwardness' – its so-called exclusion of the outer world and pursuit of aesthetic autonomy.[72] Much has been said about the defensive structures at work in the modernist text, but this book identifies a mode of receptiveness inspired by entomological 'others' that coexists alongside the more readily understood phenomenon of protectiveness and is in a sense constitutive of it.

Paying attention to insects in modernist writing can yield new insights into its ability, in the words of Rebecca West, to 'react to the external world in ways profitable to itself'.[73] As I will argue in Chapter 3, H.D.'s efforts in her inter-war prose to evolve the surface of her writing into a gauzy network of feelers capable of tuning into potential dangers offers an important insight into modernism's efforts to transform the destructive forces at work in its surroundings into a form of creative countercharge. Much of the writing under consideration exhibits an impulse to expose itself to harmful forces at work in its surroundings as a means of self-protection, be it Lewis's mimicry of the artistic adversaries that he felt posed a threat to his writing, or Lawrence's baring of his body of work to the painful sting of inter-war ideologies. In advancing this claim, this study does not shy away from the more uncomfortable aspects of modernism's entomological ideation, nor does it seek to gloss over certain troubling likenesses between writers' reactive methods and the reactionary politics of the inter-war period. Rather, in remaining attuned to moments when the modernist text risks becoming indistinguishable from the destructive ideologies against which it is attempting to protect itself, I aim to show that the writing under consideration displays an impulse to continually adapt the textual surface in response to the rapid pace of historical change, resulting in errors of judgement but also in startling innovations.

A Quick Relatedness

In a 1925 essay, Lawrence asserts that if writing is 'too human', it becomes 'lifeless'; instead, the human subject must have 'a quick relatedness to all the other things in the novel: snow, bed-bugs, sunshine' (*STH* 183). The presence of insects in the modernist text, I will argue, can also tell us something about writers' efforts to establish a level of connectedness with non-human others – a connectedness that may appear unsettling or even painful (bedbugs bite), but which can also be generative and life-sustaining. In the past few years, there have been a number of influential accounts of modernism's 'quick relatedness' to other life forms.[74] Readers such as Oliver Botar and Isabel Wünsche have helped to dispel the notion that modernism held little interest in the natural world, detailing its 'active interest in the categories of "life", the "organic", and even the destruction of the environment'. Jeffrey McCarthy has also gathered evidence of modernist writers' 'externalising attentions to the world', while Kelly Sultzbach has provided important insights into modernism's 'adaptability to other subjectivities; even trees, caves, snails, or cats'.[75]

This book builds on these existing arguments, outlining a shared concern in the work of Lewis, Lawrence, H.D. and Beckett with new modes of being and creating inspired by invertebrate life forms. It presents evidence to suggest that modernist writing is not only influenced by, but formed around a range of entomological behaviours, including mimicry, swarming and cocooning. The quiddities of insect life enabled these authors to conceive of alternative versions of selfhood, moving beyond a humanist conception of the subject as bounded, stable and autonomous, and unsettling the binary distinctions between inside and outside, self and other, human and non-human. That being said, it is important to recognise that the modernist writing under consideration does not dispense with these distinctions altogether, preferring rather to invert, unsettle and ultimately expand them. What Rosi Braidotti defines as a 'post-human interconnectedness', which marks 'the collapse of the barrier between the human and its animal and organic others', is not borne out in the work of these writers, who are interested not so much in removing as in reinvigorating the barrier between human and non-human life, maintaining the boundary between self and other while also testing its limits.[76] As Caroline Hovanec aptly puts it, modernism is 'not posthumanist in the sense of being after, or over, humanism and all its structuring binaries', but 'it did resist anthropocentrism and envision a permeable border between self and world'.[77] This is where the figure of the exoskeleton – which functions both as an intervening slash and a site of encounter – can aid our understanding of modernism's desire to connect with as well as to protect itself from the forces at work in its surroundings.

Chapter 1 examines an author whose aesthetics of the 'the *outside* of people ... their shells or pelts' has not often been read in terms of its sensitivity to external forces (*MWA* 97; original emphasis). Going beyond existing readings of Wyndham Lewis's writing as built around a hard and militaristic carapace, I argue that the author's exoskeletal defences are the sign of a heightened responsiveness to potential dangers in his cultural surroundings. After examining the author's reading of scientific studies of insect life by Fabre, John Lubbock and J. Arthur Thomson, this chapter provides evidence to suggest that the many surface alterations that Lewis made to his body of work were inspired by invertebrate behaviours such as camouflage, aggressive mimicry and autotomy (self-amputation). By drawing on the survival strategies of insects, Lewis's writing is able to shift unsettlingly between positions of opposition and similitude, attack and defence, concealment and self-exposure, exploiting its contradictions for their shock value. The chapter goes on to examine the author's aggressive imitation of his high modernist contemporaries through the lens of Joyce's fable 'The Ondt and the Gracehoper', which deploys Lewis's strategies back against him in an entomological counter-attack. Finally, I consider the author's writing alongside his self-portraits, identifying a significant shift in his formal methods from the aggressive iconoclasm of his 1920s fiction to the strategic woundedness of his 1930s writing, before exploring how this instability enabled Lewis to navigate the pressures of the literary marketplace.

Chapter 2 examines the inter-war writing of D. H. Lawrence, arguing that insects are representative in the author's work both of the insentience of modern society and its forms of expression, as well as a kind of swarming hypersensitivity capable of reinvigorating the boundaries of the self. Although, as readers of Lawrence have suggested, the insect body often appears symptomatic of the deadening effect of industrial capitalism on the individual subject, it also operates as a counterforce to this process of petrification, breaking through the 'impervious envelope of insentience' afflicting modern society and fostering new modes of feeling (*RDP* 281). Paying particular attention to the author's inter-war writing, I propose that insects can help to focalise the struggle of Lawrence's writing to maintain the liveliness of language and literary form against the deadening effects of modern life. In *Aaron's Rod* (1922) and *Kangaroo* (1923), subject and text alike are exposed to the swarming, insectile energies of social life, with both novels staging a series of itchy, formicatory encounters that appear designed to get under the skin of his readers, forcing us to experience the agonising sensations of collective life, mass culture and inter-war ideology. The final part of the chapter examines Lawrence's last novel, *Lady Chatterley's Lover* (1928), arguing that the author's depiction of transgressive sexual activity is consistent with his efforts to open up his body of work to new and uncomfortable sensations in order to provoke heightened levels of responsiveness in his readers.

Heightened awareness is also central to H.D.'s experimentation with the image of the cocoon (from the French *coque*, shell) in her writing – a temporary exoskeleton in which the caterpillar dissolves and remakes itself anew. Weaving together examples from the author's war fiction, film criticism and psychoanalytic writing, the third chapter of the study explores how H.D.'s interest in the pupal stage of the insect life cycle was mediated through the 'half finished image' of silent cinema (*MM* 119). Beginning with H.D.'s first published prose experiment, *Palimpsest* (1926), I contend that the recurring image of the cocoon can serve to illuminate the author's efforts to maintain subject and text alike in a 'fluid, inchoate' state (*A* 158), dissolving past experiences in order to reform them anew, while also resisting a state of finality and formal fixity associated throughout her writing with totalising structures. H.D.'s cocoon imagery can shed light on the author's efforts to represent an experience of trauma that is enhancing rather than simply debilitating, in which the mind is rent apart by shock, but also opened up to new ways of thinking and perceiving. The chapter goes on to examine two of the author's First World War novels, *Asphodel* (*c*.1920–7; pub. 1992) and *Bid Me to Live: A Madrigal* (1960), arguing that in addition to functioning as a protective outer layer, the cocoon resembles an intermediary channel or membrane in H.D.'s prose, through which the self is able to tune into its surroundings in new ways.

Chapter 4 examines Beckett's career-long interest in vermicular life forms – caterpillars, maggots and earthworms – arguing that the author's preoccupation with the 'worm-state' helped him to rethink the terms 'by which humanity may be thought again' in the aftermath of the Second World War (*CSP* 278).[78] It takes as its starting point the author's struggle to achieve what he describes as an 'eternally larval' form of expression by repeatedly circling back to earlier statements, ideas, characters, as well as former texts, frustrating a linear path of narrative development.[79] The chapter connects this aesthetic tendency to the author's preoccupation with instances of evolutionary divergence, including Charles Darwin's description of the regressive instincts of an 'embarrassed' caterpillar, and Henri Bergson's account of the 'crowd of minor paths in which, on the contrary, deviations, arrests and setbacks are multiplied'.[80] Focusing on Beckett's 'observations of nature' in his garden at Ussy in the 1950s, I argue that the author's flawed understanding of the reproduction of earthworms, which 'cut in two . . . at once fashion a new head, or a new tail' can offer new insights into the scissional energies of his writing from this period.[81] The chapter concludes with an examination of Beckett's final extended prose text, *How It Is* (1964), exploring how the author's worm encounters inspired him to contemplate the possibility of a generative state of self-division – in which to be cut apart is to be reborn.

The conclusion draws together the findings of the preceding chapters, arguing that the writers of this study are drawn to insects as, in the words of Robert Frost, 'things that won't quite formulate'.[82] It examines the persistence of this way of understanding the insect in a number of experimental prose texts from the late 1950s and 1960s, including Kōbō Abe's *The Women in the Dunes* (1964), William H. Gass's 'Order of Insects' (1968), Clarice Lispector's *The Passion According to G. H.* (1964) and Alain Robbe-Grillet's *Jealousy* (1957). These texts display a shared emphasis on the capacity of insects to undermine the boundaries of the human subject, opening up the self to a threatening but also potentially life-affirming otherness. Yet there is also a discernible shift towards the notion of dissolving the self and abandoning human identity entirely. This distinction, I suggest, can help to make sense of modernism's turn to the insect body in search of ways not of removing, but rather re-sensitising the border between self and world.

Notes

1. Quoted in Brenda R. Silver, *Virginia Woolf's Reading Notebooks*, 116.
2. Quoted in *Woolf's Reading Notebooks*, 117.
3. Pound, 'Translator's Postscript', *The Natural Philosophy of Love*, 208; Eliot, *The Varieties of Metaphysical Poetry*, 211.

4. Foster, *Prosthetic Gods*, 393 n. 66; Henry, *Virginia Woolf and the Discourse of Science*, 124.
5. Woolf, 'Walter Sickert: A Conversation', *Collected Essays*, Vol. 2, 233–4.
6. 'Walter Sickert: A Conversation', 233–5.
7. See Alt, *Virginia Woolf and the Study of Nature*; Kime Scott, *In the Hollow of the Wave*, 42–70.
8. Lewis, *Cambridge Introduction to Modernism*, xx, xvii.
9. Homer, *The Iliad*, 337; Shelley, *Frankenstein*, 102; Conrad, *Heart of Darkness*, 17.
10. Hollingsworth, *Poetics of the Hive*, 188, 203.
11. Warner, *Fantastic Metamorphoses*, 4, 115.
12. Kafka, *Metamorphosis*, 87, 117–18.
13. *Metamorphosis*, 115, 142.
14. Cohen, *The War Come Home*, 1.
15. *The Diary of Virginia Woolf*, Vol. 2, 93.
16. Quoted in Campbell, *Siegfried Sassoon*, 159.
17. Quoted in Saunders, *Ford Madox Ford*, 61.
18. Crawford, *The Savage and the City*, 67.
19. Langston, 'New Chemical Bodies', 267–71.
20. Howard, 'Entomology and the War', 109, 115, 111.
21. Russell, *War and Insects*, 7; original emphasis.
22. Kenner, *A Sinking Island*, 130–1.
23. Burstein, *Cold Modernism*, 93.
24. *Virginia Woolf and the Study of Nature*, 93.
25. Darwin, *Origin of Species* (1859 edn), 364.
26. Lens, 'The New Entomology', 459; *Virginia Woolf and the Study of Nature*, 146. Lens has since been identified as the eugenicist C. W. Saleeby.
27. Legros, *Fabre: Poet of Science*, 271.
28. Fabre, 'The Leaf-Cutters', 419.
29. Moore, *Complete Prose*, 668–9. Evidence of Bell and Woolf's mutual interest in Fabre can be found in a series of letters exchanged between the two sisters about an enormous moth that tapped on Bell's window late one night, Bell, *Virginia Woolf*, 126. Marcel Proust cites Fabre's account of the parasitic wasp in *Swann's Way*, 141. In a letter to John Middleton Murry, Katherine Mansfield details her observations of two wasps fighting over a leaf before signing off the letter 'Fabretta', Wilson, *Katherine Mansfield*, 207. Rebecca West refers to Fabre's insect studies in her travel memoir *Black Lamb and Grey Falcon*, 143. John Rodker quotes Fabre in an essay in *The Little Review*, 'W. H. Hudson', 21–2. For William Empson's knowledge of Fabre see Armstrong, 'The Human Animal', 111. For details of Fabre's influence on a number of surrealist artists and thinkers, including Roger Caillois, Salvador Dalí and Luis Buñuel, see Pressly, 'The Praying Mantis', 600–15.
30. Williams, *Autobiography*, xvi.
31. Pound, *Literary Essays*, 108, 343.
32. 'The Human Animal', 101–15; Hovanec, *Animal Subjects*, 159–95.
33. Sleigh, *Six Legs Better*, 72.
34. Moore, *Poems*, 34.

35. Woolf, *Diary*, Vol. 1, 134.
36. Fabre, 'The Scavengers', 239.
37. Lawrence refers directly to Fabre's study of the dung beetle in his post-war novella *The Ladybird* (1923), discussed in Chapter 2. Lewis alludes to the text in his short story 'The War Baby' (1918), describing how soldier Richard Beresin adapts to his new life in the trenches: 'He was as snug as a beetle in the midst of a trencher full of dough', *Unlucky for Pringle*, 104.
38. Fairchild and Fairchild, *Book of Monsters*, 5–6.
39. See 'Fly Nurses a Miniature Doll', *Daily Mirror*, 13 November 1908, <http://collection.sciencemuseum.org.uk/objects/co8428002/fly-nurses-a-miniature-doll-poster-advertising-poster-film-poster> (last accessed 29 October 2017).
40. A slightly later version of the film, *The Acrobatic Fly* (1910), can be viewed here: <https://www.youtube.com/watch?v=8hlocZhNc0M> (last accessed 27 March 2019).
41. For details of individual films in the series see the *National Film Archive Catalogue*.
42. Quoted in Gaycken, *Devices of Curiosity*, 87–8.
43. Marcus, *The Tenth Muse*, 266.
44. Felt, 'Bugs and Antennae', 529; Parikka, *Insect Media*, ix.
45. 'antenna, *n.*', OED.
46. Pound, *The ABC of Reading*, 73; Kenner, *The Pound Era*, 156.
47. 'Bugs and Antennae', 530.
48. Eliot, *Complete Poems and Plays*, 161.
49. 'insect, *n.*', OED.
50. Aristotle, *Historia Animalium*, 1065.
51. Brown, *Insect Poetics*, x–xi.
52. Latham and Rogers, *Modernism: Evolution of an Idea*, 1.
53. Douglas, *Purity and Danger*, 103.
54. Conrad, *Lord Jim*, 149.
55. Eliot, *Complete Poems and Plays*, 14.
56. Connor, 'As Entomate as Intimate Could Pinchably Be', para. 19.
57. Leighton, *On Form*, 3.
58. H.D., *Pilate's Wife*, 59.
59. Lawrence, *Letters*, Vol. 1, 42.
60. Quoted in Driver, *The Critical Heritage*, 219.
61. Maeterlinck, *The Life of the Ant*, 8.
62. Connor, 'As Entomate', para. 19; Burstein, *Cold Modernism*, 94.
63. Simmel, 'The Metropolis and Mental Life', 12; Nordau, *Degeneration*, 540; Weber quoted in Baehr, 'The "Iron Cage"', 153.
64. Buck-Morss, 'Aesthetics and Anaesthetics', 18; original emphasis.
65. Armstrong, 'The Self and the Senses', 93.
66. Hulme, 'Romanticism and Classicism', 75; 'Manifesto', *BLAST*, 1, 41; Pound, *Literary Essays*, 12; Lawrence, *Letters*, Vol. 1, 132.
67. Nicholls, 'Hard and Soft Modernism', 15.
68. Lewis, 'Preface', *Tarr*, 4.
69. Sheehan, *Modernism and the Aesthetics of Violence*, 169.
70. Freud, *Beyond the Pleasure Principle*, 298–9; original emphasis.

71. Woolf, *Diary*, Vol. 3, 12–13.
72. Jameson, *Fables of Aggression*, 2. For more traditional accounts of modernism's pursuit of aesthetic autonomy see Howe, *Politics and the Novel*; Huyssen, *After the Great Divide*; Carey, *The Intellectuals and the Masses*.
73. West, *The Strange Necessity*, 125.
74. Ellmann, *The Nets of Modernism*, 14–34; Hovanec, *Animal Subjects*; Norris, *Beasts of the Modern Imagination*; Rohman, *Stalking the Subject*; Ryan, 'Following Snakes and Moths'; Setz, *Primordial Modernism*.
75. Botar and Wünsche, *Biocentrism and Modernism*, 1; Sultzbach, *Ecocriticism in the Modernist Imagination*, 11; McCarthy, *Green Modernism*, 22.
76. Braidotti, *Metamorphoses*, 167, 161.
77. *Animal Subjects*, 6.
78. Beckett, *Letters*, Vol. 2, 271.
79. *Letters*, Vol. 2, 102.
80. Darwin, *Origin of Species*, 156; Bergson, *Creative Evolution*, 104.
81. Beckett, *Letters*, Vol. 2, 162, 241.
82. Quoted in Faggen, *Robert Frost*, 95.

SHELL BURSTS: WYNDHAM LEWIS

> In the art of defence, animals often employ means which our imagination would not dare to contemplate.
>
> Jean Henri-Fabre, *The Sacred Beetle and Others*, 1918

> One hides behind one's hide.
>
> Robert Musil, *Die Schwärmer* [*The Visionaries*], 1921[1]

After being faced with 'the horrible dangers of war', the French Huguenot potter and engineer Bernard Palissy worked to come up with a design for a fortress city.[2] Uninspired by existing architecture, he journeyed through woods and mountains, 'to see whether I could find some industrious animal which might give me a hint for my design'. While searching for inspiration he was brought two shells from Guinea – a murex and a whelk. Noting that the more fragile of the two, the murex, had a number of sharp spikes around its edges, Palissy decided that 'God has bestowed more industry upon the weak creatures than on the strong', and that 'the many bulwarks and defences for the fortress ... make compensation for its weakness'.[3] It was this creature, rather than the more robust whelk, that became the model for his fortress design.

Several centuries later, after facing horrible dangers as an artillery officer and war artist at the Western Front, Wyndham Lewis published his first pamphlet, *The Caliph's Design: Architects! Where Is Your Vortex?*(1919). It begins with a parable of an Eastern ruler who summons his architects,

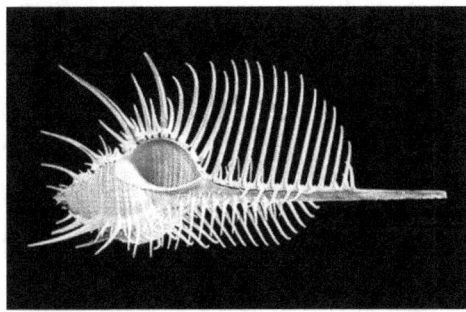
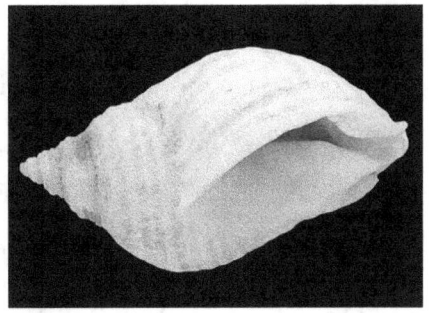

Figure 1.1 Murex shell (*Murex pecten*)

Figure 1.2 Whelk shell (*Nucella lapillus*)

informing them: 'I am extremely dissatisfied with the shape of my city, so I have done a design of a new city' (*CD* 19). By now it was clear that Lewis's 'puce-coloured cockle-shell' *BLAST* had failed to 'brave the waves of blood' and 'reach the other side of World-War' as the author had hoped it would in 1915, and now a new artistic fortification was required.[4] In the aftermath of the war, Lewis sought inspiration from another kind of 'industrious animal' encased within a protective shell – one whose vulnerability to predators has led to the development of defensive strategies, as the biologist Edward Poulton puts it, 'in number and fidelity of detail unequalled throughout organic nature'.[5]

In the second part of *The Caliph's Design*, 'The Artist Older than the Fish', Lewis likens the creation of a work of art to 'the invention of a weapon within the body of a hymenopter to enable it to meet the terrible needs of its life', adding:

> Fabre describes the creative capabilities of certain beetles, realisable on their own bodies; beasts with a record capacity for turning their form and colour impulses into living flesh. These beetles can convert their faces into hideously carved and detestable masks, can grow out of their bodies menacing spikes, and throw up on the top of their heads sinister headdresses, overnight. Such changes in their personal appearance, conceived to work on the psychology of their adversaries, is possibly not a very profound or useful invention, but it is surely a considerable feat. Any art worth the name is, at the least, a feat of this description. (*CD* 65–6)

This beetle analogy appears to be a hybrid of examples taken from Jean-Henri Fabre's popular entomological study *The Wonders of Instinct* (1918), which describes the Burying Beetle, whose abdomen is 'armed with four tiny spikes', and the Capricorn, a beetle whose 'extravagant head-dress' emerges 'from the darkness through this opening when the summer heats arrive'. Lewis may also have been thinking of Fabre's account of the Empusa, a type of mantis furnished with 'an extravagant head-dress that juts forward', as well as a 'monstrous pointed cap . . . more splendiferous' than that worn by any 'wise man of the East'.[6]

The 'feat' that Lewis is describing is a form of protective adaptation in which the insect undergoes physical changes that enable it to survive under hostile conditions. Adapting Fabre's observations to suit his own purposes, Lewis's emphasis is on the responsiveness of the beetle to an external threat, detailing its ability to 'throw up' its defences 'overnight', rapidly altering its 'personal appearance' by exuding unsettling new features. These striking modifications bear a marked resemblance to the author's aesthetic innovations. This chapter examines Lewis's 'record capacity' for transforming his body of work in response to perceived dangers, arguing that the many surface alterations that he made to his writing over the course of his career were inspired by the survival strategies of insects. What David Trotter refers to as Lewis's 'obstinate will-to-experiment' is driven, I will argue, by an excess of vigilance that seeks to protect itself from various perceived threats in its immediate surroundings.[7] Like Fabre's beetles, the author's methods are primarily visual and are designed to 'work on the psychology of . . . adversaries' by disrupting the gaze of the onlooker – the reader included.

In his essay 'Inferior Religions' (1917) Lewis cites Fabre as a key artistic influence, arguing that this 'superior being . . . knew of elegant grubs which he would prefer to the painter's nymphs'.[8] Lewis may have encountered Fabre's insect studies in *The English Review*, which published three of his early short stories, including 'Some Innkeepers and Bestre' (1909). Initially intended to feature in the journal for a 'few months' in 1912, the popularity of Fabre's articles on wasps, maggots and beetles was such that they continued to appear at regular intervals until 1922.[9] As well as holding every issue of *The English Review*, Lewis's surviving library contains the 1914 illustrated edition of J. Arthur Thomson's *Outlines of Zoology* (1895), much of which is devoted to invertebrates, and the 1915 edition of John Lubbock's study of social Hymenoptera, *Ants, Bees, and Wasps* (1891).[10] In his inter-war fiction, Lewis makes reference to Maurice Maeterlinck's *The Life of the Bee* (1901), as well as to myrmecologist Auguste Forel's *The Senses of Insects* (1908), suggesting that his entomological interest extended well beyond the work of Fabre.[11]

So far, readers have argued that Lewis's fascination with insect life informs the defensive architecture of his writing, reinforcing his own claims about his 'externalist' methods (*MWA* 121). But while much has been said about the recalcitrance of Lewis's work – the product of what Cyril Connolly describes, in terms that recall Palissy's murex shell, as the author's 'prickly and torrid sensibility' – little attention has been paid to the sensitivity of his writing to its immediate surroundings.[12] This chapter proposes that, rather than attempting simply to inure his work against a threatening outer world, Lewis's knowledge of the survival strategies of invertebrate life forms inspired him to continually adapt his writing in response to various threats from without, whether real or imagined. Throughout his post-war writing, Lewis is engaged in a struggle to protect his art from destructive forces, and like the shell of the beetle the outer surface of his writing is continually shifting, transforming and revealing concealed parts of itself in a movement that is as disturbing as it is beguiling.

A Pleasure to Be Shelled

'In writing, the only thing that interests me is *the shell*', stated Lewis in a 1931 interview, explaining the 'method preferred by me may be described as classical; it is objective, and rather scientific than sentimental'.[13] To read Lewis's body of work is to be bombarded with curious biological terms such as ossature, shield, pelt, husk, armour, carapace and 'ectodermic case', many of which describe the 'polished and resistant surfaces' of the insect body.[14] Lewis's 'external approach' to representation has been well documented (*MWA* 120): Hal Foster identifies the transformation of the human figure into a 'protective shield' as early as Lewis's paintings of the 1910s; Jessica Burstein examines the exoskeletal psychology at work in Lewis's 1932 novel *Snooty Baronet*; while Peter Nicholls argues that the author's satire involves the '"petrification" of the human into the thing-like'.[15]

Lewis's aesthetics of what he calls 'the *outside* of people . . . their shells or pelts' has often been read in relation to a passage in his first novel *Tarr* (1918), which was serialised in *The Egoist* while he was serving on the front line (*MWA* 97; original emphasis). During a conversation with the Russian socialite Anastasya Vasek, young art student Frederick Tarr outlines his theory of aesthetics:

> *Deadness* is the first condition of art. A hippopotamus' armoured hide, a turtle's shell, feathers or machinery on the one hand; *that* opposed to naked pulsing and moving of the soft inside of life. (*T* 299; original emphasis)

Tarr's remarks have often been understood as an introduction to Lewis's 'theory of the External, the Classical, approach in Art' (*MWA* 115) – a stance that was influenced by the philosophy of T. E. Hulme and which subsequently hardened in opposition to the writing of modernist contemporaries such as Virginia Woolf, D. H. Lawrence and James Joyce. Lewis was present at Kensington Town Hall in 1914 when Hulme presented his vision of a 'durable and permanent' geometrical art designed 'to be a refuge from the flux and impermanence of outside nature' and would later recall their shared preference for integumentary forms: 'We preferred a helmet to a head of hair. A scarab to a jelly-fish' (*BB* 110).[16]

The problem is that critics have tended to present Lewis's vision of an externalist art as a relatively fixed and stable concept, overlooking the ways in which Lewis modifies and complicates Tarr's conception of the armoured artwork over time, as well as the instability of the apparatus itself. As we saw in the introduction, Lewis presents a somewhat contradictory account of the shell earlier on in the same text:

> The whole of English training ... is a system of *deadening feeling*, a prescription for Stoicism ... It saves us from gush in many cases; it is an excellent armour in times of crisis or misfortune ... It would be better *to face* our imagination and our nerves without this soporific. Once this armature breaks down, the man underneath is found in many cases to have become softened by it. He is subject to shock, *over*-sensitiveness. (*T* 42; original emphasis)

How is the reader to reconcile Tarr's recommendation that mankind 'discard this husk and armour' with his subsequent championing of the 'armoured hide' (*T* 42)? This tense opposition between a conception of the outer shell as enhancing and one that is debilitating – between the desire to uphold this psychic 'armour' and the struggle not to be broken down by it – is particularly apparent in the author's war fiction. And yet, as I will argue, there is evidence to suggest that this opposition may serve a strategic purpose in Lewis's writing.

Written while the author was training as an artillery officer at Horsham, 'Cantleman's Spring-Mate' (1917) centres on a newly enlisted soldier who distracts himself from the prospect of 'death or mutilation' by wandering through the countryside near his training camp, observing 'birds with their little gnarled feet, and beaks made for fishing worms out of the mould' (*CSM* 8, 9). One definition of the verb 'to observe' is to 'maintain intact' and this meaning allows us to consider whether, by taking on the role of naturalist and thus positioning himself outside of the natural order, Cantleman may be attempting to shield himself from the threat of impending destruction.[17] In another of Lewis's war stories, 'The French Poodle' (1916), the traumatised soldier Rob Cairn derives comfort from reading 'chiefly Natural History. The lives of animals seemed to have a great fascination for his faithful, stolid thoughts.'[18] Cantleman's desire to adopt the role of detached observer is, however, complicated by his desire to 'remain amongst his fellow insects and beasts'. Lewis establishes a confusion of perspective in Cantleman's sense of himself as both a lofty naturalist and a lowly insect: despite his efforts to maintain a position of aesthetic detachment,

Cantleman soon finds himself part of 'Nature' itself, presented by Lewis as a hostile and devouring force working in cahoots with 'War' (*CSM* 9, 13).

From the outset of the text, Lewis establishes an atmosphere of excessive natural fecundity that cannot help but summon images of the ruptured bodies of nearby soldiers torn apart by exploding shells: 'the heat of a heavy premature Summer was . . . causing everything innocently to burst its skin, bask abjectly and profoundly' (*CSM* 8). Walking through the fields outside of his training camp, Cantleman experiences a frightening vision of the horrors that await him on the battlefield:

> The miraculous camouflage of Nature did not deceive this observer. He saw everywhere the gun-pits and the 'nests of death'. Each puff of green leaves he knew was in some way as harmful as the burst of a shell. (*CSM* 12–13)

Home front and front line, war and nature, self and surroundings: these distinctions appear to have 'burst' their outer shells amid this pressure-cooker atmosphere. By equating the light 'puff' of leaves with the explosive force of artillery, Lewis indicates that Cantleman's primitive survival instincts have gone into overdrive; no longer able to maintain his position as a detached observer, he appears overwhelmed by his environment, registering even the slightest movement as a deadly threat.

Perhaps most intriguing about this text is the way that it signposts the breakdown of its protagonist's psychic defences even as he struggles to reinforce them. Throughout the narrative, Cantleman's struggle to attain a sense of mastery over his surroundings is continually thwarted by the omniscient narrator's efforts to expose his powerlessness. This is particularly apparent when Cantleman seduces (or rapes) a local girl called Stella:

> The nightingale sang ceaselessly in the small wood at the top of the field where they lay. He grinned up towards it, and once more turned to the devouring of his mate . . . Cantleman was proud that he could remain deliberate and aloof, and gaze bravely, like a minute insect, up at the immense and melancholy night, with all its mad nightingales . . . and misty useless watchmen. (*CSM* 13–14)

There is a curious combination of defiance and vulnerability in Cantleman's sense of himself as a 'deliberate and aloof . . . insect' positioned beneath the predatory eye of 'mad nightingales'. Lewis's decision to align his protagonist with something so 'minute' and clearly vulnerable to the marauding instincts that he observes in the skylark gorging on earthworms earlier seems curious. In his reading of this passage, Paul Sheehan notes that Lewis appears to have set 'an aporetic trap for his hapless protagonist, whose distance or aloofness from his atavistic ancestry is underwritten by a simile eliminating that distance'.[19] Although there is undoubtedly something defiant in Cantleman's insectile gaze – a sense of boldness achieved through the contrast between so small a creature and so 'immense' a threat – it is difficult to deny his unwitting embrace of victimhood.

Earlier on in the text, perceiving himself to have been 'forced back ... among the madness of natural things', Cantleman decides that he 'must repudiate the human entirely' (*CSM* 12, 10). The ease with which he purports to discard his humanity, however, as though it too is a mere skin to be shed, suggests the opposite of reinforcement: rather than shoring up his shell against his ruin, Lewis's protagonist is gradually stripped of his defences. This dynamic becomes particularly evident towards the end of the text, when the narrator reveals that Cantleman has unwittingly impregnated Stella, thus perpetuating the very species that he seeks to 'repudiate'. Similarly, when Cantleman beats out a German's brains 'with the same impartial malignity that he had displayed in the English night with his Spring-mate', the narrator coldly rejects his belief that he was 'in some way outwitting Nature', concluding: 'evidently, the death of a Hun was to the advantage of the animal world' (*CSM* 14). The narrator's emphasis on the German soldier's gruesome fate as a source of nourishment for the animal world – food for the worms – seems particularly cruel considering that this would also have been Cantleman's and indeed Lewis's potential fate during this time.

So why might Lewis be allowing his protagonist's vulnerabilities to burst out in this way? A clue, I think, can be found in the author's war-memoir *Blasting and Bombardiering* (1937). Recalling how, after moving to a new concrete shelter, he had been subjected to relentless artillery fire, Lewis remarks with cheery stoicism: 'This [dugout] was a shell that would take some cracking. I was in it when it was hit. It was as firm as a rock. It was a pleasure to be shelled in it' (*BB* 148). These remarks establish an important tension in Lewis's shell, which functions both as a form of self-exposure that enables him to confront the source of destruction ('a pleasure to be shelled') and as a veneer of insouciance ('a shell that would take some cracking') designed to mask an underlying sense of frailty. The bravado of these remarks hints at Lewis's investment in the notion that in order to protect oneself it is necessary to hide behind the defences of language, here figured as a kind of artful punning. Not only does the above statement strike the reader with a sudden burst of dark humour, but it also seems designed to divert our attention from the vulnerable body within the 'shell'.

Here we might consider the double meaning of the verb 'to shell', which means both 'to enclose in, or as in, a shell; to encase' and 'to remove the shell, husk'.[20] Vladimir Nabokov draws the reader's attention to a similar duality in his novel *Ada or Ardor: A Family Chronicle* (1969) when the eponymous heroine observes that 'the most extraordinary word in the English language was "husked", because it stood for opposite things, covered and uncovered, tightly husked but easily husked'.[21] Like the word 'cleave', which means both to sever and to bring together, the shell is a contronym, or Janus-word, that houses opposing tendencies. Lewis's use of the term to describe both the space of safety and the threat to that safety highlights an important aspect of his oppositional thought processes. By signalling the homology of organic and artillery shells, the author reworks a threat to life into a form of self-protection. It is a strategy that recalls the phenomenon of shell-art in the trenches, where soldiers transformed discarded shell casings into decorative ornaments such as vases, lamps and ashtrays, engaging creatively with destructive material.[22] For Lewis, the 'pleasure' of the shell – as noun and verb, defence and weapon – inheres in its semantic volatility; in his war writing in particular it appears to function both as a means of self-protection and as a form of explosive energy.

Paul Edwards has written of the ways in which Lewis's war stories and paintings 'register trauma' and make 'use of shell shock'.[23] By remaining attuned to what its protagonist cannot feel, 'Cantleman's Spring-Mate' registers the explosive impact of the conflict on the individual psyche while also protecting itself behind a guise of ironic detachment. Just as Freud, after examining sufferers of shell shock, was able to develop a new understanding of the stimulus shield as comprising both a 'protective' and a 'receptive' outer layer, Lewis's wartime experiences appear to have impressed upon him a new understanding of the modern subject's psychic 'armature' – an understanding that feeds into his experimental practices.[24] Significantly, moreover, Lewis's modifications to the shell of his writing during the war resemble another form of 'miraculous camouflage' that was being experimented with by the British Army. Shortly before 'Cantleman's Spring-Mate' was published, it was decided that naval vessels should be painted 'not for low visibility, but in such a way as to break up [their] form and thus confuse a submarine officer as to the course on which [they were] heading'.[25] In a reflection of military strategy, Lewis's war writing suggests that to break up the surface of the text is also to maintain it intact.

Dazzle Defences

In April 1917, following the unprecedented success of German submarines (or U-boats) in torpedoing British ships, the artist Norman Wilkinson devised a way of reducing the vulnerability of marine vessels to enemy fire. Wilkinson was placed in charge of a naval camouflage unit based at the Royal Academy of Arts, and along with a number of fellow artists – including Lewis's friend and Vorticist contemporary Edward Wadsworth – he developed a series of geometric dazzle camouflage schemes for over two thousand war vehicles, at sea and on land. Named for its ability to 'overpower, confuse, or dim' the vision, especially 'with excess of brightness', dazzle camouflage aimed to impair the onlooker's ability to establish where a ship ended and its surroundings began.[26] As Eric. White notes, dazzle patterns made potential targets '*more* visible' to the extent that they exceeded the observer's ability to apprehend them.[27] Rather than attempting to conceal the object from view, dazzle artists worked to render the target conspicuous in order for it not to be fully seen.

Complementing the role played by avant-garde artists, two of the main innovators of dazzle camouflage were the American naturalist Abbott H. Thayer and the Scottish zoologist John Graham Kerr. In a 1914 letter to Winston Churchill, Kerr observed that certain animals are able to evade detection with the aid of 'strongly contrasting shades' and 'violently contrasting pigments' that break up the surface of their bodies.[28] Although Kerr lists the zebra as a prime example, his knowledge of this phenomenon derived from his reading of Thayer's *Concealing Colouration in the Animal Kingdom* (1909), which reveals that the most numerous and varied examples of 'dazzling colouration' occur in the insect world.[29]

Not only would Lewis have been exposed to the techniques of dazzle camouflage through his connection to Wadsworth, but as one of the founders of Vorticism, he was also a key source of inspiration behind its effects. In addition to the chaotic geometries of early paintings such as 'Composition' (1913), Lewis's attempts to confound the gaze of the onlooker are evident in *Tarr*, which he later described as an attempt at Vorticist prose.[30] Throughout the text, the volatile German painter Otto Kreisler, whose failed efforts to woo Tarr's fiancée Bertha Lunken culminate in her rape, frequently attempts to overcome his feelings of social insecurity by adopting a strategy of conspicuousness. Arriving uninvited at the prestigious Bonnington Club dance wearing inappropriately

Figure 1.3 HMS *Underwing* with dazzle camouflage pattern, c.1918

Figure 1.4 Tiger moth (*Arctia caja*)

scruffy attire, Kreisler does the opposite of attempting to blend in to his surroundings to evade detection. Joining the assembled guests on the dance floor who are 'careering, like the spoon stirring in a saucepan . . . in sluggish currents', Kreisler moves against the tide, propelling himself across the room in a jagged motion like 'a stone falling through a pond' (*T* 152, 156). By ensuring that he is ejected from the party for bad behaviour, Kreisler diverts his audience's attention away from the more embarrassing cause of his visibility – his impoverished appearance and lack of social status.

In his cultural history of dazzle camouflage, Peter Forbes discerns little connection between 'the disruptive patterns urged by [biologists] and the parallel disruption of the image' practised by Cubist and Vorticist painters beyond their convergence as a military strategy during the two world wars.[31] During the inter-war period, however, Lewis continues to deploy aesthetic strategies inspired by the 'disruptive patterns' of invertebrates, utilising various forms of insect mimicry. In April 1921, Lewis exhibited his paintings of 'Tyros and Portraits' at the Leicester Galleries in London. The exhibition consisted of a series of portraits of masked, grinning figures, including what Richard Humphreys refers to as the 'insect-like' 'Praxitella'.[32] It also featured a formidable self-portrait entitled 'Mr Wyndham Lewis as a Tyro', in which the artist's features are concealed beneath a chitinous facial armour (Figure 1.5). Lewis's 'Tyros and Portraits' coincided with the birth of his new literary magazine *The Tyro: A Review of the Arts of Painting Sculpture and Design* (1921–2), in which he explains that the 'sunny commotion in the face' of the tyro is designed 'to obtain some advantage over you'.[33] As well as recalling Fabre's morphing beetle shell 'designed to work on the psychology of adversaries', the 'sunny commotion' in the face of the tyro appears designed to dazzle and disorient the onlooker.

David Peters Corbett argues that the body of the tyro 'is hard, a carapace, a weapon itself which will refuse and frustrate the threat of destruction weighing upon it'.[34] Corbett rightly identifies Lewis's weaponising of the surface of the artwork after the war, but rather than simply functioning as a protective shield against the deleterious effects of the outer world, what is disarming about Lewis's 'carapace' is its unsettling modifications, especially the 'menacing spikes' that jut out from his chin and hat. In the aftermath of war, Lewis's writing also becomes increasingly invested in the notion that the survival of the artwork relies on the breakdown of its defensive carapace in order to facilitate unsettling acts of protrusion and eruption – shell bursts. This phenomenon can be observed in his short story 'Bestre' (1922), which was published in the second issue of *The Tyro*. It tells the tale of a hostile innkeeper, who, 'regard[ing] the material world as so many ambushes for his body', seeks to defend himself by way of attack. Waging war against long-standing neighbours and passing tourists alike, Bestre initiates a series of staring contests so hostile that they are said to resemble 'phases of a combat or courtship in the insect-world' (*B* 59–60).

The text is framed from the perspective of a passing traveller, Ker-Orr, who is struck by Bestre's extraordinary ability to utilise his gaze as a weapon: 'What he selected as an arm in his duels, then, was the Eye.' Lewis's somewhat disorientating pun on the word 'arm' to refer to Bestre's 'eye' is suggestive of the innkeeper's inversion of the function of an organ that takes in the world to one that strikes out at it. The additional connotation of 'arm' to mean weapon is also consistent with Bestre's efforts to convert his passive alertness into a form of active combat. Ker-Orr observes how: 'The eyes fix on the enemy, on his weakest spot, and do their work. He has the anatomical instinct of the hymenopter for his prey's most morbid spot' (B 60). Lewis is alluding to Fabre's account of the hairy sand wasp, an insect capable of paralysing its caterpillar prey in exactly the right spot with its sting in order to lay eggs in its body that may then feed on the living host. Like the helpless caterpillar, Fabre finds himself paralysed by the sand wasp's ability to perform its terrifying art 'without ever being taught', confessing, in terms which imply the poison has begun to take effect, that he is 'itching to explain what might well be incapable of explanation'.[35]

Fabre's account of the arresting effect of the wasp hints at an unsettling of the distinction between observer and observed, in which the entomologist suddenly finds himself identifying with the wasp's helpless prey. This reversal of roles is also suggested by the way that, despite initially apprehending Bestre 'as an entomologist would take a Distoma or a Narbonne Lycosa to study', Ker-Orr's perspective begins to break down:

> It was almost as though Fabre could have established himself within the masonries of the bee, and lived on its honey, while investigating for the human species: or stretched himself on a bed of raphia and pebbles at the bottom of the Lycosa's pit, and lived on flies and locusts. (B 56)

Despite attempting to establish a clear distinction between himself and Bestre, Ker-Orr soon finds himself drawn into 'the silken zone of his hostilities', stretching out amid his spidery lair in an apparent gesture of submission. Unable to sustain a position of aesthetic detachment, Ker-Orr attempts to reinforce his fragile position by blending, insect-like, into his environment. The breakdown of Ker-Orr's entomological gaze extends to the text as a whole: over the course of the narrative it becomes increasingly difficult to fix an image of Bestre – his presence is unmistakeable and yet curiously protean; he is both 'corpulent and ox-like' and 'nimble as a flea' (B 56). In his refusal to take on a coherent outline, Bestre could be said to exhibit a kind of dazzle camouflage, but here the objective seems to be to overpower rather than merely to confuse the onlooker.

In order to make sense of the more combative stance adopted by Lewis in 'Bestre', it is necessary to distinguish between the different kinds of mimicry adopted by insects. Like Lewis, the Surrealist writer Roger Caillois was also influenced by the discoveries of entomologists such as Fabre, which prompted him to investigate how the phenomenon of adaptive morphology in the insect world might be brought to bear on human psychology. In 'Mimicry and Legendary Psychanesthesia' (1935), Caillois writes of the butterfly that resembles the bush it most often frequents, the stick insect that simulates a twig and the spider crab that covers its shell with 'the seaweed and polyps of the milieu' in which it lives. These surface modifications may be understood as a straightforward mode of 'defensive mimicry' that enables the organism to blend into its surroundings and evade detection. Significantly, however, Caillois goes on to describe a phenomenon known as 'offensive mimicry', detailing a number of examples of insects that appear to mimic their predators. He describes the hawk moth caterpillar whose retracted rear end resembles the head of a snake, the Caligo butterfly that mimics the eyes, beak and plumage of an owl, as well as the adult hawk moth that suddenly reveals two enormous "eyes" on its hind wings, 'giving the aggressor a sudden fright' by imitating 'a huge bird of prey'.[36]

Like dazzle camouflage, offensive mimicry is a form of disguise that hinges on extreme visibility, and it is possible to discern a similar strategy at work in 'Bestre'. In particular, the unsettling effect produced by the hawk moth's imitation '"eyes"' (Caillois places them in inverted commas) bears a striking resemblance to the function of Bestre's eye as weapon: 'he seems teaching you by his staring grimace the amazement you should feel; and his grimace gathers force and . . . bursts upon you, while your gaping face conforms more and more to Bestre's prefiguring mask' (*B* 63).[37] Rather than functioning as an organ of vision, Bestre's eye is capable of arresting and even temporarily blinding the onlooker, thus inverting the power dynamics that inhere in the act of observation. Just as the Caligo butterfly's eyespots are seen to mimic those of predators, Bestre's gaze seems capable of inducing mimicry in the onlooker as it 'bursts' upon them, transforming their facial features with something akin to the force of a shell blast. Lewis's use of second-person pronouns – 'you', 'your' – implicates the reader in Bestre's threatening gaze, inscribing his eyes onto the surface of the text in an effort not to repel the readerly gaze but to seize control over it.

Like a camouflaged insect, Bestre is capable of vanishing suddenly, only to reappear just as abruptly. At one point, Ker-Orr observes that 'Bestre is *discovered* somewhere, behind a blind, in a doorway, beside a rock, when least expected' (*B* 60; original emphasis). Bestre's sudden emergence from the background 'when least expected' hinges on the transformation of defensive mimicry (dissimulation) into that of offensive mimicry (terrification). These shock-tactics seem designed to catch the onlooker out, undermining his or her powers of observation. This strategy first becomes apparent during Ker-Orr's first encounter with Bestre, in which the reader is plunged into the midst of a 'hectic assault':

> As I bent over my work, an odiously grinning face peered in at my window. The impression of an intrusion was so strong, that I did not even realise at first that it was I who was the intruder. That the window was not *my* window, and that the face was not peering in but *out*: that, in fact, it was I myself who was guilty of peering into somebody else's window: this was hidden from me in the first moment of consciousness about the odious brown person of Bestre. (B 53; original emphasis)

Bestre is at this point lying in wait for someone else, and this moment of parallel misrecognition adds to the general sense of disorientation. The experience of reading this passage may be likened to that of peering into the window in which the glass has been taken away; stylistically an 'impression of intrusion' is achieved by the sudden emergence of the 'person of Bestre' at the end of the sentence. The effect of this syntactical inversion causes the subject to burst out threateningly from the page, with the text suggesting that the forceful nature of Bestre's gaze is capable of destabilising the surrounding environment, exploding the distinction between inside and outside, subject and object, self and surroundings.

Further on in the text there is an intriguing development in Bestre's display tactics. Shortly before meeting the innkeeper, Ker-Orr encounters 'an athletic Frenchwoman', Madame Riviere, who has recently become his main adversary:

> The crocket-like floral postiches on the ridges of her head-gear looked crisped down in a threatening way: her nodular pink veil was an apoplectic gristle round her stormy brow: steam came out of her lips upon the harsh white atmosphere. Her eyes were dark, and the contiguous colour of her cheeks of a redness quasi-venetian, with something like the feminine colouring of battle. This was surely a feline battle-mask, then; but in such a pacific and slumbrous spot I thought it an anomalous ornament. (B 53)

The Frenchwoman's 'nodular pink veil' recalls the text's description moments earlier of Ker-Orr's 'composite shell' formed of 'stark calcinous segments' (B 53). Madame Riviere bears more than a passing resemblance to Fabre's armoured Coleoptera, with her rigid 'head-gear' and 'feline battle-mask' recalling Lewis's account in *The Caliph's Design* of the beetles' 'sinister head-dresses' and 'hideously carved and detestable masks', designed to 'work on the psychology of their adversaries'. Indeed, what is particularly unsettling about this 'feline battle-mask' is the way that its sculpturesque rigidity ('crocket-like', 'crisped'), belies its fluid volatility: far from being a fixed grimace, the Frenchwoman's brow is 'stormy', her gristle is 'apoplectic' and hot vapour bursts forth from her lips.

Perhaps is most striking about Madame Riviere's exoskeletal defences is the way that Bestre attempts to break them down. Initially, he responds with a gaze so hostile that it is likened to the discharge of toxic fluids: 'Excrement as well as sputum would be shot from this luminous hole.' When that doesn't work, Ker-Orr describes how Bestre 'struck the death-blow with another engine than his eye', flashing his private parts at Madame Riviere in order to shock her into submission (B 59, 62). As David Trotter notes, it is 'in accordance with a specific investment in hypermasculinity that Bestre should achieve final victory . . . by exposing himself'.[38] This is an important observation, for it suggests that exposure is the ultimate form of defence in this tense battle of wills. Trotter's reading also invites us to contemplate the possibility that Bestre's strategy of terrification may in fact be the imitation of terror felt, with him projecting onto Madame Riviere what she has already instilled in him. Confronted with this 'feline battle-mask', Lewis's protagonist strives to invert the dynamic often presented by Fabre in his observations of insect mating rituals, in which the female (including the aforementioned Lycosa) triumphs over the helpless male. By protruding his phallic weapon (his third eye), Bestre reminds his insectile assailant of her vulnerable status in the realm of gendered human relations. The innkeeper's strategic disclosure of the 'over-sensitive' organ beneath his 'armour' could therefore be read as a means of disrupting Madame Riviere's predatory stare – exposing himself in order to protect himself.

In an essay published alongside 'Bestre' in *The Tyro*, Lewis contemplates the limitations of the eye, reflecting: 'We are all, in a sense even, so thoroughly hidden from each other because we *see* each other.'[39] Seemingly, in eliciting the gaze of the onlooker, Bestre is inviting the onlooker not to see him, putting himself on display in order to disguise himself. His strategy recalls Freud's account of the sudden reversals undergone by the individual psyche in an attempt to preserve itself from harm. In 'Instincts and their Vicissitudes' (1915), Freud argues that the self-preservative instincts generated by the psyche in response to external stimuli are able to shift from active to passive positions. The essay, which informed the author's subsequent account of the protective barrier surrounding the psyche in *Beyond the Pleasure Principle* (1920), gives the example of the scopophilic instinct (taking pleasure in the exposed bodies of others), which is able to transform into a more passive state of exhibitionism (taking pleasure in exposing oneself). Such reversals, Freud notes, 'correspond to . . . attempts at defence', in which the threat of suddenly being discovered by the object of the voyeuristic gaze is negated by this act of self-exposure.[40] Freud's account of the vicissitudes of the instincts bears marked similarities to dazzle camouflage, in which the survival of the organism relies on its ability to confound the gaze of the onlooker. It also resonates with Bestre's strategy of 'provocation' (B 60), in which he allows himself to be '*discovered* somewhere' and hence dis-covered. By making himself the object of the gaze, Lewis appears to be suggesting, Bestre attains a degree of mastery over the conditions of his exposure.

In a dynamic that we saw previously in 'Cantleman's Spring-Mate', Bestre's physical act of self-exposure is reflected in the text's strategic baring of its protagonist's vulnerabilities. At one point, Ker-Orr reveals that Bestre's 'alertness, combativeness, and timidity are the result of . . . exilings and difficult adjustments to new surroundings' (B 57). The reader is suddenly confronted with a glimpse of Bestre's sensitive innards as Lewis reveals that the domineering landlord is little more than a timid outsider – an insecure immigrant. The text concludes with a final candid insight into the innkeeper's behaviour:

> I have noticed that the more cramped and meagre his action has been . . . [t]he more restrictions reality has put on him, the more unbridled is his gusto as historian of the deeds immediately afterwards. Then he had the common impulse to avenge the self that has been perishing under the famine and knout of a bad reality, by glorifying it and surfeiting it on its return to the imagination. (B 63)

Freud's account of the reversal of the instincts between active and passive positions can help to focalise Lewis's positioning of Bestre as both prey to the larger machinations of a 'bad reality', while also able to overcome this sense of disempowerment by taking on the more active role of storyteller. This strategic division of the self into both victim and victor, subject and author, appears indicative of Lewis's efforts from 'Cantleman's Spring-Mate' onwards to stage both the loss and the regaining of mastery over one's surroundings through the space of the text.

In an earlier version of the story, the narrator wonders: 'Has Bestre discovered the only type of action compatible with artistic creation?'[41] This is a telling question, because it indicates that Lewis's writing understands creativity to be a response to being under attack. From this we might venture that the author's body of work requires an external pressure in order to form itself, resembling an aesthetic outburst against the 'knout of a bad reality'. In 'Bestre', this strategy involves the disruption of stable narrative positions, with subject and object, observer and observed undergoing frequent and often disconcerting shifts. In his late 1920s writing, however, Lewis brings these disruptive dynamics to bear on his fellow modernists, exposing what he deemed to be their 'decidedly unrobust' aesthetic practices amid the 'impoverished, shell-shocked . . . and unsettled' atmosphere of the inter-war period (BB 260–1).

Mimicry as Modernist Menace

In his collection of literary criticism, *Men Without Art* (1934), Lewis details his impressions of the 'suffocating atmosphere' of the inter-war literary scene, reflecting:

> I have felt . . . very alien to all the standards that I saw being built up around me. I have defended myself as best I could against the influences of what I felt to be a tyrannical inverted orthodoxy in the making. (*MWA* 170)

After the war, Lewis soon became convinced that the formal experimentation of writers such as Pound and Eliot had grown to resemble an oppressively uniform entity – rather than challenging the status quo, their work had become indistinguishable from it. Perceiving this new 'orthodoxy' to pose a fundamental threat to artistic experimentation, Lewis launched an aggressive campaign against his fellow modernists. The primary vehicle of his attacks, *The Enemy: A Review of Art and Literature* (1927–9), cites Plutarch's assertion that in order to 'not be wounded or hurt' by wild beasts, our ancestors learned 'how to make use of them . . . arming themselves with their hides and skins'.[42] This statement marks the intensification of Lewis's strategy of offensive mimicry, with the author now utilising the methods of his contemporaries as a weapon against them.

In his critical writing from the time, Lewis highlights his opposition to a number of modernist writers, likening their 'Internalist' methods to 'the jelly-fish that floats in the centre of the subterranean stream of the "dark" Unconscious' (*MWA* 120). The author accuses James Joyce, Gertrude Stein and Virginia Woolf of participating in a time-cult influenced by the ideas of Henri Bergson which has resulted in them 'dragging the intellect with them down into their frantic maelstrom – "In the destructive element immerse"'. Yet in his fiction from this period – including his satirical novel *The Apes of God* (1930) and his fantasy novel *The Childermass* (1928) – Lewis begins to mimic these aesthetic tendencies, thus emulating the 'disintegrating metaphysic' that his non-fiction seeks to condemn (*MWA* 149). One way of understanding this tension is as part of Lewis's larger strategy of disorientation, which now involves a series of bewildering shifts between aggressive opposition and radical similitude. Indeed, the author may well have deemed mimicry to be the ultimate threat to modernism's tireless pursuit of novelty as well as its anti-mimetic approach to representation.[43] 'We believe that it is harder to make than to copy', asserted Pound on behalf of the Vorticists in 1915.[44] By embodying in order to satirise the work of his rivals, Lewis's writing exposes such aesthetic aspirations to be merely more of the same.

In other words, if modernism's 'make it new' had begun to seem derivative to Lewis, then in a reversal of this logic the author experiments with mimicry as a means of producing unalike from alike forms, achieving novelty through the act of copying. This is where the author's debt to entomology becomes particularly evident. In the insect world, the inventiveness of mimicry is everywhere apparent – from the owl-like eye-spots of the Caligo butterfly to the deceptive beauty of the orchid mantis, a deadly assassin that simulates a delicate flower. Disputing the Darwinian account of mimicry as a struggle for survival, Fabre points to the sheer variety of adaptive behaviours in the insect world, as well as their varying rates of success.[45] Vladimir Nabokov, who in addition to his literary reputation was also a respected lepidopterist, describes insect mimicry as a form of creative expression, reasoning that Darwin's theory of natural selection fails to explain the presence of a 'protective device carried to the point of mimetic subtlety, exuberance and luxury'.[46] For Fabre and Nabokov, the surplus of activity involved in insect mimicry causes it to resemble an act of making rather than mere copying.

The Childermass provides a key insight into the surface modifications that Lewis made to his body of work in the late 1920s in order to reflect, and to resist, the destructive forces that he identified in his cultural surroundings.[47] Functioning as an experimental hybrid of his fiction and non-fiction from this period, this highly exuberant text may be read as part-modernist satire, part-political tract.[48] The narrative centres on two dead First World War soldiers, James Pullman and his school fag Satterthwaite, who are attempting to navigate the shifting, illusory 'Time-flats' on their journey to the gates of the 'magnetic city'. Littered with 'exuviae', the biological term for exoskeletal remains, the shifting sands of the Time-flats are formed of the detritus of ruptured selves, with individuals reduced to calcified remnants of living beings. On their journey, Pullman (Pulley) and Satterthwaite (Satters) encounter a cast of 'peons', who resemble faceless 'halted human shells' (C 121, 5, 11, 22–3). The text is scattered with the husks of biological terms – such as 'anopheles', 'ephemerids', 'testudinate', 'funicles', 'epeira' – many of which can be traced back to Lewis's reading of the entomology of Fabre, Thomson and Lubbock (C 6, 47, 57, 310).

'The War bled the world white', Lewis reflected in 1937: 'It had to recover. While it was in that exhausted state a sort of weed-world sprang up and flourished' (*BB* 17). As well as resembling this overgrown hinterland, the 'Time-flats' bears a strong likeness to Lewis's description of the 'war-wilderness' of the front line, 'an arid and blistering vacuum' peopled with 'titanic casts of dying and shell-shocked actors' (*BB* 137–8). When Satters and Pulley find themselves in the midst of a sudden downpour, Pulley is reminded of how 'the storms in France ... used to wipe out the bombardment'. In this purgatorial climate, however, these periodical showers are formed of the bodies of dead insects, with the text explaining that occasionally, 'upon the long-winded blast the frittered corpse of a mosquito may be borne' (C 153, 6). By coldly punning on 'borne', Lewis replaces the prospect of aesthetic renewal with the drifting fragments of desiccated husks – both entomological and linguistic. In the absence of new life all that is left is a 'long-winded blast', with Lewis hinting that the explosive energy of the pre-war avant-garde has now been replaced by inert and protracted art forms.

Pulley and Satters struggle to adjust to this unpredictable environment. As they pass through a series of rapidly mutating landscapes, they frequently transform, undergoing various stages of insect-like metamorphosis. After being suddenly enveloped by 'drifting funicles' of spider's gossamer Pulley 'reduces himself to a shrunk and huddled shell' while Satters finds himself in 'animal chaos, heaving and melting' (C 57–9). Lewis appears to be revisiting his fascination with Fabre's reactive beetle shell, but rather than focusing on the responsiveness of characters to external dangers, he now presents cautionary instances of failed adaptation, in which the inter-war subject is capable of persisting only in a divided, near formless state. Reasons for this shift are not hard to find: *The Childermass* was written in the midst of a period of rapid social and economic upheaval, during which the General Strike of 1926 and the beginning of the Great Depression were contributing to the upsurge of mass ideologies. The experiences of the modern subject were also being rapidly reshaped by new technologies such as radio, telephony and cinema, with Marshall McLuhan positing that the text is concerned with the effects of 'accelerated media change . . . on psychic formation'.[49]

The author's representation of this shifting, teeming landscape with its 'heaving and melting' occupants functions as a scathing commentary on the modernist text's apparent complicity in this unstable atmosphere. As critics have noted, Satters and Pulley bear more than a passing resemblance to James Joyce and Gertrude Stein respectively, and when the pair pass through a time-vortex in the shifting Time-flats the plump Satters begins to 'stein-stammer', emulating the chiastic circularity of the author's prose rhythms. Encountering the Bergsonian figure of the Bailiff, the lean, bespectacled Pulley becomes a mindless disciple of his ideology, and later on in the text the Bailiff launches into a prolonged imitation of Joyce's *Work in Progress* (later *Finnegans Wake*) delivering a speech 'full of wormeaten wordies infant-bitten' (C 75, 215). Lewis's exaggerated mimicry of Joyce and Stein reduces their stylistic innovations to a series of regressive outbursts, with their 'wormeaten', 'infant-bitten' words (a Joycean compound of insectile and neonatal imagery) dissolving into pre-linguistic murmurs. In accordance with Satters and Pulley's unsuccessful adaptation to their surroundings, Lewis appears to be presenting the failed transformation of high modernist language into an effective mode of resistance against the pervasive influence of socio-political forces.

At one point, Pulley and Satters stumble across one of many 'optical traps' on their journey:

> There are intersections of the tunnel that are cliffs of sunlight . . . These solid luminous slices have the consistence of smoked glass: apparitions gradually take shape in their substance, hesitate or arrive with fixity, become delicately plastic, increase their size, burst out of the wall like an inky exploding chrysalid, scuttling past the two schoolboys. (C 48, 40)

In a reflection of the form of text as a whole, the exoskeletal outline of these 'solid . . . slices' soon gives way to amorphousness. Like an insect that has emerged too soon from its 'exploding chrysalid', the calcinous 'ridges' that characterise the opening lines of 'Bestre' are here rendered 'delicately plastic'. Yet as well as functioning as an image of the kind of 'jellyish diffuseness' that Lewis attributed to high modernist aesthetics, this passage may be read as a sign of the text's reaction against this state of formal fluidity. The catachresis of the phrase 'inky exploding chrysalid' evokes the defence mechanism of certain cephalopods, which release a dark pigment from their ink sacks in response to a perceived threat. *The Childermass*'s own oozing secretions of ink might therefore be read as an attempt to stave off the fluid textures of high modernist experimentation by pushing this dynamic to its extreme, with Lewis exaggerating the aesthetic tendencies of his contemporaries in order to expose their deficiencies, transforming their apparent lack into a form of aesthetic surfeit.[50]

Satters and Pulley are exhibiting signs of defensive mimicry, in which the subject passively blends into its surroundings, but the text as a whole seems to be displaying a form of offensive mimicry that enables it not only to endure this hostile terrain, but also to hit back against it. Responding to Roger Caillois's example in 'Mimicry and Legendary Psychanesthesia' of the caprella, a small crustacean that imitates a mottled surface, Jacques Lacan asserts that by mimicking its surroundings the caprella is not simply 'harmonizing with the background' but that this survival strategy is akin to 'camouflage practised in human warfare'.[51] Rather than changing itself to fit in with its surroundings, this vulnerable creature disguises itself for the purposes of ambush. Lewis's mimicry of high modernist aesthetics might be understood in a similar way: by taking on the qualities that he discerns in his literary contemporaries he inscribes himself into the scene only to then 'burst out of the wall'. Mimicry, as Homi K. Bhabha aptly puts it, is 'at once resemblance and menace'; not only does it thwart the predatory gaze of the onlooker, but it calls the appearance of things into question.[52] Having set this 'optical trap' in the text, Lewis may be attempting to foster a kind of disorientation of perspective in his readers, encouraging them to react adversely to this new literary 'orthodoxy' by bombarding them with its shifting, illusory textures.

Given the author's troubling statements about race elsewhere in his writing, the irony of citing postcolonial theory in relation to Lewis is not lost on this reader. And yet, by thinking about the ways in which Lewis's use of mimicry displays parallels with techniques deployed by the colonial subject, it may be possible to gain new insight into the author's strategy as a response to a power imbalance, in which imitation becomes the only available means of overcoming perceived victimhood. In other words, in order to make sense of Lewis's aggressive mimicry of his contemporaries, we must first recognise the threat that they posed to his artistic identity. At the same time, Lewis's lumping of his fellow writers into a single opposing force suggests that this threat also provided a means of stabilising the self. Or to put it another way, by making others homogeneous, Lewis renders his own literary output distinct. Nathalie Sarraute identifies a similar strategy in the work of modernist writers such as Marcel Proust, for whom new forms of narrative expression are only able to bubble up from beneath 'the dead surface' of everyday language. These eruptions, Sarraute argues, rely on the presence of an imagined sparring partner, who acts as a 'catalyser' or 'stimulant'. This oppositional force, she adds, functions as 'the obstacle that gives them cohesion, that keeps them from going soft'; it is 'the real danger, as well as the prey that brings out their alertness and their suppleness'.[53]

Sarraute's subtle distinction between softness and suppleness is crucial to my understanding of the way that Lewis's frequent surface modifications – the versatility of his outer shell – seem designed to stave off both the 'deadening of feeling' and the 'softening' that Tarr discerns in the shell-shocked subject. At the same time, the increasingly frenzied nature of Lewis's surface modifications is suggestive of what happens when this 'obstacle' refuses to remain constant – when the caprella's mottled background keeps changing. In his book-length essay *Time and Western Man* (1927), Lewis alerts his readers to one of the dangers of mimicry:

> Our only terra firma in a world is, after all, our boiling and shifting. That must cohere for us 'self' to be capable at all of behaving in any way but as mirror-images of alien realities, or as the most helpless and lowest organisms, as worms or as sponges. (*TWM* 132)

The defenceless anatomy of the worm corresponds to Lewis's suggestion in *The Childermass* that post-war art risked degenerating into a 'helpless' entity, unable to reinforce itself against its 'shell-shocked . . . and unsettled' surroundings (*BB* 261). By mimicking the formal methods of his contemporaries, Lewis sought to prevent his writing from morphing into a 'mirror-image' of these 'alien realities'. And yet in transforming the outer surface of his writing into the object of his criticism, Lewis also risked undermining the distinction between himself and his fellow writers on which his 'Enemy' persona had grown to depend.

Reading the Ondt Through the Gracehoper

Most of the writers targeted by Lewis refused to indulge his appetite for conflict. One of the author's more willing sparring partners, however, was James Joyce, who upon discovering that his work been subjected to a vicious assault by his former acquaintance, reacted by deploying Lewis's strategies back against him. In May 1926, Joyce wrote to his editor Harriet Shaw Weaver informing her that Lewis had requested a section from his *Work in Progress*, which later became *Finnegans Wake*, for the first issue of *The Enemy*.[54] When it appeared in January 1927 it was clear that Lewis had not only rejected the manuscript, but that he had also used sections of Joyce's material against him in a lengthy critique entitled 'An Analysis of the Mind of James Joyce'. In an allegation that recalls Tarr's account of the 'softening' of the shell-shocked subject, Lewis asserts that *Ulysses* 'imposes a softness, flabbiness and vagueness everywhere in its bergsonian fluidity'.[55] Joyce reacted by crafting a veiled counter-attack in the March 1928 edition of the literary magazine *transition*, disguising his response to Lewis behind the cautionary tale of two insects. 'The Ondt and the Gracehoper' seeks to expose the limitations of Lewis's oppositional mentality, collapsing the aesthetic distance that Lewis sought to establish between himself and his fellow modernist with a 'good smetterling of entymology'.[56]

As Fritz Senn notes, '*Finnegans Wake* teems with insects. Its hero is an earwig' and his family consist of 'three lice nittle clinkers, two twilling bugs and one midgit pucelle [flea]'.[57] Based on one of Aesop's fables, 'The Ondt and the Gracehoper' depicts a carefree grasshopper who spends the summer making merry rather than storing up food for the winter. When his supplies run low he calls on a diligent ant who rebukes him for his laziness and tells him to dance his cares away. In the figure of the 'Gracehoper', Joyce caricatures himself as a carefree figure 'hoppy, on akkant of his joyicity', who spends his time 'horing after hornests'. He is contrasted with the purposeful Lewisian 'Ondt', who spends his time 'making chilly spaces at hisphex affront of the icinglass of his windhome'.[58] If in *The Enemy* Lewis claims that Joyce 'confine[s] the reader in a circumscribed psychological space', the latter's evocation of the 'icinglass' – or isinglass, semi-transparent mica sheets used as windows – of his 'windhome' (window/Wyndham) reflects Lewis's allegation of solipsism back at him.[59]

Approaching the Ondt for help, Joyce reveals that the Gracehoper 'knew his entymology'.[60] The playful ambiguity of the possessive 'his', which could refer to either the Ondt or the Gracehoper, hints at a shared knowledge. Like Lewis, Joyce displayed more than a passing interest in entomology in his lifetime, with the author even offering to translate Maurice Maeterlinck's

La vie des abeilles [*The Life of the Bee*] (1900) for the apiculture magazine the *Irish Bee-Keeper*.⁶¹ 'Who would have guessed that Joyce knew as much about insects ... as he did about eighteenth century Irish history and late-nineteenth-century opera', remarked one critic.⁶² Incidentally, the first reader to produce an authoritative gloss of the *Wake*, Roland McHugh, was an entomologist by training, making him well suited to task of identifying the text's dense array of insect references.⁶³ Joyce's playful nod to texts by Lewis that feature a number of insect references – 'Besterfather' for 'Bestre' and 'the dresser's desdaign' for *The Caliph's Design* – suggests that this keen-eyed reader 'knew [Lewis's] entymology' too.⁶⁴ By glutting his reader on the language of invertebrate life, Joyce magnifies the 'smetterling' of insects that appear in Lewis's writing, in turn drawing attention to certain key formal and thematic parallels between himself and his rival.

That insects function as a shared currency between Joyce and Lewis is also suggested when the Gracehoper approaches the Ondt for help and finds him surrounded by the same characters who had earlier 'commence[d] insects' with him:

> Floh biting [the Ondt's] big thigh and Luse lugging his left leg and Bieni bussing him under his bonnet and Vespatilla blowing cosy fond tutties up the large of his smalls⁶⁵

The sharing of sexual partners between the Ondt and the Gracehoper harks back to Lewis and Joyce's first encounter in Paris in 1920, where the pair drank with prostitutes in local cafés.⁶⁶ There are also parasitic or even incestuous (insectuous) undertones to this transference of intimate relations with Floh (flea), Luse (louse), Bienie (bee) and Vespatilla (wasp), who are named after bugs that bite or sting.⁶⁷ These insect vectors serve as conduits between the work of the two writers, hopping back and forth between them and mingling their creative juices. In his 'Analysis' of Joyce, Lewis makes the bombastic claim that his writing 'was responsible for the manner' of parts of *Ulysses*, and readers have speculated that Lewis's epic novel of a single day, *The Apes of God* (which also contains a lengthy satire of Joyce), was his attempt at literary one-upmanship.⁶⁸ Joyce's fable may therefore be read as a stinging riposte to Lewis's allegation of plagiarism in which he presents artistic production as a process of productive parasitism.

'The Ondt and the Gracehoper' bears striking similarities to Jonathan Swift's fable of the bee and the spider in *The Battle of the Books* (1704), which mocks the dispute between two warring factions of literary production – the 'Ancients', represented by the spider, and the 'Moderns', represented by the bee. In an echo of the 'menacing spikes' of Lewis's armoured beetle, the spider, 'swollen up ... by the destruction of infinite numbers of flies' has walled himself into a citadel, a hostile fortification guarded with 'turnpikes . . . and ports to sally out upon all occasions of prey or defence'. The spider accuses the bee of plagiarism, arguing 'your livelihood is an universal plunder upon nature; a free-booter over fields and gardens'. The bee asks whether it is not nobler to roam 'by an universal range' or to fortify oneself with an 'overweening pride' that 'turns all into excrement and venom', leaving the spider, in typical Lewisian style, filled with rage and 'prepared to burst out'.[69]

Rather than simply mimicking Lewis in his depiction of the Ondt, Joyce is suggesting that their artistic output is in fact perversely similar, 'as entomate as intimate could pinchably be'.[70] Steven Connor suggests that this statement evokes 'the horror of the intimate, of the proximal, that which comes too close . . . which is represented by insects alone'.[71] Virginia Woolf records a similar sensation in her diary after reading Lewis's scathing criticism of her writing style in *Men Without Art*: 'Well this gnat [Lewis] has settled and stung, & I think (12.30) the pain is over . . . Only I can't write. When will my brain revive.'[71] Perhaps, like Woolf, Joyce is acknowledging with horror a sense of being invaded or contaminated by Lewis's satirical attack, before rising above his disgust and conceding gracefully (and hopefully, for he is a grace-hoper): 'I forgive you, dear Ondt.'[73]

Scott Klein argues that Lewis, who is also discernible in Shaun's futile attempt at 'Putting all Space in a Notshall' functions as a 'repressive authority' throughout the *Wake*.[74] Joyce's use of the 'inset' (insect) fable, a genre associated with closure, therefore appears designed to subdue and contain Lewis's enemy voice. Klein's remarks raise the possibility that, like Lewis, Joyce's literary output was also galvanised by the presence of an artistic sparring partner. Indeed, the latter's adoption of this allegorical medium is echoed by Lewis's use of allegory in *The Childermass* to contain and subdue Joyce – a parallel that highlights the way that their writing from this period simultaneously opposes and reflects one another. In this sense, Joyce's response to Lewis highlights one of the dangers of mimicry, which, like the reversal of the psyche's instinctual drives, risks having its critical gaze turned back onto itself, highlighting certain vulnerabilities that the mimic might not want to disclose.

Lewis would continue to insist that his aesthetics were fundamentally opposed to those of Joyce. In his late memoir, *Rude Assignment* (1950), the author recalls how the two men had once discussed the cathedral at Rouen together, with its 'heavily encumbered façade':

> I had said I did not like it . . . the dissolving of the solid shell – the spatial intemperance, the nervous multiplication of detail. Joyce listened and then remarked that he, on the contrary, liked this multiplication of detail, adding that he himself, as a matter of fact, in words, did something of that sort.[75]

The fundamental difference in outlook that Lewis is attempting to underline here begins to dissolve in light of his suggestion that the starting point of his and Joyce's writing is that of a 'solid shell'. As we have already seen, Lewis's account of the polished and resistant surface of his writing is not entirely borne out in his fiction, and this account of the 'nervous multiplication of detail' and 'spatial intemperance' of Joyce's writing could easily be describing the unstable, frequently mutating shell of his own body of work. Lewis's growing unease with the formal fluidity of high modernism compels him to mimic and, in a sense, contain its effects, but as is suggested by the subsequent shift in his writing towards the binding energies of fascism, this process of imitation may have begun to compromise the author's efforts to protect his writing against other, more substantial threats to artistic expression.

The 'spatial intemperance' of *The Childermass* in particular warrants further investigation. Caillois's 'Mimicry and Legendary Psychanesthesia' suggests that the protective colouration of insects may be likened to a psychological condition in which the sufferer experiences a disturbance in the 'relations between personality and space'. For humans and insects alike, Caillois posits, mimicry occurs when the individual succumbs to the temptation of space, a devouring force that undermines the distinction between inside and outside, self and surroundings. Recasting mimicry as a passive process in which the subject is gradually devoured by what it imitates, Caillois notes that while undergoing this mimetic assimilation: 'the body separates itself from thought, the individual breaks the boundary of his skin and occupies the other side of his senses. He tries to look at *himself from* any point whatever in space.'[76] There is something here akin to Freud's account of the switching of the psychic drives between active and passive positions but pushed to its extreme this process risks fragmenting the boundaries of the subject to the point of incoherence, rendering the organism unrecognisable even to itself.

In tacit recognition of this, *The Childermass* gradually moves away from the 'heaving and melting' landscape of the 'Time-flats', with the second half of the text hardening into something more sinister. During a series of debates between the Bailiff and various enemies, Lewis introduces a series of adversarial figures, Hyperides, Macrob and finally Alectryon, who forces the Bergsonian Bailiff – a figurehead of modernism's so-called 'tyrannical . . . orthodoxy-in-the-making' – to retreat back to his 'citadel of Unreality'. These figures could be said to reflect the various stages of Lewis's aesthetic modifications. The intersecting lines of Hyperides's face exhibit a kind of dazzle camouflage: 'His smashed . . . nose, with its vertical ridges of cartilage, deepset eyes, the centripetal ribs of wrinkles . . . remains stamped a mask of force'. Later, when Macrob's face 'chang[es] its colour from the pale anger of the mind to the royal scarlet of physical battle', we might recall Bestre's strategies of offensive mimicry. Finally, after Macrob is torn apart at the Bailiff's request, Lewis introduces a new and more unsettling self-image: a dark-haired figure dressed in the author's distinctive black cloak, Alectryon is descended from a 'militant epoch' and is composed of the 'severest lines' (C 400, 191, 290, 367).

Alectryon's black cloak is adorned with a swastika, a detail which may be interpreted as a commentary on the part of Lewis on the way that the absence of coherent social and cultural structures has led to the upsurge of authoritarian political movements, with the text staging the emergence of a fascist imago from the decaying chrysalis of the inter-war wasteland. At the same time, given the author's subsequent description of Adolph Hitler as a 'Man of Peace' in his swastika-adorned study *Hitler* (1931), it is important not to gloss over this troubling development. Alectryon, who in Greek mythology is transformed into a rooster that announces the arrival of the sun each morning, heralds a new and disturbing phase in the author's thinking.[77] Asserting that you 'must either explode against a thing or you must melt into it' (C 387), Alectryon's call to arms is suggestive of the efforts of *The Childermass* as a whole to 'burst out' of the molten landscape of modernist experimentation by adopting increasingly aggressive countertactics. It is also consistent with Lewis's efforts to stabilise a coherent sense of self in his writing against the 'boiling and shifting world' of his inter-war surroundings – a world that he felt his fellow writers had not only participated in, but also exacerbated.

As is illustrated by the symbol of Italian fascism – the *fasces*, a symbol of magisterial power in Ancient Rome consisting of an axe with a bundle of rods surrounding it – this movement initially strove to enact the binding of postwar society. The word fascism also recalls the anatomical term 'fascia', which denotes a sheath of fibrous tissue that envelops a muscle or organism.[78] In a parallel image, Freud's *Beyond the Pleasure Principle* asserts that the flooding of the individual's 'psychic apparatus' with an excess of stimuli can result in an attempt by the psyche to 'bind' itself by setting up an immense countercharge.[79] Although, as Laplanche and Pontalis point out, Freud's use of the verb 'binding' (*bindung*) evolves over the course of his career, here it suggests 'the idea of a whole in which a certain cohesion is maintained; a form demarcated by specific limits of *bound*aries'.[80] This defensive strategy can offer an insight into the form of *The Childermass*, which appears to dramatise the effects of psychic overstimulation in the first half of the text, before establishing a binding political countercharge in the second.

In addition to its mythological resonances, Alectryon's name recalls the biological term 'elytron' (from the Greek for sheath or cover), which denotes the hardened wing casings of beetles. The connection might seem tenuous, but in light of the preponderance of biological terminology in *The Childermass* it doesn't seem too much of a stretch to say that Lewis's language invites these kinds of associations, drawing the eye to various layers of entymological (to recall Joyce's portmanteau) wordplay. How far, though, are we to trust such resemblances? In architectural terms, a 'fascia' is also a front or covering and is linked etymological to the word façade, which denotes a false outward appearance. As well as calling into question the author's dazzling wordplay, this additional meaning invites us not to take Alectryon's political uniform entirely at face value. In a reading of *The Apes of God* (1930), Tyrus Miller provides textual evidence to support his claim that the young 'fascist' Bertram Starr-Smith 'is only *dressed* as a fascist'.[81] Miller's example tallies with Alectryon's account of the mask-like nature of his identity: 'The young male of the species today we are saying frequently resorts to protective colouring to escape attack' (C 390–1). As well as demonstrating the author's continued investment in strategies of mimicry inspired by the natural world, this statement also raises the question: just what is Lewis's writing capable of resorting to in its struggle for survival? The signs of fascism exhibited by *The Childermass* are perhaps most troubling in that they resemble little more than a superficial colouring. There is a casualness about Alectryon's fancy dress that appears symptomatic of Lewis's brash refusal, as David Dwan notes, to take the threat posed by Hitler seriously.[82]

'Contradict yourself, in order to live', Lewis wrote in a 1917 essay; 'You must remain broken up.'[83] The volatile shifts that occur in the author's fiction and non-fiction alike – between commitment and withdrawal, fierce engagement and callous indifference – appear central to the survivalism of his writing. By the late 1920s, however, having spent so much time perceiving the slightest shift in its cultural surroundings to be a deadly threat, it is as though when a true danger to artistic expression arises Lewis fails to see it for what it really is. The author's politics, like his aesthetics, are essentially reactive in nature, deriving much of their explosive energy from a sense of being under attack from all sides and needing to respond urgently and forcefully to these threats from without. At times, though, these methods can appear overreactive, as though the author's dazzle defences have begun to blind him to the more dubious aspects of his experimentation. Lewis's subsequent writing, however, demonstrates an important shift in his strategy of offensive mimicry. In *Snooty Baronet* (1932), Lewis turns his satirical gaze back upon himself, subjecting his own increasingly fragile 'Enemy' persona to intense scrutiny.

The Injured Party

Caught in the midst of the Great Depression and the rise of authoritarian regimes across Europe, the 1930s were a dark time for many writers. They were also particularly turbulent for Lewis, who referred to these years as 'a point in my career when many people were combining to defeat me'.[84] Joyce's playful mockery of Lewis the 'Ondt' was the least of these retaliations: after publishing his satirical *roman-à-clef The Apes of God*, Lewis was threatened with a series of libel suits that compounded his existing financial woes.[85] To make matters worse, following the publication of *Hitler*, Lewis was dropped by his publishers, Chatto & Windus, and perhaps most distressingly of all, rather than provoking explosive reactions from readers, the text was dismissed as 'slapdash and confused' – the primary focus of reviews being on Lewis's 'vague and insubstantial' argument rather than on his controversial ideas.[86]

During this period, Lewis turned to portraiture and commercial fiction to try and make a living, and in 1932, while composing a series of portraits entitled *Thirty Personalities and a Self-Portrait*, Lewis invited the writer Stella Benson to sit for him. While he was drawing her, she sketched out her own likeness of him:

> All the time he was drawing me he wore his hat and sat crouched over a swivelling easel; I had to keep my eyes fixed on a point above his head, but I could see his teeth gleaming . . . as he talked of all his cruel experiences of men and women.[87]

Benson's rather unforgiving portrayal of Lewis initially conforms to his earlier self-portrait of 1921, with the 'gleaming' teeth that protrude from beneath his hat harking back to the 'sunny commotion' in the face of the Tyro. The author's facial armour begins to break down, however, with Benson identifying

> something rather wistful in the look of this stout glowering snub-nosed man – sitting hunched on a too small camp stool, describing, without the slightest smile or irony, his position as the cynosure of all wickedness . . . forced into the atmosphere of battle by other people.[88]

Benson's account of this 'hunched' and 'wistful' figure reveals a side to the author that we don't often see. And yet, curiously, this frailty is reflected in the author's 'Self-Portrait' (1932) from the same series, in which he has removed his hat to reveal an exposed scalp beneath thinning hair. The author's stare is softened by a pair of moon-shaped spectacles, and the flesh on his face now appears – to recall Sarraute's term – supple, perhaps even bruised. The 'snub-nosed' Lewis no longer emits a dazzling smile; instead his lips protrude in a pout as he meets the gaze of the onlooker. Strangely, however, in its nakedness this updated image of the author appears more unsettling than the 'sinister mask' of its predecessor.

A similar set of facial features can be found in Lewis's satirical first-person narrative *Snooty Baronet* (1932). In the novel's opening lines, the eponymous

Figure 1.5 Wyndham Lewis, 'Mr Wyndham Lewis as a Tyro', c.1920–1

Figure 1.6 Wyndham Lewis, 'Self-Portrait', 1932

Baronet, Michael Kell-Imrie (nicknamed Snooty), describes his countenance as follows:

> a grim surface, rained upon and stared at by the sun at its haughtiest . . . the mouth, which did not slit it or crumple it, but burst out of it (like an escaped plush lining of rich pink), that spelled sensitiveness if anything, of an inferior order. (*SB* 15)

The surface of Snooty's face has disintegrated over time, but rather than 'crumpl[ing]' into a state of enervation its concealed contents 'burst out' (that verb again) with the force of a shell blast. The author's use of parenthesis in the line '(like an escaped plush lining of rich pink)' highlights the illicitness of these 'escaped' inner contents, as though the speaker had not meant to disclose this material. This carefully orchestrated outburst illustrates an intriguing development in Lewis's tendency to foreground his protagonists' weaknesses: Snooty's 'sensitiveness' is condemned for being of 'an inferior order', while also being conceived somewhat luxuriantly as a 'plush lining'. This discrepancy corresponds to the text as a whole, which continues to espouse an externalist aesthetic while also demonstrating a heightened sensitivity to its protagonist's inner workings.

Snooty's weather-beaten face is suffering from exposure, a term that denotes 'an unsheltered or undefended condition' as well as the act of 'unmasking or "showing up" of an error'. Exposure is also a form of publicity involving 'disclosure to view; public exhibition', and in *Snooty Baronet*, Lewis utilises the former definitions of the term as a means of achieving the latter.[89] Shortly before he began writing the text, Lewis acquired a new publisher, who had 'high hopes for it's [*sic*] popular success'.[90] The pressure that Lewis was under to produce a commercially successful novel can tell us much about the text's internal machinations: like his author, Snooty is asked by his agent, Captain Humphrey Cooper Carter (known as 'Humph'), to write a work of popular travel fiction. In real life, Lewis's publisher regarded him, presumably to the author's chagrin, 'as something in the nature of the writer to succeed D. H. Lawrence', whose travel writing had sold well.[91] From this point in the narrative, the fictional version of events departs from the reality: Humph has arranged for Snooty to be captured in Persia and held hostage as part of an elaborate publicity stunt. The operation goes wrong; Snooty is embroiled in a gunfight in the desert and shoots his agent dead, leaving his lover Val, a hack writer who has come along for the ride, to die of smallpox.

The glimmers of psychic exhibitionism seen in 'Bestre' are now a central feature of the text, with Lewis staging a series of involuntary outbursts designed to expose the chinks in his protagonist's already fragile armour. The text may be read as a form of publicity stunt, in which Lewis submits an extreme, unrepentant version of himself to intense scrutiny. It is a strategy that the author deploys in his non-fiction from this period: in a May 1932 article for the *Daily Herald*, 'What It Feels Like to Be an Enemy', Lewis describes his morning routine:

> After breakfast, for instance (a little raw meat, a couple of blood-oranges, a stick of ginger and a shot of Vodka – to make one see Red) I make a habit of springing up from the breakfast-table and going over in a rush to the telephone book. Then I open quite at chance, and ring up the first number . . . When I am put through, I violently abuse for five minutes the man, or woman . . . who answers the call.[92]

Read alongside his remarks to Stella Benson about being 'forced into the atmosphere of battle by other people', this passage demonstrates just how easily Lewis's writing slips between the role of victimiser and victim, predator and prey. Snooty too resembles a grotesque caricature of his author; not only is the writer and war veteran prone to irrational fits of rage, but he is also fascinated by insects. Appearing to parody his own preoccupation with entomology, Lewis directly references Fabre as the inspiration behind Snooty's writerly attempts to 'present (for the purposes of popular study) my human specimens', placing 'Man upon exactly the same footing as ape or insect' (*SB* 16, 64). The author now turns his entomological gaze back upon himself, with the knowing qualification of the phrase '*exactly* the same footing' appearing to condemn his previous patterning of insect behaviour onto human life as reductive, perhaps even dangerous. And yet as the text progresses, it becomes apparent that this process of self-exposure may be a new strategy of defence. In a further example of protective mimicry inspired by the insect world, Lewis's resemblance to Snooty enables him to simultaneously exaggerate and mask his by now maladapted public image.

J. Arthur Thomson's *Outlines of Zoology*, which Lewis owned and annotated, lists the 'life-saving shifts or adaptations' undergone by invertebrates as 'masking, protective coloration, surrender of parts, and "death feigning"'.[93] The final two behaviours are encompassed by the biological term self-mimesis, in which the organism ensures its survival by simulating death or injury. Self-mimesis may be contrasted with offensive mimicry in that the insect ensures its survival by cultivating a guise of defencelessness. Like an insect performing the feat known to biologists as autotomy (from the Greek *auto*, self and *tome*, severing), Snooty has surrendered his leg to the battlefield, revealing: 'I had been wounded, I had been unlimbed' (*SB* 63). This moment of passive surrender is replayed early on in the text after Snooty reluctantly seduces his 'waspish' lover Val over dinner and is quickly overpowered by his 'aggressive adversary'. Immediately after this mating ritual, Snooty describes how a 'one-legged man hopped out' of the bedroom 'and bending over the gilt-flowered slop-vessel, this man proceeded to be ill'. This stooped and naked figure, it soon transpires, 'was me' (*SB* 48–9).

This confession echoes the candid revelation at the beginning of the text, in which Snooty shyly acknowledges that the weather-beaten face described in the opening lines 'was mine'. In both instances this admission is delayed by a prolonged shift into the third person, causing it to 'burst out' in typical Lewisian fashion, 'like an escaped . . . lining'. There is thus an air of forcefulness to these expressions of vulnerability, which suggests that Lewis was experimenting with ways of transforming an admission of weakness into a means of self-empowerment. Snooty seems more than willing to expose himself to the reader, even undertaking what he describes as 'a careful study of myself'. He begins by outlining the 'surface shell' of his 'opaque and solid skull', presenting it as a disabling apparatus that prevents him from processing his surroundings. Ideas, he suggests, assail him from all sides 'like wasps . . . I can feel one strike me. Then I feel it get stuck.' The obstructive façade of this mental fortress is such that he understands 'only too well the meaning of the american [*sic*] "bonehead"' (*SB* 134). Jessica Burstein reads this passage as evidence of the author's externalist aesthetic in action, arguing that for Lewis 'any access to interiority is impossible . . . nothing quite penetrates the ossature that surrounds us'.[94] It is important to note, however, that the dense outer shell that Lewis has spent so much time espousing in his critical writing is here presented as the source of his protagonist's inner frailty. Despite continuing to promote his art of 'ossature' and 'shell' in *Men Without Art* (1934), Lewis appears to be offering a more nuanced account of the subject's 'armature' as a faulty apparatus that has left him, in the words of Tarr, susceptible to 'shock, over-sensitiveness'.

In a further twist, Lewis indicates that this disability might also be played to his advantage. In the above example Snooty is actively presenting himself to the reader as someone suffering a mental impairment and bearing in mind that the narrative is essentially a confession of his agent's murder, Lewis's signposting of this psychological defect, in addition to his physical injury, might therefore be interpreted as a strategy of self-vindication. Throughout the text, Lewis works to limit his protagonist's culpability by signposting tell-tale symptoms of shell shock, granting the reader an unusual level of access to his inner thoughts and feelings, and attributing his night terrors, disturbed thought processes and emotional numbness to 'The War' (*SB* 191). Snooty's mask of infirmity, however, gradually begins to slip. Shortly after lamenting his bone-headedness, he delivers the following outburst:

> If I could come out of this paper at you, you would find me a manner of man such as you do not expect I think, you would burst your eyes in your effort to fix me . . . that tense-as-well-as-dense expression, which when it lifts, leaves an empty face behind it – for me to grin and yawn with. (*SB* 135)

The effect of this unveiling recalls his earlier shifts from the subject to object position: 'The face was mine', 'the man . . . was me'. Snooty's direct address to the reader also recalls Lewis's unsettling use of second-person pronouns in 'Bestre': 'he seems teaching you by his staring grimace . . . while your gaping face conforms more and more to [his] prefiguring mask'. With its sinister 'grin', the arresting figure of the Tyro emerges from beneath this 'dense' carapace of infirmity. The Lewisian hawk moth, it seems, never really changes its eyespots.

Notwithstanding this apparent unmasking, it is possible to discern an additional layer of vulnerability in *Snooty Baronet* that is lacking in previous texts. While undertaking this 'careful study' of himself, Snooty is caught off guard by a sophisticated advertising stunt in the form of a hatter's automaton. Looking out from the window of a hat shop, the automaton, who bears an uncanny resemblance to his predatory agent Humph, mirrors Snooty's behaviour, causing him uncertainty as to who is mimicking who, and whether it is himself or the puppet that is the true object of the audience's attention. Unable to distinguish himself from the hatter's doll, Snooty experiences a peculiar sensation in which his inner landscape suddenly shifts:

> Do you know that sensation? When some idea with which you are perfectly familiar becomes charged all of a sudden with a far greater reality than before, or takes on other and more intensely coloured aspects? . . . I saw that I had to *compete* with these other creatures bursting up all over the imaginary landscape, and struggling against me to be *real* – like a passionate battle for necessary air, in a confined space. (*SB* 138; original emphasis)

Snooty's surroundings have begun to exhibit their own form of protective mimicry, taking on 'intensely coloured aspects'. In Lewis's description of 'creatures bursting up all over the imaginary landscape' we might recall the shifting modernist panorama of *The Childermass*, but no longer is the subject able to isolate a single force in his surroundings against which to define himself.

In contrast to Bestre's defiance when faced with 'the famine and knout of a bad reality', Snooty appears to be conceding defeat to the machinations of a 'far greater reality'. Throughout the text, Lewis's protagonist appears unable to shake off this sense of himself as falling prey to the devouring forces of commercialism and mainstream publicity. Snooty's inability to distinguish himself from the world of advertising might therefore be read as a veiled reflection on the part of Lewis on the threat of being subsumed within the landscape of capitalist production by mimicking it all too effectively. As though peeling away a previously concealed layer in its cultural surroundings, *Snooty Baronet* presents the struggle to ensure the survival of artistic expression in stark economic terms. In the inter-war period, Lewis increasingly found himself forced to '*compete*' (with the added emphasis conveying the force of his discomfort) within a crowded literary marketplace in which he was often drastically outnumbered.

By homing in on Lewis's reading of entomology during and after the war, it becomes clear that the insect body continued to shape his vision of artistic expression as unfailing in its responsiveness to external pressures. Part of this response, it seems, involved a process of acquiescence as well as resistance to its surroundings, with the author becoming cognisant of the fact that the survival of his writing relied on its growing 'suppleness' in the face of economic necessity. *Snooty Baronet* marks the end of the restless formal adaptations of Lewis's middle phase, functioning as a fault line between his aggressive pursuit of new forms of artistic expression and his capitulation to the growing demand for popular fiction. The author's struggle to reconcile his artistic vision with commercial forces in the early 1930s is suggested by his decision to produce a popular edition of *The Apes of God* featuring adverts of 'Steamship Lines, tooth-pastes, and lawn-mowers', which he felt would 'arouse a great deal of interest and result in a wide publicity'.[95] At the same time, what Miller characterises as Lewis's 'practical manipulation of publicity' may be seen as a continuation of his strategies of dazzle camouflage and offensive mimicry – a form of commercial subterfuge.[96]

As though commenting on his capitulation to a more popular mode of literary representation, self-mimesis plays a prominent role in Lewis's later work. In *The Revenge for Love* (1937), protagonist Percy Hardcaster, who is also missing a leg, tends 'towards liquefaction, upon cuticle and upon intestine', coming to resemble 'an aqueous shell' (*RL* 45). In his final novel *Self Condemned* (1954), Rene Hardcaster, whose circumstances mirror Lewis's own during the Second World War, ends up 'a glacial shell of a man' following the suicide of his wife.[97] In his late writing, however, the extent to which Lewis's foregrounding of his protagonist's weaknesses functions as a form of self-condemnation (as his title suggests) remains tantalisingly unclear. A key instance of this ambiguity can be observed at the end of *The Revenge for Love*, a work of political satire set during the Spanish Civil War. In the final moments of the text, communist agitator Percy Hardcaster suddenly realises that his actions have resulted in the death of an innocent young woman, Margot Stamp. Receiving news of her demise in his prison cell, the text describes how Percy 'proceeded to give a sculpturesque impersonation of THE INJURED PARTY' to his cellmates. He is unable to sustain this deception, and moments later 'the eyes in the mask of THE INJURED PARTY dilated in a spasm of astonished self-pity. And down the front of a mask rolled a sudden tear, which fell upon the dirty floor of the prison' (*RL* 380; original emphasis).

This ending has astonished critics, with Fredric Jameson even making the somewhat gushing claim that 'before our astonished eyes there hangs and gleams forever the realest tear in all literature'. In a similarly extravagant claim Hugh Kenner states that 'the one thing recalcitrantly real in the universe of the book remains Margot's love'.[98] What is particularly striking about these critical responses is just how unguarded they are, suggesting that Lewis was able to break down the defences of even his more discerning readers. *The Revenge for Love* is undoubtedly more sentimental than Lewis's earlier fiction. Intriguingly, however, Jameson's use of the verb 'gleams' to describe Percy's display of emotion calls to mind Stella Benson's account of Lewis's 'gleaming' teeth – a resemblance that warns us not to take this dazzling display of remorse at face value. In his autobiographical poem *One-Way Song* (1933), Lewis encourages the reader to question appearances in his writing: 'Take binoculars to these nests of camouflage – I Spy out what is *half-there* – the page-under-the-page'.[99] By instructing his readers to look beyond the illusory façade of his late style, Lewis reminds us not to mistake these surface appearances for anything remotely or 'recalcitrantly' real.

As is the case in *Snooty Baronet*, it is possible to view Percy, who shares his author's first name, as a kind of exaggerated self-portrait. Lewis makes this likeness increasingly explicit towards the end of the novel when Percy embarks on a process of self-evaluation:

> For this man of truth was not in the habit of sparing himself. Indeed, he somewhat enjoyed exercising his incorruptible intellect upon the dissection of Percy Hardcaster. He was like a painter fond of self-portraiture: and his self-portraits were not chocolate-boxes! He hit hard when he hit Percy. (*RL* 377–8)

The teasing nature of the simile 'he was *like* a painter fond of self-portraiture, which flashes a knowing wink to the reader, combined with the final statement: 'He hit hard when he hit Percy' recalls the sudden reveal of Snooty's post-coital confession: 'The face was mine', 'The man was me'. Percy is me, Lewis seems to be saying, I want you to see that he is me. And yet these exposing self-portraits involve a masking of the self: by detaching parts of his 'Enemy' persona and offering them, like a quivering limb, to the reader, Lewis may have been attempting to evade a more painful process of critical evaluation at the hands of those around him.

Having adopted the guise of the injured party in *The Revenge for Love*, Lewis produced one of his most critically acclaimed novels. In doing so, he transformed a growing sense of fallibility into an integral feature of his late style. By espousing an art of 'the *outside* of people . . . their shells or pelts', Lewis has often succeeded in distracting the reader's attention from the sensitivity of his writing. And yet, just as *The Caliph's Design* constructs a new artistic vision based on Fabre's morphing beetles, the ingenuity of Lewis's writing lies in its frequent shifts between 'sculpturesque' hardness and surprising suppleness. The author's body of work is inscribed with the cost of survival, its rougher textures and weaker patches a mark of the many explosive battles waged against external forces, threatening or otherwise. Yet these rich and varied surface modifications are also suggestive of the unyielding campaign waged by Lewis's writing to develop beyond the limitations of its surroundings, as well as its own weaknesses.

Paying attention to insects can help to overcome some of the more fixed ideas about Lewis's work, complicating but also enriching our understanding of his 'art of defence'. The author appears to have been particularly drawn to the dynamism of the insect body – its responsiveness to its surroundings, its surface modifications, its ability to startle and disorient predators. Despite its tendency to mimic breakdown, however, Lewis's writing is ultimately geared towards self-preservation: by staging a series of controlled explosions (or carefully orchestrated outbursts) it seeks to maintain itself intact. In the work of

D. H. Lawrence, on the other hand, insects are instrumental to a more drastic unsettling of the boundaries between inside and outside, self and surroundings, in which subject and text alike are exposed to an unsettling but potentially transformative otherness.

Notes

1. The original quotation reads: 'Man verkriecht sich hinter seiner Haut'. The English translation is by Claudia Benthien, *Skin: On the Cultural Border Between Self and World*, 22.
2. Quoted in Bachelard, *The Poetics of Space*, 146.
3. Quoted in Brightwell, *Palissy: The Huguenot Potter*, 184, 187–8.
4. Lewis, 'Editorial', *BLAST* 2, 5.
5. Poulton, *The Colours of Animals*, 264–5.
6. Fabre, *The Wonders of Instinct*, 73, 54, 32.
7. Trotter, *Paranoid Modernism*, 289.
8. Lewis, 'Inferior Religions', 8.
9. The editorial note accompanying the first of these articles states: '*The English Review* has acquired the sole right of publishing serially the portions of Henri Fabre's lifework that have not yet appeared in England; and a series of six chapters from his "epic of the insect world" will be published in these pages in the course of the next few months', 'The Weaving Spider', 519.
10. Wyndham Lewis's surviving library is searchable through the University of Texas at Austin's online database, available at: <http://catalog.lib.utexas.edu/search/x> (last accessed 14 March 2019).
11. Lewis makes reference to Maeterlinck's *The Life of the Bee* (1901) in *The Roaring Queen*, 65. He also makes detailed reference to Forel's *The Senses of Insects* (1908) in his 'Essay (entomology) for Semester VI', which features in his unpublished manuscript *Joint*. I am grateful to Kevin Rulo for drawing my attention to this document.
12. Connolly, 'The Wild Body', 358.
13. Quoted in Deming, 'Wyndham Lewis on James Joyce', 552; original emphasis.
14. Lewis, *The Art of Being Ruled*, 121.
15. Burstein, *Cold Modernism*, 75–81; Foster, *Prosthetic Gods*, 137; Nicholls, *Modernisms*, 292.
16. Hulme, 'Modern Art and Its Philosophy', 86.
17. 'observe, *v*.', *OED*.
18. Lewis, 'The French Poodle', 40.
19. Sheehan, *Modernism and the Aesthetics of Violence*, 133.
20. 'shell, *v*.', *OED*.
21. Nabokov, *Ada or Ardor*, 210.
22. Isyanova, 'The Consumer Sphinx', 134.
23. Edwards, 'Lewis and the Uses of Shellshock', 228, 240.
24. Freud, *Beyond the Pleasure Principle*, 298–9.
25. Wilkinson, *A Brush with Life*, 79.
26. 'dazzle, *v*.', *OED*.

27. White, 'Technicities of Deception', 39; original emphasis.
28. Quoted in Murphy and Bellamy, 'The Dazzling Zoologist', 177.
29. Thayer, *Concealing Colouration*, 225.
30. Lewis, *Letters*, 552.
31. Forbes, *Dazzled and Deceived*, 104.
32. Humphreys, *Wyndham Lewis*, 43.
33. Lewis, 'Note on Tyros', 2.
34. Corbett, 'Grief with a Yard-Wide Grin', 119.
35. Fabre, 'The Modern Theory of Instinct', 15.
36. Caillois, 'Mimicry and Legendary Psychanesthesia', 28, 18–19.
37. Lisa Siraganian discerns 'eye-like spots' on Lewis's cover image for the first issue of *The Enemy* that 'might also serve to frighten potential predators', *Modernism's Other Work*, 73.
38. *Paranoid Modernism*, 310.
39. Lewis, 'Essay on the Objective of Plastic Art in Our Time', 36; original emphasis.
40. Freud, 'Instincts and their Vicissitudes', 129.
41. Lewis, *The Complete Wild Body*, 321; Klein, *Monsters of Nature and Design*, 27.
42. Lewis, *The Enemy*, 1, ii.
43. For a more detailed account of modernism's vexed relationship with mimesis and Lewis's use of mimetic satire see Nicholls, 'Apes and Familiars', 421–38.
44. Pound, *Ezra Pound and the Visual Arts*, 6.
45. Fabre, *The Mason-Bees*, 200–10.
46. Nabokov, *Speak Memory*, 91.
47. *The Childermass* is the first part of an incomplete tetralogy entitled *The Human Age*. Lewis later published two sequels, *Monstre Gai* and *Malign Fiesta* (1955), but the final text in the series remained incomplete at the time of his death in 1957.
48. The text's formal hybridity is partly due to the fact that *The Childermass* and *Time and Western Man* were initially conceived as part of a single text, *The Man of the World*. See Edwards, 'Afterword', in *TWM* 488–93.
49. McLuhan, *Understanding Media*, 29.
50. Nicholls, 'Apes and Familiars', 428.
51. Lacan, 'The Line and the Light', 99.
52. Bhabha, 'Of Mimicry and Man', 127.
53. Sarraute, 'Conversation and Subconversation', 94.
54. Joyce, *Letters*, Vol. 1, 241.
55. *The Enemy*, 1, 122.
56. Joyce, *Finnegans Wake*, 417.
57. Senn, 'Insects Appalling', 39; *Finnegans Wake*, 29.
58. Joyce, 'Continuation of a Work in Progress', 16, 17.
59. *The Enemy*, 1, 110; McHugh, *Annotations to Finnegans Wake*, 415.
60. 'Work in Progress', 18.
61. Ellmann, *James Joyce*, 141; Murray, 'Beelines', 1–14.
62. Bonheim, 'Review of *A Wake Bestiary*', 235.
63. See McHugh, *Annotations to Finnegans Wake*.
64. 'Work in Progress', 17; *Finnegans Wake*, 153.

65. 'Work in Progress', 17–18.
66. Ellmann, *James Joyce*, 515; O'Keeffe, *Some Sort of Genius*, 231–2.
67. There is also the suggestion that the men may have contracted an itch (i.e. a venereal disease) from these women in Joyce's reference to the Ondt 'spizzing' (*spiz*, Italian dialect for itch), as well as 'crabround' and 'tickling Luse' (louse), 'Work in Progress', 17; *Finnegans Wake*, 417.
68. *The Enemy*, 1, 127.
69. Swift, *The Major Works*, 7–9.
70. *Finnegans Wake*, 417.
71. 'As Entomate', para. 33.
72. Woolf, *Diary*, Vol. 4, 252.
73. 'Work in Progress', 19.
74. *Finnegans Wake*, 455; Klein, *Monsters of Nature*, 194.
75. Lewis, *Rude Assignment*, 56.
76. 'Mimicry and Legendary Psychanesthesia', 128; original emphasis.
77. Lewis, *Hitler*, 4.
78. 'fascia, *n*.', OED.
79. *Beyond the Pleasure Principle*, 302.
80. Laplanche and Pontalis, *The Language of Psychoanalysis*, 52; original emphasis.
81. Miller, *Late Modernism*, 116; original emphasis.
82. Dwan, 'The Problem of Romanticism in Wyndham Lewis', 184.
83. Lewis, *The Code of a Herdsman*, 36.
84. Lewis, *Letters*, 206.
85. Meyers, *The Enemy*, 184.
86. Quoted in O'Keeffe, *Some Sort of Genius*, 301–2.
87. Quoted in *Some Sort of Genius*, 319.
88. Quoted in *Some Sort of Genius*, 319.
89. 'exposure, *n*.', OED.
90. Quoted in Smith, '*Snooty Baronet*: Satire and Censorship', 195.
91. Quoted in '*Snooty Baronet*: Satire and Censorship', 183. Lewis and Lawrence first met in 1914, after which Lawrence reported that he soon found himself engaged in a 'heated and vivid discussion' with his fellow modernist, *Letters*, Vol. 2, 193. The heat intensified when Lewis launched a bitter attack on Lawrence's writing in *Paleface: The Philosophy of the Melting Pot* (1929), to which Lawrence retaliated in a review of Edward Dahlberg's *Bottom Dogs*, *Introductions and Reviews*, 117–24.
92. *Wyndham Lewis on Art*, 266–7.
93. Thomson, *Outlines of Zoology*, 798.
94. Burstein, *Cold Modernism*, 77; 'Waspish Segments', 145.
95. Lewis, *Letters*, 196.
96. *Late Modernism*, 93.
97. Lewis, *Self Condemned*, 464.
98. Jameson, *Fables of Aggression*, 177; Kenner, *Wyndham Lewis*, 130.
99. Lewis, *One-Way Song*, 33; original emphasis.

2

FORMICATION: D. H. LAWRENCE

Mr. Edison, I was informed, had been up the two previous nights discovering 'a bug' in his phonograph – an expression for solving a difficulty, and implying that some imaginary insect has secreted itself inside and is causing all the trouble.

'bug, *n.*²'[1], *OED*

This flea is you and I

John Donne, 'The Flea'

After checking into the Grand Hotel in Syracuse, Sicily in May 1920, D. H. Lawrence observed signs of a recent struggle between man and insect: 'It is a rather dreary hotel – and many squashed bloodstains of mosquitoes on the bedroom walls. Ah vile mosquitoes!'[1] Written in the midst of this battleground, or shortly after departing from it, Lawrence's poem 'The Mosquito' is a 'paean of derision' to the 'pointed fiend' caught sucking the speaker's blood. Unfolding in the present tense, it describes the state of profound irritation induced by this 'hateful little trump | . . . Which shakes my sudden blood to hatred'. The speaker is particularly troubled by the mosquito's ability to get under his skin – literally and figuratively – expressing a sense of horror at its 'obscenity of trespass' (*TP* 288–9). Responding to the remorseless squashing of the creature at the end of the poem, Keith Sagar argues that in contrast to the other poems in his 1923 collection *Birds, Beasts, and Flowers*, 'Lawrence makes no attempt to enter into the mosquito, or to take its otherness into himself. By violating his own separateness it has crossed a forbidden frontier, and that is obscene.'[2] Sagar rightly identifies the speaker's resistance to being contaminated by the mosquito's 'otherness', but there are also moments in the poem when the fear of violation gives way to a fantasy of breaking out of one's skin – of becoming mosquito. At one point the speaker wonders wistfully: 'Am I not mosquito enough to out-mosquito you?' A powerful sense of aversion is now replaced by something approaching longing, as the speaker's eagerness to destroy this threat to separateness becomes a desire to emulate its 'imponderable weightlessness' (*TP* 288–9).

Lawrence's speaker also refers to the mosquito's 'suspended transport', with the word 'transport' denoting both a physical carrying across from one place or person to another – from man to mosquito – as well as the sensation of being carried away 'with the strength of some emotion; to cause to be beside oneself, to put into an ecstasy, to enrapture'.[3] The term carries an important sense of the role played by the mosquito in the poem. By provoking a fierce rage, this tiny creature generates much of the strength of feeling that fuels the speaker's creative response – while gorging on his blood, it feeds his imaginative processes. Beneath the surface of this exchange lies a productive commingling of self and other, human and insect. In the final lines of the poem: 'Queer, what a big stain my sucked blood makes | Beside the infinitesimal faint smear of you', the speaker finds himself quite literally beside himself, with the mosquito's 'filthy magic' inducing an alteration of perspective that is at once profound and deeply unsettling (*TP* 287–9).

When he wrote 'The Mosquito', Lawrence would have been all too aware that the insect's diminutive devilry was not only irritating but potentially deadly. At the turn of the twentieth century the link between mosquitoes and malaria was finally made, and the author contracted the disease in Ceylon less than two years later.[4] At the same time, the poem's repeated transgression of the 'forbidden frontier' between self and insect – as though enacting the very 'obscenity of trespass' that it fears – discloses an important tension in Lawrence's work. The author's writing, I will argue, is caught between an anxiety of contamination that compels the subject to recoil into separateness, and a contrary desire to break out of the confines of the self by forging a tactile intimacy with this corrupting influence. So far, critics have tended to read Lawrence's insects as symbols of the modern subject's imprisonment within a 'carapace of industrialism', in which human life is rendered 'mechanical, insect-like'.[5] While not discounting the largely negative connotations of insect life in the author's work, I want to suggest that by filling his writing with things that prickle and sting, Lawrence is also drawing on the energy of what Jean-Michel Rabaté, in a reading of lice in Joyce, characterises as 'life-affirming vermin'.[6] In other words, if insects represent the negation of human life in Lawrence's writing, in which the individual is encased within an 'impervious envelope of insentience', a 'shell . . . insulated from life', then they may also function as the counterforce capable of breaking through this inert casing and provoking new forms of responsiveness (*RDP* 281).

Lawrence's body of work plays host to an array of entomological sensations that are suggestive of the infiltration of individual life by a threatening multitude – from Ursula's horror at the 'insect-like intentness' of the crowds at Ostend in *Women in Love* (1920) to Kate's phobic perception of the Mexico City masses gathered in 'terrible swarms, like locusts' in *The Plumed Serpent* (1926).[7] The author's non-fiction discloses a similar anxiety: after stumbling across a troop of trainee soldiers at Worthing in 1915, Lawrence reflected: 'they remind me of lice or bugs . . . They are teeming insects.'[8] In his wartime essays and correspondence, soldiers, critics, divorce lawyers, fellow artists, Bloomsbury homosexuals and perhaps less obviously Cornish people, are frequently likened by Lawrence to 'teeming insects', 'creeping . . . bugs' and, with an almost pathological frequency, 'black-beetles'.[9] Such is the intensity of this state of psychic unease that it can resemble a cutaneous hallucination known as formication (from the Latin *formīcāre*, to move like ants), a sensation akin to the crawling of ants over and under the skin. In *Mr Noon* (1920–1; pub. 1984), the eponymous protagonist is beset by a tickling sensation 'worse than fleas, worse even than mosquitoes on a sultry night', while at a climactic moment in *The Trespasser* (1912), the distressed Siegmund experiences a 'horrible tickling' comparable to 'a myriad quivering tracks of a myriad running insects over his hot, wet, highly-sensitised body'.[10]

Formication is suggestive of the experience of the self as a multiplicity, a breakdown of the subject's physical borders that corresponds to a breach (or trespass) in the mind's defences. Significantly, however, Lawrence's interwar fiction appears to embrace this state of epidermic dissolution, at times displaying a formal impetus akin to formication, in which the language of the text quakes, shudders and writhes at the touch of a threatening otherness that it actively seeks and yet recoils from in horror. This otherness is often located in the urban masses, the exponential growth of which was felt by many during this period to pose a major threat to individual subjectivity. As Simon King notes, human swarms are everywhere in modernist writing – from Baudelaire's 'Fourmillante cité' in *Les Fleurs du mal* (1861), to the 'hooded hordes swarming | Over endless plains' in Eliot's *Waste Land* (1922).[11] My sense, however, is that rather than simply describing the encroachments of mass existence in entomological terms, Lawrence's writing explores the bristling excitations generated by these epidermic encounters between self and swarm through the form of the text. For Lawrence, this process of exposure may provide an antidote to the deadening effects of industrial modernity, restoring the vitality of subject and text alike by placing them into contact with the disruptive energies of mass culture and inter-war politics. Rather than excluding what it cannot cope with, the author's work continually rubs up against the forces in its surroundings which it finds discomforting, renewing itself through this often painful interaction with what lies beyond its borders.

Lawrence's efforts to expose his work to the source of its unease may account for the sense of almost physical discomfort that tends to surface in critical responses to his writing. 'His novels do not leave you where they found you', remarked one contemporary reviewer: 'They have designs on you. They quicken your consciousness, enlarge your capacity for feeling. They invade you, pluck at you, pervade you.'[12] More recently, Anne Fernihough notes that there 'seems to be hardly anyone else who has generated such extreme reactions in his readers, from people at one end of the spectrum who have tried to "become" Lawrence, to people who have felt contaminated by reading him.'[13] These readings evoke the boundary-threatening nature of the author's writing – not only does it allow itself to be infiltrated by the forces at work in its surroundings, but it also subjects its readers to this process of contamination. In both instances, there are shades of the transgressive dynamics of the human-insect encounter in 'The Mosquito', suggesting that the tendency of Lawrence's writing to inflame the sensibilities of his readers is bound up with its efforts to induce a level of feeling which, as another critic puts it, 'is almost painful in its fierceness'.[14] Focusing on a number of inter-war texts – including *The Ladybird* (1923), *Kangaroo* (1923) and *Lady Chatterley's Lover* (1928) – this chapter will argue that Lawrence's use of entomological figures is central to his vision of the literary text as a lively and disruptive force capable of stinging characters and readers alike into a new awareness of themselves and the world around them.

Casting Off the Shell

After sending a copy of his new novel, *Sons and Lovers* (1913), to his publishers in November 1912, Lawrence was anxious to defend the novel from allegations that it lacked shape. In an impassioned letter to his editor David Garnett, he insisted: 'I tell you it has got form – *form* . . . The son casts off his mistress, attends to his mother dying. He is left in the end naked of everything.'[15] For Lawrence, the form of the novel emerges from a process of casting off, in which the subject is gradually stripped of the vestures of his or her social identity in order to reveal the essential self beneath. *Sons and Lovers* concludes with Paul Morel's epiphanic realisation that he is merely 'one tiny upright speck of flesh' in a vast and terrifying universe, 'infinitesimal, at the core a nothingness, and yet not nothing'.[16] There is a glimmer of hope in these final lines: having lost everything that defines him, Paul can finally make something, or at least 'not nothing', of himself. Lawrence's vision of casting off resurfaces in his next novel, *The Rainbow* (1915), at the end of which Ursula fantasies that the local colliers 'would cast off their horny covering of disintegration, that new, clean, naked bodies would issue to . . . a new growth' (*R* 459). The phrase 'covering of disintegration' can tell us much about the author's exoskeletal aesthetic: here and elsewhere in his writing, the shell is not what keeps the subject together, but rather apart, lacking cohesion, divided.

Lawrence's vision of casting off is symptomatic of the modernist tendency to present identity as a series of exuviations. In remarks that recall Lewis's deceptive self-portraits, Pound revealed that when writing his poetry collection, *Personae* (1909): 'I began . . . casting off, as it were, complete masks of the self in each poem.'[17] Woolf's essay 'Street Haunting: A London Adventure' (1930) describes how, on stepping out of the house, 'we shed the self our friends know us by and become part of that vast republican army of anonymous trampers'.[18] In Joyce's *Portrait of the Artist as a Young Man* (1916), Stephen's spiritual progress involves the sloughing of a former identity: 'as if his very body were being divested with ease of some outer skin or peel'.[19] There is, however, a sense of 'ease' to these sudden transformations that is not borne out in Lawrence's writing. More often than not, the subject struggles to break out of his or her shell, or the process is delayed indefinitely. In *The Rainbow*, for instance, Ursula can only hope that the miners 'would', at some stage, 'issue . . . to a new growth', while in *Women in Love*, the narrator describes how Ursula's own 'active living was suspended, but underneath . . . something was coming to pass. *If only* she could break through the last integuments!' (*WIL* 9; emphasis added). More often than not, the shell functions as a restrictive outer casing that suspends 'active living' and inhibits personal growth. Yet just as Lewis's work often seems to require an oppositional force in order to define itself, the exoskeleton functions as a source of external pressure in Lawrence's writing, against which it is able to form itself anew. Like the mosquito, this 'horny covering' galvanises the author's body of work, provoking a creative response that is born out of a sense of struggle and resistance.

The act of casting off, which involves the sloughing of a skin in the process of growth, is known to biologists as ecdysis. The term derives from a compound of the Greek *ek*, or 'out', and *dúō*, 'I get in', which hints at the idea that getting out of one form may entail getting into another. In the case of invertebrates, ecdysis involves the periodic moulting of the exoskeleton, during which the organism emerges from beneath its outer shell in a soft and vulnerable state known as the instar phase. Although Lawrence's work is often hostile to scientific systems of knowledge, his vision of literary form as a process of shedding can be traced back to his early interest in studies of biology. The author's enthusiasm for botany has been well documented, as has his reading of a number of works of evolutionary theory – including Charles Darwin's *On the Origin of Species* (1859), Herbert Spencer's *Principles of Biology* (1863), T. H. Huxley's *Man's Place in Nature* (1863) and Ernst Haeckel's *The Riddle of the Universe* (1901).[20] In addition to his expertise in identifying local flora, a close childhood friend from his Nottingham days, G. H. Neville, revealed that Lawrence had 'a very profound knowledge of the insects of the locality'. Although he was reluctant to collect these creatures as was customary during this period, Lawrence accompanied Neville on numerous expeditions that resulted in 'the mounting and dressing of specimens'.[21]

Lawrence's aversion to insect collecting suggests that he was in favour of Jean-Henri Fabre's alternative approach to the study of nature. In order to understand 'the habits of insects', Fabre writes in *The Life of the Caterpillar* (1912), 'one must observe them long and closely . . . in the place where their habits have full and natural play'.[22] Lawrence alludes to Fabre's writing on a number of occasions in his writing, and the latter's emphasis on observing the 'full and natural play' of insect life resonates with the author's assertion in his literary criticism that 'only in the novel are *all* things given full play' (*STH* 198; original emphasis). Elsewhere in his critical writing, Lawrence expresses disdain towards an understanding of living organisms that is divorced from a sustained engagement with them in their natural surroundings, writing contemptuously of people who 'study entomology and think they "know" insects' in the way that people 'go to Spain and "know" Spain' (*RDP* 215). For Lawrence, the novel provides an ideal space in which to 'know' a creature – whether human or non-human – in its life-world: it is '*only* in the novel', he posits, that '*all* things' are given free play. 'If you try and nail anything down in the novel', he adds, 'either it kills the novel, or the novel gets up and walks off with the nail' (*STH* 174). These remarks present an image of the text as a kind of insect, but crucially one that refuses to be pinned down by the taxonomic methods of nineteenth-century entomology.

Much to the author's chagrin, Garnett failed to be convinced by Lawrence's vision of literary form as a process of casting off and a month later he vented to a friend: 'They want me to have form: that means they want me to have *their* pernicious ossiferous skin-and-grief form, and I won't.'[23] Responding to this passage, Andrew Harrison argues that Lawrence's search for a 'new idea of form' involves a rejection of the 'conventional forms' associated with the Edwardian novel, forms which 'lay behind his own youthful works'.[24] Seemingly, then, Lawrence was not only attempting to cast off '*their* . . . form', but also his own formal methods. The author's unusual phrasing bears out his resistance to traditional modes of expression: the curious compound 'skin-and-grief' appears to be his own coinage, while the geological term 'ossiferous', meaning containing or yielding deposits of bones, takes the place of the more commonly used adjective 'ossified', which describes living matter turned to bone as well as a rigid and inflexible outlook. Lawrence's struggle to maintain the vitality of words against the stultifying effect of inveterate use – what the poet W. S. Graham refers to as 'the caught habits of language' – is reflected in his offbeat phrasing and misshapen metaphors, which contort stock images into unusual shapes.²⁵ Consistent throughout the author's work – and indeed through all of the writing examined by this study – is a resistance to what H.D. refers to as 'the stark rigidity of words' (*H* 75). For, Lawrence, the 'life-motion' of the literary text can only be maintained through a series of restless formal strategies, a 'frictional to-and-fro' of language that seeks to stave off the mortification of meaning (*WIL* 313, 486).

Lawrence's antipathy towards 'ossiferous . . . form' speaks to a concern raised frequently in his essays and correspondence regarding the deadening effects of modern civilisation on individual subjectivity. In two early war essays, Lawrence asserts that British society has become imprisoned within a 'glassy envelope, the insect rind', living 'safe and atrophied . . . as dying chrysalides' (*STH* 16–17). During the initial stages of the conflict, Lawrence was hopeful that this cataclysmic event might reinvigorate British society, enacting a metamorphosis of humankind. The author saw the outbreak of the First World War as an opportunity for writers and readers alike in order to 'break the shell, the form' constraining the modern subject and its forms of expression and 'creep forth' from this abandoned husk, 'tender and overvulnerable, but alive'.²⁶ In a further entomological analogy, Lawrence asserts that man must 'yield himself up to his metamorphosis . . . and so come to his new issuing, his wings, his resurrection, his whole flesh shining like a mote in the sunshine'. By the end of 1915, however, not only had the devastating consequences of the war become apparent, but *The Rainbow* had recently been suppressed by the literary censors on the grounds of obscenity, with an instruction issued that all available copies were to be hunted down and destroyed. 'My dear nation is bitten by a tarantula', Lawrence lamented in a letter to Cynthia Asquith, 'and the venom has gone home at last.' This analogy of bodily contamination is telling: by now the stress of the conflict had compounded Lawrence's already fragile health to the extent that he found himself temporarily paralysed 'all down the left side'.²⁷

Unable to enlist for active duty because of a pre-existing health condition, the author was subjected to a series of invasive physical examinations in order to determine his level of fitness for non-military duties. After moving to the furthest reaches of Cornwall to escape the conflict, Lawrence and his wife Frieda found themselves under constant surveillance from neighbours and local authorities, who suspected that they were German spies. As a testament to these various obscenities of trespass on his body and mind, Lawrence's letters from this period teem with insect imagery. 'They creep in', he wrote of the summer tourists at Zennor, 'like bugs that creep invidiously in, and they are too many to crush.' After visiting Duncan Grant and Maynard Keynes in Cambridge, Lawrence wrote that they made him dream of 'a beetle that bites like a scorpion'. What these 'swarming selves' appear to have in common is the perceived threat that they posed to the author's sense of self during a period when he was often in low spirits and poor health.²⁸ As Rick Rylance notes:

'Beetles are at work in psyche *and* society' in Lawrence's war writing, which often blurs the distinction 'between "character" and "milieu"'.[29] Intriguingly, however, rather than attempting to exclude this anxiety of infiltration from his fiction, the author allows it to enter his body of work, experimenting with ways of overcoming the disintegrative effects of war on the individual psyche by utilising rather than attempting to exclude its negative force.

In December 1921, having extricated himself from the English hordes and settled into a new life in rural Italy, Lawrence began work on a novella that diagnoses an ailing wartime Britain. *The Ladybird* (1923) begins by chronicling the plight of Lady Beveridge, who has been pierced by the 'agony of the war': 'It was the winter of 1917 – or in the late autumn. She had been a fortnight sick, stricken, paralysed by the fearful death of her youngest boy' (*L* 157–8). Lady Beveridge's condition is presented as symptomatic of a state of wartime paralysis afflicting the entire nation, with the text going on to introduce a host of pierced and war-torn bodies, including Lady Beveridge's tubercular daughter, Daphne Apsley, her shrapnel-scarred husband Basil, as well as the bullet-ridden Count Dionys Psanek. Early on in the narrative, Daphne becomes reacquainted with injured war veteran Dionys, who is an old family friend, after visiting a London military hospital for prisoners of war. She agrees to sew him a shirt emblazoned with his 'family insect', an armorial ladybird crest, using a thimble engraved with a scarab that he had given her years earlier as a gift, and this act of embroidery knits the couple together in an unspoken intimacy (*L* 175).

Explaining the significance of the ladybird, the Count describes it as 'the beetle of Our Lady' (*L* 209). Named in the Middle Ages after Mary's wearing of red garments to represent the blood of Christ, the religious symbolism of the ladybird hints that the puncturing of the body may function as a necessary precursor to its renewal.[30] The introduction of the thimble symbol coincides with the gradual return of feeling (pins and needles) to bodies left paralysed by war, and this is reflected in the host of formicatory sensations that suffuse the text. When Daphne imagines herself 'giv[ing] way to that relaxation that the Count wanted of her', for instance, 'some hypersensitive nerve started with a great twinge in her breast', while he too 'suffer[s]' a tingling sensation when faced with the 'hot-house delica[cy]' of her skin (*L* 182, 208). Similarly, when the Count touches Daphne's skin for the first time she responds with a 'shudder'; far from being repulsed by contact with this foreign body (as she is by her husband's touch), her shudder response corresponds to the shedding of a state of infirmity: 'she had suddenly collapsed away from her old self' (*L* 214, 219). Lawrence's use of the verb 'collapse' to describe Daphne's sloughing of her previous identity seems somewhat curious, with the verb appearing to signify the opposite of recovery. And yet just as the 'horny covering' that envelops the miners results in a state of 'disintegration', the text invites us to consider the possibility that by falling apart in this way the self may be brought back together.

The tingling sensation experienced by both Dionys and Daphne is closely linked to another type of transgression that lurks beneath the surface of their interactions: fornication.³¹ Although it remains unclear whether the couple consummate their relationship, when Basil returns from the front halfway through the text he is forced to accept that his wife's intimacy with Dionys has had a restorative effect, breathing new life into her 'nerve-worn' body. Lawrence presents the Count as a Dionysian figure capable of releasing the 'wild energy' that is 'dammed up' within Daphne's ailing body, a dynamic that is particularly evident during their lively verbal exchanges (*L* 160–1). When Dionys is attempting to persuade Daphne to sew him a shirt, he remarks: 'There will be a ladybird on your finger when you sew, and those who wear the ladybird understand.' She responds playfully: 'I suppose . . . it is as bad to have your bee in your shirt as in your bonnet', resulting in a quick-fire back and forth between the couple arising from his confusion over the meaning of this English idiom (*L* 175). Seeing the expression through the Count's eyes calls to mind the frequent approximation in everyday speech between insects and states of agitation – to be bitten by the bug, to have ants in your pants, to stir up a hornet's nest. Daphne and Dionys's verbal frisson also recalls the enlivening wordplay of Gudrun and the 'insect-like' German sculptor Loerke in *Women in Love*: 'The whole game was one of subtle inter-suggestivity . . . From their verbal and physical *nuances* they got the highest satisfaction in the nerves' (*WIL* 452, 448; original emphasis). Indeed, the erotically charged subtext of these 'half-suggested ideas, looks, expressions, and gestures' is suggestive of the transgressive tendencies of *The Ladybird* as a whole, which at times resembles what Lawrence refers to later on in his writing as 'an infinite fornication of words'.³²

Quick Little Beetles

Basil fails to recognise the extent of his wife's recovery at the hands of Dionys, just as he underestimates the significance of his family insect, wondering: 'isnt it an odd thing to have a ladybird on your crest? . . . The Americans would call it a bug' (*L* 209, 195). According to the *OED*, the primary American definition of the term 'bug' is any 'small insect or larva that is considered to be a pest', suggesting that the symbolism of the ladybird is lost on the somewhat obtuse Basil.³³ Lawrence, on the other hand, appears to be employing the term far more suggestively: as well as denoting an imaginary spirit or evil creature, from the late nineteenth century a 'bug' denoted a fault in a machine, and by the early twentieth century its use had expanded to include a microbe or germ, as well as a person obsessed by an idea.³⁴ Crucially, these meanings correspond to states in which the boundaries of the self are threatened in some way – by disease, by a disruptive foreign element or creature, or by an idea that troubles the mind. *The Ladybird* appears to intermingle these definitions: over the course of the narrative, malfunction, contamination and states of mental excitation are all encompassed within the talismanic power of the Count's 'spotted beetle' (*L* 209).

Perhaps the most intriguing example of the evolving meaning of the word 'bug', cited in the opening epigraph to this chapter, is the *Pall Mall Gazette*'s description of Thomas Edison's bug in the system: 'an expression for solving a difficulty, and implying that some imaginary insect has secreted itself inside and is causing all the trouble'. This definition can help to make sense of the troublesome role played by Dionys in the text. Throughout the narrative, the Count's controversial views of natural aristocracy, female subservience, as well as his worship of 'the God of anger', have a tendency to rub his British contemporaries up the wrong way, resulting in a series of uncomfortable exchanges. His disruptive influence is most apparent during a visit to Daphne's father, Lord Beveridge, on his country estate. The initial meeting between the two men results in a prickly exchange between the Lord and this 'little alien enemy', in which the Count probes at the hidden, hostile meanings beneath his polite speech until he 'flush[ed] dark, with all his native anger offended' (*L* 205–6). Lord Beveridge's inflamed complexion suggests that Dionys, like the 'pointed fiend' in 'The Mosquito', is able to get under the skin of his host, with this foreign body bringing to the surface feelings that usually lie concealed beneath the 'class armour' of English relations (*RDP* 384).

Dionys's disruption of the status quo is particularly apparent during a dinner table discussion with the Beveridges and the Apsleys, in which he explains that his family emblem is the descendent of the Egyptian scarab, known as the sacred beetle:

> 'The scarab *is* a piquant insect,' said Basil.
>
> 'Do you know Fabre?' put in Lord Beveridge. 'He suggests that the beetle rolling a little ball of dung before him, in a dry old field, must have suggested to the Egyptians the First Principle that set the globe rolling. And so the scarab became the symbol of the creative principle – or something like that.'
>
> 'That the earth is a tiny ball of dry dung is good,' said Basil.
>
> 'Between the claws of a ladybird,' added Daphne.
>
> 'That is what it is, to go back to one's origins,' said Lady Beveridge.
>
> 'Perhaps they meant that it was the principle of decomposition which first set the ball rolling,' said the Count.
>
> 'The ball would have to be *there* first,' said Basil.
>
> 'Certainly. But it hadn't started to roll. Then the principle of decomposition started it.' The Count smiled as if it were a joke.
>
> 'I am no Egyptologist,' said Lady Beveridge, 'so I can't judge.'
>
> The Earl and Countess Beveridge left next day.
>
> (*L* 209–10; original emphasis)

The beetle analogy is introduced following a heated discussion about the war, during which Dionys refuses to accept the view that it has been a 'valuable thing' (*L* 198). In the article to which Lord Beveridge is referring, which was published in *The English Review* in September 1917, Fabre claims that the Egyptians 'saw in the rolling sphere' of the dung beetle 'an image of the world performing its daily evolution'.[35] Lord Beveridge's introduction of Fabre's argument appears designed to reinforce his vision of war as a force of evolutionary progress – what Basil, in agreement with his father-in-law, describes as a 'higher state . . . of life' emerging from the 'ordeal one had to go through' (*L* 198). The text's resistance to this interpretation of war is reflected in the chaotic ricocheting of ideas between the speakers, which speaks of a disruptive incomprehension of its own material. After Lord Beveridge gets the ball rolling, Basil turns Lord Beveridge's analogy on its head, before Daphne connects the scarab to its present-day ancestor and Lady Beveridge rolls the analogy back to its 'origins'. What might appear to be a lively exchange of ideas quickly degenerates into a series of repetitive echoes that run counter to the notion of narrative progress or productive intellectual discussion. This is until the Count cuts through the crap, so to speak: in a formulation that recalls Ford's atavistic account of himself as a dung beetle 'rolling backwards, clinging on to his pellet of dung', Dionys introduces a more radical, anti-modern interpretation of human progress as a 'process of decomposition' or devolution.

An earlier version of this argument is presented in *Women in Love*, while Birkin is recollecting a West African statue of a female figure:

> He remembered her: her astonishing cultured elegance, her diminished, beetle face . . . Thousands of years ago, that which was imminent [*sic*] in himself must have taken place in these Africans: the goodness, the holiness, the desire for creation and productive happiness must have lapsed, leaving the single impulse for knowledge . . . in disintegration and dissolution, knowledge such as the beetles have, which live purely within the world of corruption and cold dissolution. This was why her face looked like a beetle's: this was why the Egyptians worshipped the ball-rolling scarab: because of the principle of knowledge in dissolution and corruption. (*WIL* 253)

Written in the midst of what the author described as the 'bitterness of the war', this entomological ekphrasis repeatedly circles back to the same terms, dissolving the possibility of linear development.[36] There is a thick and stodgy feel to Lawrence's use of synonymy – 'disintegration and dissolution', 'corruption and cold dissolution' – that is akin to being stuck in the mud (or worse). Troubling racial overtones aside, Birkin's perspective is indicative of a shift in Lawrence's war writing towards a negative understanding of human progress and yet the pejorative undertones of words such as 'cold' and 'corruption', coupled with the unrelieved agitation of the passage's 'slightly modified repetition', suggests that this 'knowledge . . . in disintegration and dissolution' has not yet been recognised in terms of its potential to enact positive social change.

If we compare Birkin's analogy to the beetle passage from *The Ladybird*, it is possible to observe a livelier, dialogic opposition in the later text between the 'creative principle' and the 'principle of decomposition'. This opposition may be related to Fabre's discovery that the 'Sacred beetle[s]' of Ancient Egypt are 'none other than Dung Beetles, the dealers in ordure, the scavengers of the cattle-fouled meadows'. Fabre goes on to explain that these abject muck-dwellers are integral to the fertility of the soil: 'Out of the filth she creates the flower; from a little manure she extracts the thrice-blessed grain of wheat.'[37] This may be what Dionys means by the 'principle of decomposition': the beetle's filthy work is what makes life possible. Fabre's study of the dung beetle provides an important insight into Lawrence's exploration of the idea that there may be knowledge 'in', as opposed to out of, dissolution and corruption. At the core of this debate about the 'First Principle' seems to lie a bigger question about whether, in the aftermath of the war, the possibility of artistic and social renewal may depend on the disintegration of existing forms – on breaking things down in order to set them rolling again. Fabre's emphasis, moreover, on the paradoxical status of the dung beetle as both sacred and profane, symbolic of death and new life, is also useful as a means of identifying the role played by insects in Lawrence's writing more generally, which appear at once representative of the decay of modern civilisation and of the creative force capable of counteracting this state of decline.

Lady Beveridge's terse response to Dionys – 'I'm no Egyptologist' – followed by the abrupt departure of the couple signals that his perspective is unwelcome, and yet it appears to be the only one capable of breaking the deadlock of tautologous statements. The few readers who have responded to *The Ladybird* over the years have tended to share Lady Beveridge's sense of unease. Julian Moynahan is perturbed by the destructive political implications of the text, describing it as Lawrence's 'ugliest story', while Colin Clarke argues that the centrality of the theme of 'self-destruction' in the text results in its 'failure'.[38] Part of this discomfort appears to stem from the author's sloughing of an earlier optimism; no longer does Lawrence's writing offer the hope of renewal (or not one that readers tend to recognise as such) suggested by Ursula's pre-war fantasy of 'clean, naked bodies' issuing to 'a new growth'. The critical condemnation of Dionys's destructive logic, however, has meant that his enlivening effect on other characters, as well as on the text as a whole, has largely been overlooked.

The Count's invigorating function is further indicated by the host of foreign words that Lawrence introduces into the body of the text. Dionys explains that his surname, Psanek, is Polish for 'outlaw', and he is later sent to a convalescent home called 'Voynich Hall' (*L* 172, 177). The editor of the Cambridge edition of *The Ladybird*, Dieter Mehl, suggests that Lawrence may have been alluding to Ethel Voynich's best-selling novel *The Gadfly* (1897), which the author read and admired.[39] The novel centres on the life of a young revolutionary in 1840s Italy, and according to H.D. it so influenced Pound that he began to sign his books with a gadfly symbol.[40] A term originally attributed to Socrates, who characterised himself as a social agitator capable of stinging people and whipping them into a fury in the service of truth, the gadfly is a lone figure who attacks prevailing social norms and intellectual orthodoxies in order to spur individuals into action. In a role at times reminiscent of Lewis's self-styled Enemy persona, Lawrence's inter-war writing emulates the spirit of the gadfly, with its prickly methods designed to provoke heightened levels of responsiveness in its readership. The author would even refer to himself in this way, characterising himself in a late autobiographical poem, 'Song of a Man Who Is Not Loved' as a 'gadfly in the dusk'.[41]

Significantly, however, *The Ladybird* is framed not from the perspective of Dionys but of Daphne, who 'disliked his words intensely, but she liked him' (*L* 201). By establishing this critical distance, Lawrence appears to be asking the reader to examine the function rather than merely the content of these unlikeable words and the uncomfortable sensations that they are capable of provoking in others. A figure closely related to the gadfly is that of the devil's advocate, who takes a disagreeable stance in social situations in order to stimulate debate. Early on in *The Ladybird*, the Count complains that he has 'a devil in my body, that will not die', to which Daphne responds: 'Must one hate a devil that makes one live?' (*L* 169). This is an important question raised by the text, as well as the author's writing more generally: in a strategy that recalls the 'devilry' of the mosquito, Lawrence appears to be asking the reader to recognise the importance of engaging with destructive views as a means of generating new ideas. During the war, Lawrence remarked in his critical writing: 'My form and shape . . . depend on the virtue of resistance', adding: 'I am like one of the cells in any organism, the pressure from within and the resistance from without keep me as I am' (*RDP* 49). In an analogy that marks a shift from the author's earlier emphasis on 'casting off', form is here presented as a kind of resistant membrane or skin – an outer shell that remains permeable but protective. These remarks also provide an important insight into *The Ladybird*, which allows itself to be infected by destructive ideas, seemingly with the notion of building up a strain of resistance – in itself and in its readers.

In a letter to John Middleton Murry, Lawrence described the text as having 'the quick of a new thing'.[42] The author often uses this word in his writing, most notably to describe the 'quick relatedness' of the novel to 'snow, bed-bugs, sunshine' (*STH* 183). It also surfaces in the manuscript draft of *The Ladybird* when Basil likens the Count to a 'quick little beetle' (*L* 267). The word 'quick' denotes that which is living and 'capable of sensation, sensitive to pain', as well as that which is 'reinforced', and this double meaning can shed light on Lawrence's efforts to cultivate a form of representation that remains in touch with its surroundings but also robust enough to endure them.[43] It also evokes the increasingly insectile diffuseness of Lawrence's language as it deviates and proliferates over the surface of the text, refusing to progress in a 'straight line' or to settle into a final form. Readers must be quick if they want to keep up with Daphne and Dionys's lively back and forth about bees, for instance, which follows a similarly chaotic trajectory to the discussion of the scarab's ball of dung. Daphne playfully suggests that having a bee or a ladybird in your bonnet is a sign of being 'out of your wits', to which the Count responds: 'give me the madness of the ladybird' (*L* 175). Both conversations veer from a positive to a negative interpretation of an idea, before their conclusions convert these terms into something positive – madness as an enlivening state, destruction as a source of creative energy.

In his essay *Fantasia of the Unconscious* (1922), which he wrote shortly before *The Ladybird*, Lawrence indicates that insects had begun to play a pivotal role in his thinking:

> We are all very pleased with Mr Einstein for knocking that eternal axis out of the universe. The universe isn't a spinning wheel. It is a cloud of bees flying and veering round . . . So that now the universe has escaped from the pin which was pushed through it, like an impaled fly vainly buzzing: now that the multiple universe flies its own complicated course quite free, and hasn't got any hub, we can hope also to escape. We won't be pinned down, either. We have no one law that governs us . . . There is no straight path between you and me, dear reader, so don't blame me if my words fly like dust into your eyes and grit between your teeth, instead of like music into your ears. I am I, but also you are you, and we are in sad need of a theory of human relativity.[44]

Adapting Einstein's theories of relativity to suit his own purposes, Lawrence extends his account of the universe in flux to the workings of literary form. The frenetic energy of the passage, which deviates rapidly from atomic to entomological to linguistic matter, is pivotal to an understanding of the formicatory impulses of *The Ladybird*, as well as the author's body of work as a whole. Lawrence is presenting the text as a form of irritant ('my words fly like dust into your eyes') that goads readers to react forcefully to this threatening otherness, reasserting the boundaries of the self by way of their resistance to his linguistic assault. Yet in statements such as '[w]e won't be pinned down' and 'we have no one law that governs us', the text is attempting to dissolve the boundary between self and other, liberating itself and its readers from the constraints of these categories.

The passage highlights the frequent oscillation in Lawrence's inter-war writing between celebrating the limitless possibilities of being ('We have no one law that governs us'), while also aggressively reasserting the distinction between self and other ('I am I', 'you are you'). The author's insect imagery helps to capture the back and forth, 'frictional to-and-fro' movement of his writing between the loss and the renewal of self-definition. These shifts can be disconcerting and, as will become apparent later on in this chapter, profoundly irritating for some readers. And yet they are also suggestive of a renegotiation of the human subject and its place in the 'multiple universe'. Einsteinian overtones aside, Lawrence's emphasis on 'human relativity' hints at a complex form of relatedness that veers away from anthropocentric modes towards the loose unity of the swarm. In their study of organisational networks, Alexander Galloway and Eugene Thacker argue that the swarm combines qualities of 'formlessness and deliberate strategy, emergence and control, or amorphousness and coordination'.[45] By modelling his writing on 'a cloud of bees' – a construct which privileges flux over fixity, and which is neither completely bound nor entirely diffuse – Lawrence experiments with an aesthetic formation that emulates the unsettled energy of this entomological assemblage.

Swarming Forms

The word swarm, which denotes a body of social insects that gather in 'a compact mass ... and fly off together in search of a new dwelling-place' as well as a 'dense crowd or throng' of people, contains a multitude of etymologies. Deriving from Sanskrit, Latin and German words for a sound or hum, the term has also been linked to the Norwegian dialect word *svarma*, which means to be giddy or to stagger, and *svarva*, 'to turn, go in a circle ... be agitated'.[46] The association between swarming and unsettled movement is reflected in the German term *Schwärmerei* (from *schwärmen*, to swarm, rove and rave) which has played a long-standing role in political discourse. First used as a term of opprobrium by Martin Luther in the early sixteenth century to describe the riotous energies of extremist mobs, the term proliferates in eighteenth-century philosophical writing. As Richard Porteous notes, however, the *Schwärmerei* takes on a countervailing import in the work of writers such as Goethe and Walter Pater, denoting enthusiasm, literary passion and the sensuous appeal of 'unruly, Dionysian behaviour'.[47]

By the time that Lawrence began his writing career, the swarm had become a highly unsettled concept, shifting between human and non-human referents, external forces and inner states, as well as between pejorative and favourable imports. In a further indication of its mutability, the *OED* speculates that the words 'swarm' and 'swerve', meaning to turn aside or deviate from a course, 'might arise from parallel formations on the same base'.[48] Nicholas Royle has examined how the 'figure of the swerve or clinamen', the term given by Lucretius to the unpredictable swerving of atoms, operates at a formal level in Lawrence's writing, exploring the ways in which the author's work frequently veers off course through stylistic deviations, repetitions and non-sequiturs.[49] In a parallel formation, I want to suggest that Lawrence's inter-war writing, following its exposure to the collective energies of the masses, strives to emulate the restless dynamism of the swarm, transforming its anxieties regarding the inescapability of social life into a galvanising force in his writing.

Begun in 1918 and published in 1922, *Aaron's Rod* charts the journey of Nottinghamshire miner and flautist Aaron Sisson, who leaves his job and his young family behind to pursue a career as a professional musician in Europe. While he was writing the novel, the itinerant Lawrence was exposed to a number of inter-war mass movements, documenting a series of unsettling encounters with socialist and fascist ideology during his travels through Italy and Germany in the early 1920s. 'There swarmed the *ferrovieri* like ants', the author would later recall as he overlooked Rome: 'There was democracy, industrialism, socialism, the red flag of the communists and the red white and green tricolor of the fascisti.'[50] These experiences inform key passages of the novel, such as when Aaron witnesses 'a sea of black hats' processing through the square from his hotel window in Florence, with Lawrence likening their frenzied movement in an earlier draft of the text to 'the swarming of bees' (*AR* 183, 305). Dressed in green, the members of the Carabinieri who confront the crowd are likened to 'green-flies on rose-trees, smother-flies. Europe's got the smother-fly in these infernal shoddy militants' (*AR* 236). The growth of this simile mimics the rapid spawning of mass movements in the early inter-war period – what begins as a minor infestation on 'rose-trees' quickly expands to blight all of Europe. It is also suggestive of the ways in which Lawrence, positioned during this time as an onlooker to these new movements, allows their frictional energy to proliferate in his writing.

Aaron's highly-strung friend Rawdon Lilly is horrified by this sudden upsurge of mass activity, proclaiming: 'All I want is to get *myself* out of their horrible heap: to get out of the swarm. The swarm to me is nightmare and nullity – horrible helpless writhing in a dream' (*AR* 119; original emphasis). Aaron too appears anxious to maintain a safe distance from this 'helpless writhing', often observing the masses from up high rather than moving among them. Yet as Michael Bell notes, *Aaron's Rod* centres on its protagonist's efforts to 'protect himself from the various forces that threaten to overwhelm him', but it also dramatises his failure to sustain this ideal of 'sheer, finished singleness'.[51] Towards the end of the novel, a bomb explodes in the middle of a cafe where Aaron and Lilly are dining, and Lawrence's narrator describes how: 'Out of this shock Aaron felt himself issuing amid a mass of terrible sensations'

(*AR* 282). In contrast to Ursula's hopes that the miners would 'issue to . . . a new growth' in *The Rainbow*, the unusual prepositional phrasing of this statement hints at the idea that Aaron's efforts to get '*out of* the swarm' only serve to place him 'amid' its destructive energies. Although he survives with all but his flute intact, Aaron's 'terrible' rebirth amid the masses suggests a drastic modification of Lawrence's pre-war vision of transformation. Having cast off his former life as one the masses of 'stiffened bodies' that Ursula observes from her bedroom window, ex-miner Aaron now finds himself once again caught up in the collective energies of social life (*R* 459).

Human swarms feature heavily in Lawrence's next novel *Kangaroo* (1923). Written during a three-month stay in Australia over the summer of 1922, it is perhaps the author's most experimental text – part thought experiment, part travel narrative, part political allegory. The narrative follows English writer Richard Somers, who arrives in Sydney with his wife Harriet at the end of the war in search of a society capable of 'grow[ing] into new forms' (*K* 69). Somers initially experiences 'a great relief in the atmosphere' of Australia: 'a relief from tension, from pressure. An absence of control or will or form.' It is not long, however, before he discovers that there is little to distinguish the '[g]reat swarming teeming Sydney' from 'the old closing-in of Europe' with its mass of metropolitan bodies:

> How I detest this treacly democratic Australia . . . It swamps one with a sort of common emotion like treacle and before one knows where one is, one is caught like a fly on flypaper, in one mess with all the other buzzers. (*K* 27, 66)

Somers's sense of being 'caught' recalls Ursula's carapaced existence in *Women in Love*, in which her 'active living was suspended', her inner being 'caught, meshed' (*WIL* 9). His outlook also recalls that of the 'war-bitten' young veteran Angus in *Aaron's Rod*, who explains his decision to enlist as a front-line officer after being overwhelmed by the dominant public mood:

> The feelings all came on to me from the outside: like flies settling on meat. Before I knew where I was I was eaten up with a swarm of feelings . . . And ever since [the war] I've been trying to get out of my swarm of feelings, which buzz in and out of me, and have nothing to do with me . . . It's exactly like trying to get out of a swarm of nasty dirty flies. And every one you kill makes you sick, but doesn't make the swarm any less. (*AR* 193)

These entomological analogies are reminiscent of Lawrence's wartime correspondence, in which the fear of physical and psychological violation is evoked with a phobic intensity. In both passages, the 'swarm' is comprised of the carrion of 'common emotion' or 'feelings', suggesting that Lawrence's disdain is not directed towards the masses per se but rather the dehumanising social atmosphere that threatened to infiltrate the individual psyche during and after the war.

By placing these fly passages side by side, it is possible to identify a subtle development in Lawrence's thinking. While in *Aaron's Rod* Angus likens himself to 'meat' or dead flesh that is assailed by an invasive 'swarm' of alien sensations that 'have nothing to do with me', for Somers there is no 'outside', only a sticky mass of 'common emotion' that he shares '*with* all the other buzzers'. Having only recently emerged from the war, Angus is in the process of passing over into the swarm of collective life – his assertion that 'every one you kill makes you sick' is indicative of a growing uncertainty in Lawrence's work about whether lashing out at one's social surroundings may be a form of self-mutilation. In *Kangaroo*, on the other hand, the move towards socialisation is more complete; by likening himself to one of many 'caught like a fly on flypaper', Somers resigns himself to a lack of clear distinction between himself and his fellow 'buzzers'. The shift in outlook that appears to have taken place between the two passages suggests that for Lawrence the survival of the postwar self may now depend on the acquiescence of the individual to collective life in all its sticky discomfort.

In a reading of the Symbolist poet Arthur Rimbaud, Kristin Ross argues that the swarming energies of collective life result in the 'dispersion of the body's surface into a thousand microsensations'. In poems such as 'Les Chercheuses de poux' ['The Lice-Hunters'] the riotous energies of the masses are experienced at both a macro- and a micro-level as a series of entomological incursions, 'as if the body itself were peopled by multiplicities'. Crucially, however, rather than evoking the dissolution of the subject under modern capitalism, Ross suggests that Rimbaud's poetry seeks to 'forestall the erosion of individuality' by calling for a 'hypersensorial, more-than-human perception'. Rimbaud's transformation of the horrors of mass existence into a productive force in his writing – what Ross helpfully calls his 'swarm poesis' – helps to focalise the change that takes place in Lawrence's inter-war writing.[52] If, in *Aaron's Rod*, the swarm functions as an obstacle against which the text struggles (and fails) to reassert the boundaries of the self, in *Kangaroo* Lawrence seems to be attempting to harness its turbulent energy.

This swarming aesthetic becomes particularly apparent halfway through the text, when Somers sits reading *The Sydney Bulletin* over breakfast – 'a lively creature', made up 'all of bits' (*K* 269). After faithfully transcribing several fragments of local gossip, recipes, advertisements and trivia from this popular newspaper, the narrator remarks:

> Bits, bits, bits. Yet [Somers] read on. It was not mere anecdotage. It was the sheer momentaneous life of the continent. There was no consecutive thread. Only the laconic courage of experience. (*K* 272)

Somers's decision to immerse himself in this document of mass culture causes the relatively 'consecutive thread' of *Kangaroo*'s narrative to break down, with the text descending into a series of snippets of advertising and local gossip, disjointed thoughts, emotional outpourings and narratorial intrusions. That this process of disintegration is a deliberate strategy (rather than a product of authorial carelessness as some have suggested) is hinted at by Lawrence's use of the archaism 'momentaneous'.[53] Two years earlier, in his 'Preface' to the American edition of his *New Poems* (1920), Lawrence advocates a 'seething poetry of the incarnate Now', consisting of 'the rapid *momentaneous* association of things' and characterised by a poetics of 'haste, not rest, come-and-go, not fixity, inconclusiveness, immediacy'.[54] In 'Bits', Lawrence appears to be experimenting with a similar incarnation of the 'Now', plunging the text into the midst of its immediate surroundings in order to generate a 'seething' mass of images and sensations.

Somers's 'restlessness' drives him outdoors on a day trip with Harriet to the coastal town of Wolloona, where he is confronted with a series of shop signs: '"Smashed to Bits", "Prices Smashed to Bits", in big labels' (*K* 272). Published in 1928, Walter Benjamin's fragmentary account of urban life, *One-way Street*, describes how the written word has been 'ruthlessly dragged out into the street by advertisements and subjected to the brutal heteronomies of economic chaos', adding that: 'Locust swarms of lettering, already darkening the sun of the supposed mind of the city dweller, become thicker with each successive year'.[55] In *Kangaroo*, on the other hand, Lawrence seems to be contemplating the possibility that being exposed to this swarm of signifiers may have an enlivening effect on subject and text alike. Travelling home from his shopping trip, Somers allows himself to be transported along the streets with these 'careless Australians' amid the 'pantechnicon of civilisation', expressing a sense of admiration for these 'bright, quick' people 'so alert and alive' (*K* 272, 275). Tony Pinkney has likened 'Bits' to the 'Aeolus' section of Joyce's *Ulysses*, identifying 'a notable sense of narrative relief, a sudden access of energy arising from this excursus into the mass-cultural world of the contemporary'.[56] Significantly, however, while Joyce's incorporation of fragments of advertising and popular song has been celebrated by critics, Lawrence's parallel technique has often been dismissed.[57]

Rather than conceding defeat to the forces of mass culture, my sense is that *Kangaroo* seeks to revitalise itself by means of its exposure to the 'locust streams' of commercial language and the swarming streets of Sydney. Throughout the text, Somers is engaged in a frenzy of reading, not only of commercial signs, but also the 'disintegrative, elemental language' of the shoreline and the 'weird, wordless cries' of animals. Somers's frequent turning of his attention outwards to the life of the Australian wilderness is indicative of a 'quick relatedness' in the novel between human and non-human worlds that feeds into Lawrence's entomological wordplay. At one point, the eponymous Kangaroo, who is discussed further on in this chapter, refers to the 'ant-tactics' of the Sydney masses, 'all antics and ant-tricks'. Somers also describes Kangaroo as a 'queen bee buzzing with beatitudes. Beatitudes, beatitudes. Bee attitudes'. All this punning is exhausting – 'It made Richard feel tired' – yet it bespeaks a certain defiance in the face of overstimulation, evoking a mind that remains alert and alive to the generative possibilities of this state of linguistic hypersensitivity (K 154, 133, 123, 283).

Written at breakneck speed, *Kangaroo*'s quick energy causes it to resemble a swarm of miscellaneous elements that threaten to swerve out of control. What are we supposed to do, for instance, with a bizarre recipe for curing mange in horses or a callous anecdote about domestic violence? One way of understanding Lawrence's inclusion of such incongruous and jarring elements is as an attempt to maintain the liveliness of the literary text or, to think of it another way, to maintain the liveliness of readers in response to these 'biting comments' (K 270). Lawrence is not alone in figuring language as a kind of swarm: there are the words that 'swarm and jostle like ants' in Beckett's *The Unnamable* (TN 326), as well as the 'swarm of highly evocative admirable words' that appear in Lewis's 'A Soldier of Humour'. And who could forget the teeming word-life of Joyce's *Finnegans Wake*, a text described by Marcel Brion as 'a swarming of the lowest Brownian movements under the lens of the microscope'.[58] The modernist language of the swarm conjures an image of textual unruliness in which words jostle on the page, generating a host of associations. It is a form of literary expression that has slipped the pin and now flies 'its own complicated course quite free', thwarting our best efforts to grasp its myriad meanings.

Kangaroo's 'swarm poesis' conveys a kind of 'knowledge ... in disintegration', in which the breakdown of the shell of narrative conventions gives rise to an immediate, and almost unmediated, sense of the 'incarnate Now' in all its seething intensity. In this dissolute state, however, the text can provide little resistance against the more sinister forces at work in its surroundings. As Maud Ellmann aptly notes, the idea of the swarm suggests a world in which 'things can no longer be contained by thought' and where language as a coherent system 'falls apart, leaving only isolated words'.[59] This state of collapse is a far cry from Lawrence's vision of literary form as a kind of resistant membrane. Indeed, while 'Bits' derives a 'bright, quick' energy from its exposure to the teeming energy of collective life, the text as a whole is far from at home in the swarm.

The Envelope of Suffering

Towards the end of 'Bits', Somers's growing sympathy for his fellow city-dwellers is suddenly replaced by a cold hatred for the masses:

> It takes how many thousand facets to make the eye of a fly – or a spider? . . . Well, all these people are just facets: just bits, that fitted together make a whole. But you can fit the bits together time after time, yet it won't bring the bug to life. (*K* 277)

Somers's shattered optic may be linked to his own dipteran status: moments later he likens himself to a fly trying to crawl out of a pot of ointment. The protagonist's fragmentary perspective also hints at a wider uncertainty on the part of Lawrence as to whether exposing his writing to the swarms of sociality serves a revitalising function, bringing the self (and the text) 'to life', or whether this process of exposure will inevitably give way to the same kind of deathly insentience that his writing is attempting to resist.

This tension is most apparent in Somers's fraught interactions with charismatic lawyer Benjamin Cooley, known as Kangaroo, the leader of a proto-fascist paramilitary group called the Diggers.[60] Lawrence describes the growing appeal of Kangaroo's fantasy of imperviousness to Somers, who informs him:

> I have been like a man buried up to his neck in an ant-heap: so buried in the daily world, and stung and stung and stung again . . . till now their poison is innocuous, and the formic-acid of social man has no effect on me. (*K* 122)

Over time, Kangaroo's skin has hardened, like proud flesh, into a carapace, with Lawrence indicating that his prolonged exposure to the masses has resulted in an increasingly callous attitude towards his fellow man. Immersive sociality here gives way to a version of extreme isolation, as overexposure comes to resemble a form of 'ossiferous' non-exposure. Kangaroo's outlook is consistent with his extremist politics: in his sociological study of the rise of National Socialism, Klaus Theweleit draws on Freud's account of the protective barrier surrounding the psyche to describe how the cultivation of the fascist ego hinges on an extreme form of masochism:

> Painful encroachments by external agencies on [the fascist male's] bodily periphery . . . are integral to the process whereby the not-yet-fully-born acquires something approaching the psychic agency of . . . a 'stable' body-ego.[61]

Theweleit's account of ego-formation by way of a quasi-entomological invasion of the flesh bears striking similarities to Kangaroo's strategy of self-inurement by way of exposure to the 'formic-acid of social man'. Although he is advocating a way of resisting the deleterious effects of social life on individual identity, Kangaroo's protracted immersion in the myrmecological masses – which resembles an extreme form of formication – has resulted in the anaesthetising of his flesh into precisely the kind of 'envelope of insentience' that Lawrence's writing seeks to discard.

Following his prolonged absorption in the masses in 'Bits', Somers's thoughts undergo a similar process of hardening as he longs to return to the 'central isolate, absolute self' and coldly fantasises that a sudden volcanic eruption might exterminate the 'teeming absolute of the . . . ant-heap' and purify the world. Somers's murderous musings echo Kangaroo's earlier diatribe against the 'ant-men and ant-women' who 'swarm over the face of the earth', suggesting that his thoughts have been infiltrated Kangaroo's destructive rhetoric (*K* 280, 282, 121). These analogies also indicate that Lawrence may have been influenced by Wilfred Trotter's sociological study, *Instincts of the Herd in War and Peace* (1916), which draws overt parallels between modern civilisation and 'the hive and the ant's nest'. Alluding to the work of contemporary entomologists, Trotter writes:

> A study of bees and ants shows at once how . . . [t]he individual in such communities is completely incapable, often physically, of existing apart from the community, and this fact at once gives rise to the suspicion that even in communities less closely knit than those of the ant and the bee, the individual may in fact be more dependent on communal life than appears at first sight.[62]

This account touches on one of *Kangaroo*'s deepest anxieties, namely that human beings are social creatures at heart and that the lure of collective existence is strong enough to subsume individual identity. In December 1916, Lawrence returned Trotter's study to a friend, complaining: 'I cannot stand this scientific talk of instincts and bee communities . . . as if everything worked from a mechanical basis'.[63] Yet in an early version of *Lady Chatterley's Lover*, members of a dinner party discuss a book about the 'ant-heap psychology', suggesting that Trotter's writing continued to permeate his thinking well into the 1920s.[64] As Rachel Crossland observes, Lawrence's frequent references to the 'mass-spirit' and the 'herd instinct' in *Kangaroo* 'suggest a greater internalization of contemporary ideas on crowd psychology than he would perhaps have been willing to admit'.[65]

Although Somers is not entirely taken in by Kangaroo's 'ant-tricks' and 'bee attitudes', Lawrence establishes a causal link between his protagonist's growing susceptibility to extremist ideology and the trauma of his wartime experiences. Returning home from a meeting with Kangaroo through the crowded Sydney streets, Somers suddenly remembers how during the war every individual was 'swept away with the ghastly masses', likening this fevered atmosphere to a kind of 'blood-poisoning and mortification' (K 214, 217). In the extended wartime flashback that follows, which is entitled 'The Nightmare', Somers recalls how his own tortured alienation came to a head during the final of a series of invasive medical examinations. In an ordeal closely based on Lawrence's own experiences, he is pricked, probed and prodded in his private parts with the 'poisonous bite' of this encounter such that he longs never to be touched again. Lawrence describes how the return of this repressed wartime memory is so forceful that Somers 'trembled helplessly under the shock of it', with the text diagnosing this formicatory sensation as a result of 'contact with Kangaroo and [socialist leader] Willie Struthers, contact with the accumulating forces of social violence' (K 259–60). Positioned at the centre of the narrative, 'The Nightmare' resembles the reopening of a psychic wound that leaves the text open to ideological contamination.

When Somers visits Kangaroo in private to tell him that he has decided to distance himself from contemporary politics, Kangaroo follows him to the door 'like a spider, approaching with awful stillness. If the stillness suddenly broke, and he struck out!' Intriguingly, however, while enveloped in his embrace, Somers realises: 'He wouldn't be hugging me if I were a scorpion', before deciding, 'And I *am* a scorpion' (K 211, 208–9; original emphasis). Steven Connor has described the sensation of feeling one's skin crawl as an imitation of the threat felt, with the skin 'borrowing a survival from the very kind of life that it fears will carry it away piecemeal'.[66] In this first moment of physical contact between the two men Lawrence demonstrates how an arachnidan mode of defence (spiders and scorpions both belong to the arachnid class) passes from one body to another. Earlier on in the text, Kangaroo reveals that he too has been transformed at the touch of the ant-like masses, remarking: 'I can fight them with their own weapons: the hard mandibles and the acid sting of the cold ant' (K 121). These examples, which recall Lewis's strategies of offensive mimicry, can help to shed light on the mimetic strategies at work in *Kangaroo*. Rather than simply conceding to the forces at work in its surroundings, the text actively mutates into a swarming multiplicity in order to stave off the hypertrophy of sensation in its surroundings – be it the onslaught of mass culture, the 'poisonous bite' of war or the steady creep of inter-war ideology.

Throughout *Kangaroo*, Lawrence appears to be working through a dilemma as to whether being exposed to the destructive political energies of the inter-war period is able to strengthen the resistance of the subject, or whether the self is irrevocably contaminated by these interactions, mutating into what it fears. The novel gains much of its momentum from its vexed efforts both to withdraw from and engage with the source of its discomfort. When Somers attempts to retreat from human contact into the 'sacred separateness' of the Australian outback, he soon realises that his ability to write depends on the 'agony of irritation' that he feels when he is 'caught up in the rush' of social life. Significantly, when Harriet asks him why he can't simply retreat from the world and live in peace with her, Somers responds: 'Because I feel I *must* fight something out with mankind yet ... I've got a struggle with them yet' (*K* 155, 68; original emphasis). Unlike Kangaroo, who submits himself to the source of his discomfort until 'it has no effect', Somers continues to veer wildly towards and away from the Sydney crowds, with the text appearing to recharge (as opposed to overcharging) itself through this 'frictional to-end-fro'. In this way, the novel refuses either to inure itself to its surroundings or to disintegrate at their touch into a mere word heap, remaining instead an antsy, agitated surface – a swarming without settling.

An important insight into this busy movement may be found in Didier Anzieu's psychoanalytic study *The Skin Ego* (1985). Drawing on Freud's account of the stimulus shield in *Beyond the Pleasure Principle*, Anzieu argues that in some cases the pursuit of physical pain may serve to mitigate the effects of psychic distress: 'inflicting a real envelope of suffering on oneself can be an attempt to restore the skin's containing function.'[67] Anzieu's account helps to make sense of the almost pathological tendency of Lawrence's inter-war fiction to expose itself to that which it finds disturbing, renewing the boundaries of the self through these painful interactions. To suffer 'an agony of irritation', Lawrence's writing often seems to suggest, is to return to one's own skin, in contrast to the debilitating numbness that marks Somers's post-war isolation. Ostensibly, there is little to distinguish Anzieu's 'envelope of suffering' from the masochistic impulses that Theweleit attributes to the fascist ego. But while Somers's intermittent exposure to the masses functions as a necessary, albeit painful, means of resensitisation, Kangaroo's extreme pursuit of suffering leads only to the bug-like insentience that brought society to war in the first place.

Kangaroo allows itself to be contaminated by the rhetoric of fascism to the point that it risks succumbing to its 'poisonous bite' and 'mortification'. Yet in staging these painful interactions at the level of form, the text also exerts a relentless pressure on itself as well as its readers, demanding a response that entails an active sense of resistance. 'An author should be in among the crowd, kicking their shins', Lawrence declared in 1925.[68] Echoing his earlier account of the swarming energies of the text that 'fly like dust into your eyes', *Kangaroo* assails its readers with a series of aggressive statements and bewildering formal shifts, forcing us to recoil and thus reassert our singularity in response to this unpleasant encounter. It is undoubtedly a risky strategy, which coupled with taunting outbursts from the narrator – 'If you don't like the novel, don't read it' – increases the likelihood of alienating the reader to the point of their giving up on the text (*K* 284). At times, moreover, the authoritarian stance adopted by the narrator exposes the novel's proximity to the very rhetoric it is attempting to expose. Tony Pinkney argues that *Kangaroo*'s narrator 'turns aggressively and tauntingly on its reader', leaving us 'stung, hurt, angry' and inclined to react with 'irritation and frustration'.[69]

The confrontational stance that Pinkney discerns in the text may be understood as an ambitious move on the part of Lawrence to make readers experience the calamitous effects of inter-war ideology, as well as to suffer the acute isolation and displacement of the post-war subject. In other words, rather than simply being irritating, the text deploys irritation as an aesthetic strategy. In her study of negative emotions, *Ugly Feelings*, Sianne Ngai notes that irritation tends to 'apply equally to psychic life *and* life at the level of the body – and particularly to its surfaces or skin'.[70] Ngai's emphasis on the slippage between psychic and somatic sensations is consistent with the way that Somers's 'agony of irritation' often seems to extend from his mental state to the body of the text. In his account of Lawrence's most 'irritating' text, John Worthen argues that *Kangaroo* attains its status as a modernist text in its depiction of 'alienation which struggles against itself but does not wish to be relieved'.[71] Rick Rylance likens the novel to '*The Waste Land* in prose; a critical cultural enquiry whose shape comes from the distress of its personally felt predicament'.[72] These readings describe a form of literary representation that is borne out of its own psychic distress, and yet rather than provoking sympathy in the onlooker the text's tonal shiftiness and restless wordplay seem designed to rub readers up the wrong way, forcing them to experience an unrelieved irritation in the hope that this discomfort may forestall a more dangerous state of psychic numbness.

Kangaroo is uncomfortable in its own skin but refuses either to retreat from or inure itself to the contemporary social and political formations that it finds so distressing. Instead, it antagonises its readers, bugging us at every turn, refusing either to let us be or to drop our guard against it. Like the swarms it depicts, we cannot settle either. Perhaps understandably, this bold strategy has led some readers to conflate Somers's more aggressive statements with the author's own views. As John Humma notes, other than *The Plumed Serpent*, '*Kangaroo* is probably Lawrence's most thoroughly disliked novel'.[73] As is also evident in critical responses to *The Ladybird*, readers of *Kangaroo* have tended to bristle at Lawrence's incorporation of uncomfortable views into the body of the text, perceiving them to be a corrupting influence. One reviewer, the American writer Alyse Gregory, was particularly disturbed by *Kangaroo*, writing of her wish to erase the text from her mind and lamenting: 'Would that [Lawrence] himself had remained uncorrupted by the disease of ideology which so exasperates him in others and in the throes of which he likewise now lies prostrate.'[74] Gregory's analogy of prostration evokes a wider sense of unease in

Lawrence criticism regarding the author's apparent failure to reinforce his writing against 'the disease of ideology'. Despite Somers's gradual realisation that the revolutionary cure proffered by both Kangaroo and Struthers is really a continuation of the 'blood-poisoning' of war, like a mosquito, the text appears to feed on the volatile energies of these movements, tapping into their aggressive ideals. The uncertain nature of the text's engagement with right-wing extremism in particular, the value of which it neither fully endorses nor entirely rejects, invites readerly frustration due to its refusal to adopt a coherent stance, instead vacillating between extremes in its agonised pursuit of 'a new life-form, a new social form' (*K* 86).

'To read a really new novel will *always* hurt', Lawrence insisted in 1925, 'there will always be resistance' (*STH* 175; original emphasis). Following the completion of *Kangaroo*, however, there are signs that Lawrence was beginning to tire of this strategy of readerly provocation. In his next novel, *The Plumed Serpent* (1926), one character remarks wearily to another: 'the agitators go round and infect the peons. It is nothing but a sort of infectious disease . . . all this revolution and socialism.'[75] In 1928, the author announced a new phase in his thinking, writing that 'the leader-cum-follower relationship is a bore', and that 'the new relationship will be some sort of tenderness, sensitive, between . . . men and women'.[76] When he made these remarks, Lawrence was in the process of publishing *Lady Chatterley's Lover* (1928), which he briefly considered calling *Tenderness*. As well as evoking a quality of gentleness and compassion, the word denotes a state of epidermic frailty – a skin that is sensitive and easily hurt.[77] In his final novel, Lawrence continues to inflame the sensibilities of his readers, while also dispensing with the swarming formations that characterise his middle phase in favour of a gentler, more tender mode of expression.

Insex

Lady Chatterley's Lover tells the story of the ailing Constance Chatterley, who casts off her physically and emotionally paralysed husband Clifford after experiencing the restorative touch of gamekeeper Oliver Mellors. Clifford, a wounded war veteran and industrial magnate who is likened to an 'invertebrate' comprised of a 'hard, efficient shell of an exterior and a pulpy interior', epitomises the 'negation of human contact' that Lawrence saw as afflicting inter-war Britain (*LCL* 100, 256). Connie and Mellors's sexual relationship (their fornication) is presented as the antidote to Clifford's carapaced existence, with the text presenting the couple's intimacy as a force capable of breaking through the inertness of post-war society. The novel advocates a new form of 'bodily awareness' based on 'natural physical tenderness', drawing on the author's belief that sex, 'the closest of all touch . . . keeps us tender and alive at a moment when the great danger is to go brittle, hard, and in some way dead' (*LCL* 203, 16).[78]

Lawrence completed a first draft of *Lady Chatterley's Lover* in late 1926, before rewriting the novel from scratch twice in 1927. As Michael Squires notes, Lawrence's revision of the novel 'impressively parallels his theme'. With each version, he 'breaks out of the prison of his own work by recreating it anew, vicariously breaking the form of his earlier self'.[79] Squires's reading highlights Lawrence's continued efforts to prevent his writing from hardening into an 'impervious envelope of insentience'. Indeed, as he redrafted *Lady Chatterley*, Lawrence began to strip away the formicatory sensations that characterise his middle phase, as though sensing that they had begun to harden into a set feature of his writing. In the first version of the text, Parkin (an early version of Mellors) describes falling in love with a woman as 'worse than that malaria as some chaps got so bad out there in Gallipoli. It comes on in bouts and all your insides turn over'.[80] Connie's desire for Parkin also leaves her with 'an inflamed place which she could not smear with forgetful ointment'.[81] These analogies of bodily discomfort are removed from the final version of the novel and replaced with an emphasis on the couple's 'live, warm beauty of contact' (*LCL* 125). Crucially, though, the text's gradual shedding of an aesthetic of itch and disintegration coincides with the arrival of a host of stinging obscenities that function in a similarly disquieting manner. Ever the gadfly, Lawrence continues to push up against social and novelistic conventions in controversial ways, with the final version of the text going to extreme lengths in its depiction of a 'new relationship' between men and women.

One of the most striking passages in the text is an apparent description of anal intercourse between Connie and Mellors that appears to have bypassed the censors during the *Lady Chatterley* trial. In an uncomfortable instance of free indirect speech, the narrator discloses Connie's perspective on the act:

> And what a reckless devil the man was! really like a devil! One had to be strong to bear him . . . And how he had pressed in on her! . . . Now suddenly there it was, and a man was sharing her last and final nakedness, she was shameless. What liars poets and everybody were! They made one think one wanted sentiment. When what one supremely wanted was this piercing, consuming, rather awful sensuality. (*LCL* 247)

Although the passage makes no direct reference to what is taking place, Lawrence's use of deixis ('there it was') combined with short sharp exclamations ('really like a devil!') serves to impress upon the reader, in rather a visceral way, what is occurring. The dynamics of opposition at work in the passage – between attraction and repulsion, pleasure and pain, disintegration and renewal – are consistent with Lawrence's efforts to expose the subject to a piercing but potentially life-affirming otherness. The repetition of the word 'devil', in particular, transports us back to the 'devilry' of the mosquito with its 'obscenity of trespass', as well as to Daphne's question to Dionys: 'Must one hate the devil that makes one live?' Now it is Mellors who takes on this insect-like role, breaking through Connie's outer defences to reveal her 'last and final nakedness'.

The text's representation of a sexual activity that, due to its lack of procreative function, was considered by many during this time to be a deviant practice, celebrates the generative possibilities of sex as 'sheer sensuality' rather than as a social good (*LCL* 248). That being said, it is important to acknowledge that this celebratory attitude is confined to the realm of heterosexual intercourse. Frank Kermode observes that as far back as *Women in Love*, Lawrence had 'tried to distinguish between buggery which was wholly dissolute and buggery that was initiatory, the symbolic death before rebirth, the cracking of the insect carapace'.[82] As well as drawing attention to the limitations of Lawrence's sexual politics, Kermode's remarks suggests that his thought processes have been infiltrated by Lawrence's entomological imagery. Indeed, this exoskeletal analogy helps to connect the transgressive eroticism of *Lady Chatterley* to the role of insects as boundary-threatening entities in the author's body of work. The term 'buggery', in particular, recalls the bug-like figure of Dionys, as well as the excremental figure of Fabre's dung beetle with its counterbalancing of the 'creative principle' and the 'principle of decomposition'.

Just as Daphne's intimacy with Dionys enables her to 'collapse away from her old self', Connie's relationship with Mellors serves to restore her waning vitality: 'She was her sensual self, naked and unashamed.' The text likens Connie's 'piercing' sensation to the release of contaminants, describing how the couple's transgressive union is able to 'burn out false shames and smelt out the heaviest ore of the body into purity' (*LCL* 247). According to Claudia Benthien, the words 'shame' and 'skin' share the same Indo-Germanic root, which means 'to cover'.[83] Lawrence's molten analogy suggests that the frictional heat generated by this sexual encounter is able to dissolve the shameful connotations of sex, purging the couple's physical intimacy of its disreputable associations. At the same time, as the text's reference to 'pressing in' implies, Lawrence continues to rely on the notion of a restrictive outer shell to exert a form of external pressure on the subject. Rather than simply merging together into two formless blobs, the emphasis is on Connie's resistance to the threat of dissolution posed by Mellors – 'one had to be strong to bear him'. Elsewhere in the text, Lawrence describes how, after enduring the intrusive gossip of hostile locals, Connie is able to convert this social animosity into an invigorating substance: 'it was a sort of tonic, something to live up against' (*LCL* 14).

In the author's late writing, the possibility of self-renewal continues to depend on the presence of a negative counterforce. Connie's vehement assertion that poets are 'liars' is consistent with Lawrence's efforts to break through the conventions of literary form in his portrayal of sex, attempting, as Barbara Hardy puts it, to 'tell the whole uncomfortable truth'.[84] This candidness extends to the text's bold use of four-letter words: 'A woman's a lovely thing when 'er's deep ter fuck, and cunt's good', Mellors states bluntly to Connie after she presses him to articulate his feelings for her. The explicitness of this statement appears designed to restore the connection between words and the objects to which they refer: moments later, the narrator describes how Mellors 'softly . . . laid his hand on [Connie's] mound of Venus' (*LCL* 212), with the act of touch bridging the divide between signifier and signified. Roland Barthes defines obscenities as 'a mode of writing whose function is no longer only communication or expression, but the imposition of something beyond language'.[85] Barthes's use of the term 'imposition' is suggestive of the role played by insects in Lawrence's writing – their ability, like words such as 'cunt' or 'fuck', to produce an intense, almost physical reaction, as well as the way that their diminutive status belies their curious strength.

'How can you put so much devilry', wonders the speaker of 'The Mosquito' to his anopheline assailant, 'Into that translucent phantom shred | of a frail corpus?' (*TM* 287). *Lady Chatterley*'s use of four-letter words poses a similar question, reasserting the affective power of words as frail yet forceful entities. That insects and sex are intimately connected in Lawrence's writing is also hinted at in his novel *The Boy in the Bush* (1924), which he co-wrote with the Australian author Mollie Skinner. Early on in the text, hardened veteran of the outback Len instructs wide-eyed protagonist Jack to wrap up his 'meat . . . against th' ants . . . against th' insex'.[86] Like Mellors's Nottinghamshire dialect ('when 'er's deep'), this unusual orthography pertains to regional pronunciation, but it also evokes the transgressive nature of Lawrence's wordplay. By advising Jack to guard his meat (and by implication his flesh) 'against th' insex' Len's remarks serve to highlight the shared function of insects and sex, formication and fornication, as forces capable of breaking down the subject's defences. And yet, as is so often the case in Lawrence's writing, this threat of dissolution also functions as a means of renewing the boundaries of the self against this all-consuming threat.

Despite its emphasis on transgression, *Lady Chatterley's Lover* is careful to maintain an air of discretion – to not give way to the prurience of which it was inevitably accused. The candidness of Mellors's assertion that a 'woman's a lovely thing when 'er's deep ter fuck, and cunt's good' is perhaps less disturbing than the use of lewd euphemisms by other characters such as Connie's father Sir Malcolm, who praises Mellors for having set his daughter's 'stack on fire' before boasting of his powers of sexual harassment: 'The test of a woman is to pinch her bottom.' By attempting to initiate Mellors into what the narrator refers to as 'the old free-masonry of male sensuality', Sir Malcolm demonstrates that discussions of sex are essentially hiding in plain sight (*LCL* 283). In a late essay entitled 'Pornography and Obscenity', Lawrence argues that sex has become 'a kind of hidden sore or inflammation which . . . becomes more and more secretly inflamed, and the nervous and psychic health of the individual is more and more impaired'.[87] By stripping it of this itchy skin of secrecy, *Lady Chatterley* attempts to purge sex of its destructive influence on the psyche, replacing the covert reference with a form of straightforward honesty.

To a certain extent, the use of obscenities in *Lady Chatterley* resembles the authorial abuse of *Kangaroo*; in both novels there is a hint of self-sabotage in Lawrence's introduction of elements designed to unsettle and discomfort the reader that is akin to the placing of a bug in the textual system.[88] Yet, it is important to acknowledge the marked shift in Lawrence's final novel towards a more conciliatory mode of expression. In a letter to Connie at the end of the text in which he struggles to articulate his feelings, Mellors breaks off suddenly, remarking: 'so many words because I can't touch you. If I could sleep with my arm round you, the ink could stay in the bottle' (*LCL* 301). This sudden shift into second person address recalls the aggressive authorial outbursts of *Kangaroo* ('if you don't like the book, don't read it'), as well as the unsettling eye-contact of Lewis's protagonist in *Snooty Baronet* – 'If I could come out of this paper at you' (*SB* 135), but this instance constitutes a more tender transgression of the fourth wall. Mellors's struggle to substitute touch for language is symptomatic of the efforts of the text as a whole to instigate 'a new relatedness' between writer and reader – to comfort as well as to discomfort (*STH* 174). In its attempts to reach beyond the existing parameters of literary representation, *Lady Chatterley's Lover* reaches out to its readers in a way that many found deeply unsettling. Evidently, Lawrence intended to shock his readers, writing with characteristic impudence of his decision 'to publish 1000 copies of the unexpurgated edition, and fling it in the face of the world'.[89] What is striking, therefore, is the way that the text refuses the sense of unease that it seems designed to provoke, 'burn[ing] out false shame' in its bold depictions of sex in a manner that forces readers to re-examine the source of their unease.

The text's denial of discomfort is reflected in Lawrence's confidence in the integrity of his novelistic vision, asserting in one letter: 'to me it is beautiful and tender and frail as the naked self is'.[90] Consistent throughout *Lady Chatterley* is an emphasis on the ability of the human body to persist and even thrive in a 'frail' and often vulnerable state – the instar phase of insect life as opposed to the 'hard . . . shell'. The novel establishes a close connection between Connie and Mellors's 'new nakedness' and their natural surroundings, with the couple's burgeoning relationship coinciding with the arrival of spring:

> Everything came tenderly out of the old hardness. Even the snaggy craggy oak-trees put out the softest young leaves, spreading thin, brown little wings like young bat-wings in the light. (*LCL* 125, 184)

No longer is the emergence of the self from beneath its 'horny covering' confined to some unspecified point in the future; now the 'old hardness' has finally been vanquished. Elsewhere in the text, Connie informs Mellors that what sets him apart from other men is 'the courage of your own tenderness' (*LCL* 277). Just as the word 'tender' recurs over fifty times over the course of the text, courage is also a defiant mantra – 'the courage' of Tommy Dukes 'to say "shit" in front of a lady', or of Mellors's naked body, 'courageous and full of life' (*LCL* 39, 248). The marriage of 'courage' and 'tenderness' is, I want to suggest, central to Lawrence's achievement of a form of representation that is both sensitive and robust – one that remains exposed to its surroundings so as not to be destroyed by them.

For all its emphasis on frailty, *Lady Chatterley* is perhaps the most resilient of Lawrence's novels, suffering decades of notoriety and neglect before finally emerging onto the literary scene after the 1960 trial. Despite having previously suffered the censorship of *The Rainbow*, Lawrence bared the novel to the world in its original form, only to undergo a series of wounding encounters with typesetters, censors and outraged reviewers, as well as the disfiguring effects of piracy. In the decades since its trial, *Lady Chatterley's Lover* has gradually been accepted into literary circles, but as a mark of the difficulty in transforming social attitudes it has still yet to fully cast off its reputation as a salacious novel. 'In the popular imagination', wrote Doris Lessing recently, the novel remains 'a period sex romp'.[91] Considering all it has been through, Lawrence's final novel may be said to exemplify the courageous vulnerability of the author's post-war writing – its willingness to expose itself to the hostile forces in its external surroundings, as well as its readiness to endure these excoriating encounters.

Reviewing Lawrence's poetry in October 1916, the literary critic Arthur Waugh bristles at the author's use of 'symbols from the natural world to illustrate a degree of self-abandonment which is so invertebrate as to be practically abnormal'.[92] Waugh is attributing a lack of moral backbone to Lawrence's work, but his analogy highlights an important connection between the author's insect imagery and his experimentation with various forms of self-abandonment – from the sloughing of a former identity to the forsaking of the subject's 'sheer finished singleness' for the life of the swarm. These states of being are suggestive of Lawrence's efforts to renegotiate the boundaries of individual identity in his writing, redefining what it means to have a self in an age of collectivity. Such states are not easily settled: in the author's inter-war prose in particular, insects appear to be representative of seemingly irreconcilable notions of decay and renewal, egotism and deindividuation, numbness and hypersensitivity, contamination and healing. But just as Edison's 'bug' in the phonograph is defined not only as the cause of the problem, but also as 'an expression for solving a difficulty', Lawrence's insects can help us to come to terms with some of the more troublesome aspects of his writing, allowing us to see that its tendency to aggravate and disturb readers is also the sign of its ability to transport us beyond ourselves. H.D. also turns to the insect world in search of strategies of self-renewal. The next chapter considers the author's aesthetic interest in the cocoon, examining her efforts to craft a form of literary expression that is able at once to dissolve and recreate the self.

Notes

1. Lawrence, *Introductions and Reviews*, 51.
2. Sagar, *D. H. Lawrence*, 62.
3. 'transport, *v.*', OED.
4. Jones, *Mosquito*, 73–103; Ellis, *Dying Game*, 235.
5. Pinkney, *Lawrence and Modernism*, 138; Fernihough, *Aesthetics and Ideology*, 52.
6. Rabaté, 'Theory's Slice of Life', 106.
7. WL 389; *The Plumed Serpent*, 106.
8. *Letters*, Vol. 2, 331.
9. *Letters*, Vol. 2, 331, 650, 321. In *Women in Love*, Lawrence incorporates his fear of black beetles into the character of the Pussum, who lisps: 'I'm not afwaid of anything essept black-beetles . . . If one were to crawl on me, I'm *sure* I should die.' WL 69–70; original emphasis.
10. *Mr Noon*, 245; *The Trespasser*, 199.
11. Baudelaire, *Complete Poems*, 230; Eliot, *Complete Poems and Plays*, 73; King, *Insect Nations*, 21.
12. Sherman, *The Critical Heritage*, 252.
13. Fernihough, 'Introduction', *Cambridge Companion*, 1.
14. Chevalley, *The Critical Heritage*, 156.
15. The letter includes a note from his German partner Frieda, who asks: 'why are you English so keen on [form?]', adding that 'form wants smashing in almost any direction, but they can't come out of their snail house', *Letters*, Vol. 1, 476–7, 479; original emphasis.
16. *Sons and Lovers*, 464.
17. Pound, *Gaudier-Brzeska: A Memoir*, 85.
18. Woolf, *The Death of the Moth*, 23.
19. Joyce, *Portrait of the Artist*, 149.
20. Burwell, 'A Checklist', 66–70.
21. Neville, *The Betrayal*, 40. Neville also recalled that the young Lawrence was an avid reader of the scientific magazine *The Nature Book*, 187 n. 18.
22. Fabre, *The Life of the Caterpillar*, 1.
23. *Letters*, Vol. 1, 492; original emphasis.
24. Harrison, *Lawrence and Italian Futurism*, xv.
25. Graham, *Collected Poems*, 153.
26. *Letters*, Vol. 2, 285, 426.
27. *Letters*, Vol. 2, 266, 600, 526.
28. *Letters*, Vol. 2, 650, 319.
29. Rylance, 'Lawrence's Politics', 168; original emphasis.
30. Marren and Mabey, *Bugs Britannica*, 349.

31. Beckett was alert to the similarity between the two terms. In *Happy Days* (1961), Winnie points out 'an emmet' (an ant) carrying the egg of its offspring, to which her husband Willie responds: 'Formication'. Winnie appears to mishear Willie, and their shared laughter indicates that she heard the word 'fornication', *CDW* 150.
32. *The First and Second Lady Chatterley's Lover*, 183.
33. 'bug, *n.*²', *OED*.
34. 'bug, *n.*², *n.*¹', *OED*. It wasn't until after the Second World War that the word 'bug' was used to describe the use of covert audio surveillance, or the act of annoying or pestering someone, 'bug, *v.*¹', *OED*.
35. Fabre, 'The Scavengers', 240.
36. Lawrence, 'Foreword', *Women in Love*, 485.
37. Fabre, 'The Scavengers', 239.
38. Moynahan, *The Deed of Life*, 178; Clarke, *River of Dissolution*, 113.
39. See *The Ladybird*, 177 n. 36; *Letters*, Vol. 1, 525.
40. H.D., *End to Torment*, 23.
41. Lawrence, *Poems*, Vol. 1, 181.
42. *Letters*, Vol. 4, 447.
43. 'quick, *adj.*, *n.*¹, *adv*', *OED*.
44. Lawrence, *Fantasia of the Unconscious*, 72.
45. Galloway and Thacker, *The Exploit*, 66.
46. 'swarm, *n.*', *OED*.
47. Porteous, 'The Disappearing "Swarm"', 29; see also La Vopa, 'The Philosopher and the *Schwärmer*', 85–115.
48. 'swarm, *n.*', *OED*.
49. Royle, *Veering*, 178.
50. Lawrence, *Introductions and Reviews*, 33.
51. Bell, *Language and Being*, 145.
52. Ross, 'The Swarm', 110, 133, 102, 133.
53. See, for instance, Sagar, *Art of D. H. Lawrence*, 131; Kermode, *D. H. Lawrence*, 100.
54. Lawrence, *Poems*, Vol. 1, 646–7; emphasis added.
55. Benjamin, *One-way Street*, 66.
56. *Lawrence and Modernism*, 115.
57. Frank Kermode, for instance, alleges that several pages of the text are 'simply copied out of the *Sydney Bulletin*' because Lawrence 'wrote on and on without cease, even when uncertain of what to do next', *D. H. Lawrence*, 100.
58. Lewis, *Complete Wild Body*, 37; Brion, 'The Idea of Time', 31.
59. *The Nets of Modernism*, 29.
60. The word 'digger' was Australian military slang for soldiers during the First World War and is connected to ideas of male camaraderie, hardiness and fighting spirit. See 'Mateship, Diggers, and Wartime', <http://www.australia.gov.au/about-australia/australian-story/mateship-diggers-and-wartime> (last accessed 23 July 2017).
61. Theweleit, *Male Fantasies*, 289.
62. Trotter, *Instincts of the Herd*, 91, 167, 19–20.
63. *Letters*, Vol. 3, 59.
64. *The First and Second Lady Chatterley's Lover*, 275–6.

65. Crossland, *Modernist Physics*, 141.
66. Connor, *The Book of Skin*, 244.
67. Anzieu, *The Skin Ego*, 201.
68. *Letters*, Vol. 5, 201.
69. *Lawrence and Modernism*, 122–3.
70. Ngai, *Ugly Feelings*, 184; original emphasis.
71. Worthen, *Idea of the Novel*, 143.
72. Rylance, 'Lawrence's Politics', 171.
73. Humma, *Metaphor and Meaning*, 30.
74. Gregory, *The Critical Heritage*, 222.
75. *The Plumed Serpent*, 101.
76. *Letters*, Vol. 6, 321.
77. This double meaning is hinted at during Mellors's description of his relationship with his soldiers during the war: 'I had to be in touch with them, physically . . . I had to be bodily aware of them – and a bit tender to them – even if I put them through hell', *LCL* 277.
78. *Late Essays*, 224.
79. Squires, *The Creation of Lady Chatterley*, 105.
80. *First Lady Chatterley*, 202.
81. *First Lady Chatterley*, 266.
82. *D. H. Lawrence*, 141.
83. Benthien, *Skin*, 100.
84. Hardy, *The Appropriate Form*, 162.
85. Barthes, *Writing Degree Zero*, 7.
86. *The Boy in the Bush*, 62.
87. *Late Essays*, 243.
88. Pinkney, *Lawrence and Modernism*, 146.
89. Quoted in Worthen, *Idea of the Novel*, 178.
90. *Letters*, Vol. 6, 29.
91. Lessing, 'Testament of Love', para. 1.
92. Waugh, 'The New Poetry', 155.

3

COCOON STATES: H.D.

> Man cannot purge his body of its theme,
> As can the silkworm, on a running thread,
> Spin a shroud to re-consider in.
> Djuna Barnes, 'Rite of Spring'

> A dim capacity for Wings
> Demeans the Dress I wear –
> Emily Dickinson, 'My Cocoon tightens –'

Pat Barker's novel *Regeneration* (1991) centres on the pioneering methods of the British psychiatrist W. H. R. Rivers, who treated a number of shell-shocked soldiers – including Wilfred Owen and Siegfried Sassoon – during the First World War. After meeting with a severely traumatised young veteran who is beginning to show signs of a 'complete disintegration of personality', Rivers recognises something hopeful in his patient's declining mental state:

> Rivers knew only too well how often the early stages of change or cure may mimic deterioration. Cut a chrysalis open and you will find a rotting caterpillar. What you will never find is that mythical creature, half caterpillar, half butterfly, a fit emblem of the human soul . . . No, the process of transformation consists almost entirely of decay.[1]

The pupal stage of insect life is here called upon to express a curious psychic phenomenon, in which the mind of the shell-shocked subject appears to degenerate further during the initial stages of recovery. As the passage indicates, there are long-standing associations between the 'human soul' and lepidopteron life forms: Aristotle first attested that the word psyche, meaning soul, mind or spirit, is also Greek for butterfly or moth.[2] The physicality of Barker's 'rotting' chrysalis, however, with its suggestion of knowledge gained through observation ('Cut a chrysalis open and you will find . . .'), is perhaps more in keeping with Rivers's frequent recourse to entomology in his writing. In her cultural history of myrmecology, Charlotte Sleigh identifies 'numerous references' to studies of insect life in Rivers's published works, arguing that 'for him . . . Insecta were illustrative of the deeper recesses of the human psyche'.[3]

Published in 1920, Rivers's study *Instinct and the Unconscious: A Contribution to a Biological Theory of the Psycho-Neuroses* outlines a theory of nervous disorder that results from the disruptive resurfacing of primordial instincts, such as immobility, aggression and nervous collapse, in response to danger. Building on the findings of Fabre and others, Rivers likens this phenomenon to the way that certain butterflies preserve responses to stimuli that were aroused during the caterpillar stage. Memories of a particular plant, he reports, 'were liable to intrude into the consciousness of the fully-developed butterfly with its vastly different needs and interests', causing it to seek out this earlier food source.[4] Initially perplexed by this behaviour, which presents no obvious benefit to the adult insect, entomologists concluded that the resurfacing of this earlier instinct allowed the butterfly to lay eggs close to where its caterpillar young would feed, thus ensuring the survival of its offspring. Applying this principle to cases of shell shock, Rivers posits that the resurfacing of suppressed instincts in traumatised soldiers serves a similar function, giving rise to physical symptoms such as paralysis and anaesthesia that prevent the sufferer from being returned to the front line. These symptoms, though debilitating, may be understood as a form of self-preservation: in appearing to 'mimic deterioration', the psyche ensures its survival.

H.D.'s First World War writing also discerns structural similarities between insect metamorphosis and the early stages of psychic recovery. In her novel *Asphodel* (*c*.1920–7; pub. 1992), protagonist Hermione Gart senses a change coming over her as she recovers from the traumatic birth of her stillborn child during an air raid: 'She was being disorganised as the parchment-like plain substance of the germ that holds the butterfly becomes fluid, inchoate' (*A* 158).[5] Writer Hermione's sense of amorphousness represents a shift in her mental state from a kind of psychic paralysis, to a visionary, albeit disorderly, state of consciousness that marks the return of her creative powers. Like Rivers, H.D. was aware that in order to reform itself anew, the caterpillar must first dissolve itself entirely. The process of liquidation that takes place within the cocoon involves the grouping together of 'imaginal cells', which cluster and vibrate together to create the organs of the adult insect.[6] As well as pertaining to the imago stage, the name given by scientists to this biochemical phenomenon harks back to an earlier definition of imaginal: 'Of or 'relating to the imagination . . . a mental image'.[7] This double meaning provides a useful way of thinking through H.D.'s pupal imagery. Throughout the author's war writing, I will argue, the cocoon functions as a space of imaginative possibility in which debilitating psychic states are recognised in terms of their aesthetic potential, and where trauma is reconceived as a source of creativity.

Having already established a reputation as an Imagist poet, H.D. began experimenting with prose during a series of cataclysmic wartime events. Following the miscarriage of her first child in 1915, which she attributed to the shock of hearing of the German torpedoing of the RMS *Lusitania* (a British passenger ship carrying 1,200 civilians), the author suffered the loss of her brother Gilbert in action in France in 1918, as well as the sudden death of her father shortly afterwards. This sequence of shocks coincided with the breakdown of her marriage to fellow writer and serving soldier Richard Aldington and culminated in the flu epidemic that nearly proved fatal to her and her second unborn child in the winter of 1919. Largely centred on these events, although often registering their effects obliquely, H.D.'s war novels – which include *Palimpsest* (1926) and *Bid Me to Live: A Madrigal* (1960) – are first and foremost narratives of trauma, a liminal psychic state located, as Andreas Huyssen puts it, on the 'threshold between remembering and forgetting, seeing and not seeing, transparency and occlusion'.[8] Huyssen's remarks evoke the implicit likeness, discernible throughout the author's war fiction, between the experience of trauma and the in-between stage of being that takes place within the cocoon. Explaining her decision to begin experimenting with prose in a letter to fellow Imagist poet John Cournos, H.D. stated: 'Writing poetry requires a clarity, a clairvoyance almost . . . But in the novel I am working through a wood, a tangle of bushes and bracken out to a clearing, where I may see again.'[9] Here and elsewhere in her writing, H.D. presents her prose as a kind of middle space in which to work through a 'tangle' of experiences that cannot easily be rendered into the 'clarity' of verse.

As a testament to this, many of H.D.'s novels remained in an in-between stage of composition during the author's lifetime – written but unpublished – while the few that were released are often described by critics as having the appearance of something provisional or incomplete. This is partly down to the generic instability of H.D.'s prose, which occupies an uncertain threshold between fiction and autobiography, and partly the result of the author's reiteration of her traumatic wartime experiences over several narratives, which have the effect of blurring into one another. The indeterminacy of these texts is exacerbated by their densely woven, reticulated style, consisting of strategies of repetition, layered voices, frequent temporal ruptures, as well as the destabilising of referents. Readers of H.D.'s fiction have tended to interpret these stylistic features as part of an attempt by the author to represent the disfiguring effects of war on the individual psyche.[10] Weaving together examples from her fiction, film criticism and psychoanalytic writing, I want to suggest that H.D.'s cocoon imagery can shed light on her efforts to represent an experience of trauma that is enhancing rather than simply debilitating. Connecting the recurrence of this exoskeletal structure in the author's war writing to its linguistic and formal excesses, this chapter proposes that the cocoon can serve to illuminate the author's efforts to maintain the text in a 'fluid, inchoate' state, dissolving past experiences in order to rearticulate them anew and ensuring that the self is preserved by its disintegration, remade by what it makes.

The Celluloid Cocoon

Hearing that she had begun work on a novel, Richard Aldington wrote to H.D. from the front line in the summer of 1918, protesting: 'Prose? No! You have so precise, so wonderful an instrument – why abandon it to fashion another perhaps less perfect?'[11] Aldington's assessment echoes the terms often used to describe H.D.'s writing. After emerging onto the literary scene in 1911, the author quickly became renowned in literary circles for her compressed 'crystalline' verse, with reviewers frequently characterising her as 'the perfect Imagist'.[12] As well as judging something to be superlative, perfection describes that which is absolute, complete or final: entomologists characterise the fully developed insect (or imago) as being in its 'perfect' form due to the fact that it has emerged from a state of amorphous provisionality into one of clear definition.[13] H.D. understands perfection in a similar way: in a 1916 review, she describes how the poet Marianne Moore turns her 'perfect craft as the perfect craftsman' to an art that is 'clear' and 'absolutely hard'.[14] The author's assessment is complimentary and could easily be describing her own Imagist poetics, but it also indicates that she understands the 'perfect' form to be fixed in its outline, leaving little room for further growth. Indeed, H.D. would come to find her reputation for perfection constraining, complaining of her critics: 'They squeal that H.D. is no longer the pure crystalline. I suppose there's nothing for it but a shell of water-tight and fool proof M[arianne] Moore variety.'[15] In her interwar writing, therefore, the author begins to fashion a looser, more provisional form of expression.

Further insight into H.D.'s experimentation with a 'less perfect' medium can be found in her essay 'The Mask and the Movietone', which appeared in the film journal *Close Up* in November 1927. Criticising the 'mechanical perfection' of the new Movietone system capable of synchronising images with audio, she asserts: 'If I see art projected too perfectly . . . don't I feel rather cheated of the possibility of something more divine behind the outer symbol of the something shown there?' The audience of the 'talkie', H.D. argues, is 'paralysed before too much reality', adding that as a viewer: 'I want to help to add imagination to a mask, a half finished image, not have everything done for me' (*MM* 120, 119). Likening silent cinema to the masked spectacle of Ancient Greek theatre, H.D. details its effect on the onlooker:

> Our censors, intellectually off guard, permitted our minds to rest. We sank into this pulse and warmth and were recreated . . . Into this layer of self, blurred over by hypnotic darkness or cross-beams of light, emotion and idea entered fresh as from the primitive beginning. (*MM* 116)

Enabled to function in several layers, the 'self' is creatively renewed, with the senses of the viewer paradoxically sharpened by the limitations of the medium. This is a far cry from the Imagist mantra that the artwork must be 'hard and clear, never blurred or indefinite'.[16] For H.D. this 'half-world of lights and music and blurred perception' functions as a form of intellectual cocoon in which the mind enters into a period of active dormancy, before emerging transformed like a 'moth' that floats 'into summer darkness' (*MM* 120).

In his phenomenological study of spaces associated with retreat – including nests, cottages and dovecotes – Gaston Bachelard argues that within the chrysalis 'two dreams are joined together, dreams that bespeak both the repose and the flight of being'.[17] Bachelard's interest in the cocoon as a site of imaginative possibility resonates with H.D.'s description of the paradoxical combination of rest and recreation experienced by the cinema-goer. By indicating that two distinct processes are taking place in the mind of the spectator of silent cinema, resulting in the 'blurr[ing] over' of a fixed and stable perspective, H.D. presents a vision of a creative psyche that remains stubbornly out of sync with itself. The essay concludes with the statement: 'We want healing in the blur of half tones and hypnotic vibrant darkness', thus consolidating the notion that the imperfections of the artwork – the things it lacks, or leaves 'half finished' – may have a restorative effect on the onlooker. 'The Mask and the Movietone' can tell us much about the author's approach to literary representation in the 1920s: H.D.'s inter-war prose is interested in the aesthetic possibilities of the 'half finished image' offered by nascent visual technologies, with her experiences of the 'hypnotic darkness' of the cinema prompting her to cultivate a multi-layered textual space in which subject and reader alike are able to be 'recreated' anew.

'The Mask and the Movietone' also discloses one of the sources of H.D.'s aesthetic interest in insects. Visiting the cinema, she notes: 'One laughs (or used to) at scientific projections, lizards like dinosaurs, beetles exaggerated out of recognition, gargantuan night-moths' as well as 'the exaggerated antics of enormous ants and hornets' (*MM* 118–19).[18] Between 1922 and 1933, more than 140 short nature documentaries were screened in British cinemas

Figure 3.1 The cocooning of the ailanthus silk moth in *Skilled Insect Artisans*, 1922

as part of the educational film series 'Secrets of Nature'. Although they showcased a wide variety of life forms – ranging from micro-organisms to exotic mammals – many of the films in the series focused on the insect world. By the time H.D. wrote 'The Mask and the Movietone', there had been at least six films devoted solely to lepidoptera, offering intimate access to the life cycle of organisms such as the comma butterfly, the red admiral and the ailanthus silk moth. These 'scientific projections' magnified and accelerated their developmental stages (larva, pupa, imago), offering audiences an unprecedented insight into the formation of the cocoon.[19] As a result, some viewers were quick to discern parallels between the natural processes depicted and methods of artistic production, including the art critic Huntly Carter, who marvelled at the ways in which 'natural objects unfold and clothe themselves in their own aesthetic, through the exercise of the power of art expression inhering in themselves'.[20]

The revelatory optics of 'Secrets of Nature' seem to have inspired H.D. to exercise her artistic powers in new ways. Completed in 1927, the same year that she wrote 'The Mask and the Movietone', the author's experimental bildungsroman *HERmione* (also known as *Her*) features extreme close-ups of a 'giant night-moth', a 'fibrous peony stalk with a snail clinging underneath it', as well as the 'magnified magnificent underbelly' of a bee (*H* 55, 13). Although the novel is based on events that took place in the author's youth, it describes how subsequent footage of natural forms 'magnified out of proportion' would serve to clarify the images and patterns of thinking that lay dormant in protagonist Hermione Gart's '[p]recinematographic conscience':

> She would later have seen form superimposed on thought and thought making its spirals in a manner not wholly related to matter but pertaining to it. (*H* 60)

These cognitive circumvolutions call to mind the coiling of tendrils in the series' numerous depictions of plant growth, as well as its accelerated footage of caterpillars spinning cocoons, clothing themselves in silken spirals. Hermione's subsequent exposure to these magnified life forms helps her to define her literary craft: 'writing had to do with the underside of a peony petal that covered the whole of a house like a nutshell housing woodgnats' (*H* 71). These delicate shells appear to have aided H.D. in her efforts to craft a form of expression capable of housing the 'underside' or hidden layers of experience.

H.D.'s exposure to insects on screen also fuelled her ambivalence towards the notion of a reality 'projected too perfectly' and thus stripped of its mysteries. In the same essay, the author likens the 'scientific projections' of moths and hornets to the aggressive realism of the 'talkie', arguing: 'We are used to nature, expanded and ennobled past all recognition, now we must again readjust and learn to accept calmly, man magnified' (*MM* 119). Although she doesn't elaborate further, H.D. appears to be alluding to the dangers of cinema as a vehicle of propaganda, in which, like the 'exaggerated antics of ants', human existence is 'ennobled past all recognition'. The essay's cryptic reference to 'man magnified' might therefore be interpreted as a nod to the political gigantism of extreme right-wing ideologies that were pupating across Europe during this period. Years before Theodor Adorno argued that the aesthetics of fascism 'combine the utmost technical perfection with complete blindness', H.D. appears cognisant of the fact that cinema – in its enlargement both of natural and human forms – was in danger of distorting the reality that it purported to enhance.[21]

H.D.'s ambivalent response to 'Secrets of Nature' may be linked to its combination of aesthetic experimentation and scientific didacticism. Caroline Hovanec argues that many of the films in the series

> stage an encounter between two modes of representation: the natural history narrative, which presents information about the biology and life history of nonhuman species in a domestic, anthropomorphic wrapping, and the cinematographic image, which presents mimetic yet defamiliarizing views of these species.

While the former mode dates back to the taxonomic methods that dominated natural history during the Victoria era, the latter exhibits something akin to a 'modernist visual register'.[22] In the 1922 film *Skilled Insect Artisans*, for example, prosaic inter-titles such as 'Inside the cocoon the caterpillar is changing into a moth, but the exterior remains unaltered', belie the strangeness of quivering leaves captured by time-lapse photography, as well as the play of light and shadow over the image as it lurches forward in sudden jump cuts.[23] Such textual intrusions draw attention to what cannot be captured by the camera, positioning the human spectator on the outside of events, unable to penetrate the mysteries of the outer shell. The cryptic nature of the cocoon is not only down to the limitations of early film technology; as the entomologist A. D. Imms explains, the changes that take place within the pupa remain 'only imperfectly understood, notwithstanding the efforts of some of the most famous biologists to unravel them'.[24] Yet this footage can help to explain why the cocoon exerted such a strong hold over the author's imagination: part of its appeal seems to lie in this tension between revelation and concealment, with its refusal to fully disclose itself meaning that, as is the case with silent cinema, the onlooker is forced to 'add imagination' to a 'half finished image'.

Hovanec's distinction between the natural history narrative and the cinematographic image helps to bring into focus an important aspect of H.D.'s insect imagery, which resists a taxonomic approach to the natural world in favour of a more defamiliarising modernist optic. The author's anti-classificatory stance is particularly apparent in her account of a half-remembered entomological incident from her childhood, in which she placed an enormous cocoon in her father's study for safekeeping. Initially identifying her find as a butterfly pupa, she describes how one evening an 'exotic and enormous . . . moth' suddenly hatched out and 'crawled or fluttered' around the room before settling on an old Indian skull. Horrified by the emergence of this gargantuan creature, which she likens to a 'not-so-small bird', H.D. flings open the window in the 'hope that it will fly out' (*TF* 127). The incident, which the author details in *Tribute to Freud* (1956), a memoir of her analysis with Sigmund Freud in 1933 and 1934, resurfaces in her experimental novella *Mira-Mare* (1934), where it becomes 'a sort of Arabian Nights roc-moth, a creature of imagination'.[25] In a similar vein, H.D.'s purported ignorance regarding the contents of the cocoon serves to amplify her imaginative response to the emerging moth. The author is unwilling even to attempt to classify the moth that emerges in her father's study, remarking: 'I had had some slight converse with amateur experts, though I myself knew the name of not one butterfly' (*TF* 127).

One amateur expert was H.D.'s maternal grandfather Francis Wolle, a respected naturalist who was responsible for the classification of thousands of species of freshwater algae.[26] In *Asphodel*, after referring vaguely to 'several types of butterflies', Hermione notes: 'you know my grandfather always knew them – all their names. We had a glass case of them hanging over his desk' (*A* 188). Another was lifelong bug-collector Richard Aldington, who shared his enthusiasm for 'fritillaries' and 'swallowtails' in letters to the author.[27] H.D.'s claim not to know the name of a single butterfly does indicate a slight masking of the true extent of her knowledge, for in the same text she refers to the 'death-head moth' and the 'sphinx moth' (*TF* 117). Spurred on by her father, Charles Doolittle, who was Professor of Astronomy and Mathematics at the University of Pennsylvania, the author enrolled at Bryn Mawr College in 1904 with the aim of becoming a scientist, before dropping out after a year of study. Alluding to her incompatibility with taxonomic ways of thinking, H.D. describes how the protagonist of *Her* had 'grappled with . . . biological definition' and 'found the whole thing untenable' (*H* 5–6). The author's aversion to scientific ways of thinking was not absolute; as Adalaide Morris notes, her writing 'bristles with terms from biology, chemistry, physics, and astronomy'.[28] Yet H.D.'s preference was for a somewhat bleary half-knowledge of entomology, an imperfect understanding of insects mediated through the shadowy cinema screen or the murky depths of childhood memory – one that seeks to maintain their strangeness as well as the mysteries of their growth.

In *Tribute to Freud*, H.D. recalls how when she was five years old her older brother Eric had dislodged a previously 'immovable' log in their garden, and the pair had stood 'spell-bound' at the revelation of 'unborn things' beneath it, which resemble 'white slugs' or 'cocoonless larvae'. Not knowing what they were, H.D. reflects that these mysterious forms had opened up a new dimension in her developing mind, as she realises: 'There were things under things, as well as things inside things.' The impact of these creatures on the author's psyche may extend in part from their appearance as 'unborn things' – 'they might "hatch" sometime', she notes, with apparent trepidation. Like the gauzy blur of the cinema screen, these 'half finished' insects contain more than can be seen; the young H.D. can only wonder 'what they might portend' (*TF* 20-1). This formative episode provides a powerful insight into the role of entomological life forms in enlarging the author's understanding of herself and the world around her, affording her a multi-layered perspective that feeds into her creative processes. As we shall see, insects are often central to these moments of sudden, revelatory understanding in H.D.'s writing, in which seemingly immovable ways of thinking are suddenly dislodged.

A Creature Half Formulated

The various threads of connection in H.D.'s writing between images of half-finished insects, the aesthetic imperfections of early cinema and the shadowy workings of the psyche are perhaps best illustrated by an incident that took place in the author's life shortly after the war. In 1920, while recovering in Corfu from the trauma of her wartime experiences, H.D. experienced a prolonged hallucination of writing on a wall, which resembled 'a sort of pictorial buzzing . . . like ants swarming, or very small half-winged insects' (*TF* 47–8). As well as anticipating her subsequent exposure to insects at the movie theatre, the phrase 'pictorial buzzing' evokes the teeming overlay of dust and scratches on analogue filmstrips – a phenomenon alluded to by fellow cinema-goer Virginia Woolf in her 1926 essay 'The Cinema' when she refers to film as an art form 'covered over with accretions of alien matter'. An imperfect medium, the gauzy celluloid of early film stock tended to throw up anomalous hallucinatory elements, such as the 'monstrous quivering tadpole' that Woolf apprehends in the corner of the screen during a performance of *The Cabinet of Dr Caligari* (1920).[29]

After realising that this frightening spectre was an 'unintentional' effect of the film, Woolf decides that this amorphous intrusion expressed the protagonist's disturbed imagination more effectively than words ever could:

> It swelled to an immense size, quivered, bulged, and sank back again into nonentity. For a moment it seemed to embody some monstrous diseased imagination of the lunatic's brain. For a moment it seemed as if thought could be conveyed by shape more effectively than by words.[30]

Woolf's recourse to this larval form may have been informed by her exposure to actual larvae on screen. The London Film Society, where the author is known to have watched *The Cabinet of Dr Caligari*, screened a range of avant-garde films alongside early nature documentaries, including 'The Comma Butterfly' and 'The Dysticus and Its Larvae'.[31] The notion that thought could be 'conveyed by shape more effectively than by words' resonates with H.D.'s description of the cinematograph's magnified images of nature as 'form superimposed on thought'. Woolf's emphasis, moreover, on the expressive power of the damaged surface of the celluloid strip bears a marked parallel to H.D.'s response to her 'pictorial buzzing' in Corfu. When Freud diagnoses this entomological hallucination as a 'dangerous symptom', H.D. rejects his interpretation, wondering instead whether it might be 'a high-powered *idea*' – not so much a 'symptom' as a form of 'inspiration' (*TF* 51; original emphasis). With this alternative reading in mind, it becomes possible to develop a more multi-layered understanding of trauma in the author's war fiction as a sign of psychic impairment that is also a form of creative stimulus.

H.D.'s first published novel *Palimpsest* (1926) is comprised of a triptych of narratives set in ancient Rome, wartime London and contemporary Egypt respectively. Nestled at the centre is 'Murex: War and Postwar London (circa A.D. 1916–1926)', the events of which take place on an afternoon in 1926. Having recently returned to London and eager not to recollect the trauma of her wartime experiences, Raymonde welcomes the inner fog that the city imposes on her 'too alert perception' and 'too keen thinking', describing how 'it soothed her nerves', propelling her into 'a sort of half-state, a state of half-thought'. The text likens its protagonist's state of mind to the motion of 'some swift cinematograph' where images 'were superimposed and showed dark shadows where the outlines held' (*P* 95–8, 163). This description recalls the novel's opening epigraph, which reads: 'palimpsest, i.e., a parchment from which one writing has been erased to make room for another'. H.D.'s definition of the palimpsest echoes her description in *Asphodel* of 'the parchment-like plain substance' of Hermione's 'cocoon state' (*A* 179). In both examples, the author's use of the word 'parchment', which denotes a skin, membrane or husk, as well as a page or manuscript, creates an intriguing overlap between the material surface of the page and the stages of erasure and self-renewal that take place within the pupa.³²

Throughout the text, H.D. experiments with an imperfect form of psychic erasure where, in a phenomenon not dissimilar to the 'accretions of alien matter' on a strip of celluloid, ghostly traces of a former self remain visible. The narrator details the efforts of Raymonde Ransome to maintain a 'cocoon-blur of not thinking', a 'silken mesh . . . of her own self-obliteration' (*P* 96, 114). So far, readers have tended to interpret Raymonde's 'cocoon-blur' as a symptom of suppressed trauma, solipsistic withdrawal and artistic paralysis. Crucially, however, Raymonde's psychic bleariness bears a marked resemblance to H.D.'s account of her 'over-mind' in 'Notes on Thought and Vision' (1919), a state of heightened consciousness associated with artistic creativity, in which 'things about me appear slightly blurred as if seen under water'.³³ As well as harking back to this state of visionary bleariness, H.D.'s use of the compound 'cocoon-blur' evokes her combined interest in the pupal stage of insect life and the bleary optics of early cinema. With recourse to the author's contention in 'The Mask and the Movietone' that silent film offers 'healing' in the 'blur of half-tones', it becomes possible to identify an important connection between her protagonist's filmy 'over-layer of blurred reminiscence' and H.D.'s interest in the restorative effects of silent cinema (*P* 112).

Early on in 'Murex', Raymonde's private reverie is punctured by a visit from Ermentrude Solomon, known as Ermy, another member of Raymonde's 'still-born generation'. Ermy has just found out that her husband Martin has been seduced by a woman called Mavis, who previously had an affair with Raymonde's former husband Freddie during the war. Ermy's arrival results in the painful resurfacing of Raymonde's suppressed memories of Freddie's infidelity, which occurred while she was recovering from the birth of her stillborn child. The narrator describes how Ermy's tale of a parallel betrayal causes an 'unexpected breach in [Raymonde's] armour' (*P* 117, 106). H.D.'s exoskeletal analogy bears a striking similarity to Freud's definition of trauma in *Beyond the Pleasure Principle* as a 'breach . . . in the protective shield against stimuli'.³⁴ In an earlier essay, Freud argues that the force of 'psychical trauma' is such that it can only make itself known to the subject retrospectively as a form of belated understanding or 'deferred action'.³⁵ Applying Freud's formulation to the act of storytelling, trauma theorist Cathy Caruth suggests that the self is capable only of 'belated experience' of trauma experienced as an act of narrative repetition or 'double telling'.³⁶ Caruth's reading helps to focalise the experience of trauma in H.D.'s writing as being out of sync with oneself – of being unable to access one's initial shock except through a secondary medium.

In 'Murex', the notion of trauma as a kind of palimpsestic 'double telling' is suggested by the way that Raymonde's suppressed memory of her husband's betrayal only becomes available to her, as well as to the reader, during Ermy's account of an almost identical seduction. Listening to her tell the tale over and over again, Raymonde realises that there may be something to be gained from listening to Ermy's ramblings:

> For of all the tangle of over-detail Ermy had spun . . . each time Ermy told the story, some fine detail detached itself as one may detach some tiny delicately detailed shell or golden fruit from some over-worked Carlo Crivelli that at first seems a blur of too extraneous detail. (P 129)

By enveloping Raymonde's experiences within the elaborate wrappings of Ermy's parallel ordeal, H.D. indicates that Raymonde's trauma may only be registered obliquely through the kind of 'half state' fostered by the text. In the above passage, the act of storytelling resembles a process of cocooning, as Ermy circles round and round the situation rather than addressing it head on, resulting in a bewildering 'tangle of over-detail'. Curiously, however, Ermy's drawn-out narrative is able to generate moments of sudden clarity for Raymonde, who, while listening to Ermy's 'hopelessly involved' tale, is able to recall details of her own husband's affair during that 'distant devastating decade' for the first time (P 120, 129).

H.D.'s allusion to Carlo Crivelli is a detail that may be detached from the text and used to focalise some of its aesthetic strategies. An Italian Renaissance painter famed for his ornamental extravagance, Crivelli is renowned for what Susan Sontag refers to as his *'trompe-l'oeil* insects and cracks in the masonry', overlaying flies and beetles onto his religious scenes in order to disrupt their gleaming façade.[37] Like Woolf's 'quivering tadpole', these alien elements add a new dimension to the image, puncturing an otherwise unblemished surface. Norman Land suggests that Crivelli's illusory insects demand a form of involvement on the part of the viewer, who is forced to engage with the object of deception and reject its devilry.[38] A similar dynamic is discernible in 'Murex': over the course of the text, suppressed memories from Raymonde's wartime past begin to intrude into the present-day narrative, including memories of soldiers marching off to troop trains and of nurses informing her that her child is stillborn. As is the case with Crivelli's devilish diptera, these temporal disruptions serve as untimely reminders, forcing the reader to engage with that which, having been brushed away, settles once more on the surface of the page. And yet, crucially, these intrusions also provide moments of unexpected lucidity, bringing the suppressed contents of Raymonde's wartime experiences back into focus.

Towards the end of the narrative, Raymonde begins to refine her memories into verse for the first time, and it becomes clear that the text's title, 'Murex', symbolises the poetic distillations of her trauma: 'Verses were the murex' (P 160). In light of H.D.'s characterising of her prose as a process of 'working through an old tangle' so that she 'may see clearly again', Raymonde's shift from prose to poetry might be said to resemble a transition from a cocooned state of traumatised 'half thought' to the 'crystalline' lucidity represented by this spiky marine exoskeleton (Figure 1.1). At the same time, 'Murex' simultaneously undermines this progression from gauzy nebulousness to hard clarity, raising questions about the compatibility of a lyric medium 'strung too high' and 'too polished' to represent the persistent formlessness of Raymonde's 'post-war Limbo'. Like her author, poet Raymonde has begun to experiment with prose, spending her time 'grubbing at odd manuscripts' (P 152, 124, 116). H.D.'s use of the loaded term 'grubbing' evokes a playful uncertainty as to whether Raymonde's (and indeed her own) transition from poetry to fiction resembles a descent into the hack domain of the Grub Street writer, or a more incipient, grub-like form of expression.

That the text cultivates a kind of 'half state' between poetry and prose (between murex and cocoon) is suggested by H.D.'s use of amorphous run-on sentences interspersed with snatches of verse from Robert Browning, as well as the spondaic march of 'Feet – feet – feet – feet – feet –' that punctuate the narrative. The volume (in both senses) of these 'muffled treadings' gradually increases over the course of the text, before being explicitly associated with Raymonde's repressed memory of the march of soldiers en route to the 'troop trains' at Victoria (P 98, 110, 114). The compressive effect of these bodily and metrical feet functions as a metonym for all that has been systematically stamped out in Raymonde's mind, as well as in wider society, by the conflict. This militarised march also resonates with Raymonde's memories of soldier Freddie's pressuring of her to cultivate the 'beat and throb of metre' of her early verses, becoming a 'hateful metronome' of her poetic identity during the war. In Raymonde's tortured recollection of the '[m]etres in her head that beat and beat and beat' the reader is presented with both a violent analogue of the conflict, as well as with a distressing image of a winged creature (perhaps a 'gargantuan night-moth') confined in too narrow a space (P 146, 149, 159). Raymonde's association of her poetic identity with her soldier husband is indicative of a growing discomfort in the author's post-war writing with the apparent complicity between avant-garde aesthetics – her own included – and militarist aggression.[39] Consequently, although H.D.'s protagonist refines her experiences into verse, transforming her complex feelings about Mavis's betrayal into a simple plea to 'be free | of all my old compunction', the narrative as a whole raises questions about Raymonde's willingness to compress her imperfectly formed experiences into what she calls the 'absolute form' of poetry (P 151, 165).

The text appears to be asking whether it is possible or even desirable for Raymonde to 'be free' of her war trauma. Of the existing readings of 'Murex', however, the majority have tended to attribute something of an absolute formula to Raymonde's reluctant concession to poetic form. Sarah Dillon, for instance, identifies 'a shift in her mental state from a feeling of blurred obliteration to one of acute perceptiveness' resulting in 'a return to poetic creativity', while Susan Stanford Friedman discerns a 'linear direction and tenuous resolution' to the text.[40] The reality is blurrier and in a sense more troubling than these readings will allow: although 'Murex' concludes with Raymonde's first poem about her war experiences, it is not without an underlying sense of coercion: 'I don't want to write it' (*P* 146). At this early stage in her prose career, H.D. appears to be resisting the trappings of her earlier Imagist aesthetic while also struggling with her new, 'less perfect' formal instrument. This is suggested by the way that, while listening to Ermy's tale unfold, Raymonde repeatedly criticises her narrative methods:

> a vague Frankenstein, a creature half formulated . . . It was a vague monster that rose from all her ramblings . . . 'How *could* she? *Why* did she,' was the eternally recurrent . . . wail into a room shadowing her odd form, her hunched and solitary degradation. (*P* 107; original emphasis)

Although Raymonde quickly tires of the 'overworked obvious situation' depicted in Ermy's excessive tale, she could easily be describing her own stylistic vagaries, as well as the 'odd form' of *Palimpsest* as a whole (*P* 126). Indeed, Raymonde's account of Ermy's 'tangle of over-detail' echoes the language used by H.D. to justify her turn to prose: 'in the novel I am working through . . . a tangle of bushes and bracken out to a clearing, where I may see again'. Implicit in this statement is the notion that, in the aftermath of the war, the possibility of artistic clarity is now contingent on the embrace of uncertainty and confusion – blurred as opposed to crystalline vision.

The above passage is also suggestive of the ways in which trauma manifests in H.D.'s writing both as a kind of 'half state' ('vague', 'half formulated'), as well as a repetitive 'double telling' ('ramblings', 'recurrent', 'shadowing'). Readers of *Palimpsest* have expressed a similar sense of frustration when describing the novel's formal textures: Deborah Kelly Kloepfer describes it as a 'difficult, disorientating' text, while Conrad Aiken, in his review of the text, complained of the 'fragmentary and chaotic and repetitive welter of the interior monologue'.[41] Even H.D., upon re-reading the text later in her career, would concede that it is 'sometimes difficult to disentangle the central theme from the turnings and involutions'.[42] In a definition that recalls the enveloping layers of the cocoon, the word 'involution' refers to a state of being 'enfolded, enwrapped', as well as to an 'intricacy of construction or style'.[43] Significantly, however, H.D. was also surprised to note that the text 'held and astonished' her, adding 'it is hallucinated, and I must become hallucinated in order to read it.'[44] The author's emphasis on being 'held' by the text is, I think, key: to enter into the 'cocoon-blur' of *Palimpsest* is to be captivated as well as taken captive, enraptured by its formal intricacies as well as tangled in its 'weedy and involved' threads.[45] In an observation that recalls the 'hallucinated writing' on the wall at Corfu comprised of half-winged insects, H.D. indicates that it may be possible to capture an iteration of trauma in her writing which, though disabling, may also serve to enhance the workings of the creative mind.

The Middle Voice

H.D.'s war novel *Asphodel* is split into the 'pre-chasm' years of American writer Hermione Gart's emergence into the avant-garde circles of pre-war London, followed by the sharp decline in her mental health after the birth of her stillborn child during an air raid in 1915. While recovering from her ordeal, Hermione attempts to articulate the 'sort of half-state, the sort of Limbo that she was in', with her mind flitting between a series of analogies before settling on the image of the cocoon: 'she was . . . holding herself in so many layers, so carefully housed, self and self and all confused and blurred by the cocoon state that she was in' (*A* 144, 179). H.D.'s use of the imperfect tense to describe her protagonist's mental condition is suggestive of a self that maintains itself by virtue of its refusal to come together, with Hermione 'holding herself' in a state of palimpsestic layeredness. Hermione's state of mind is reflected in the indeterminate status of the text, which H.D. chose to maintain in a middle stage of composition – written but unpublished – later referring to the manuscript as an early version of her later war novel *Bid Me to Live*. The cover sheet to *Asphodel* contains an instruction, written in the author's handwriting, to 'DESTROY' it, and yet H.D. held on to the text for the rest of her life, even housing it for posterity in her archive at Yale.[46] This discrepancy imbues the novel with a curious ontological status, as though, like a dissolving caterpillar, it has survived its own attempts at erasure.

Hermione's 'cocoon state' coincides with her discovery that she is expecting a second child: 'It seems to me that I must be having . . . a butterfly.' Understanding her condition in this way is consoling:

> Men could do nothing for her for a butterfly . . . a soft and luminous moth larva was keeping her safe. She was stronger than men, men, men – she was stronger than guns, guns, guns. (*A* 160, 162)

Hermione's recourse to insect metamorphosis to describe her second pregnancy enables her to distance herself from human modes of reproduction that have so far failed to come to fruition, with the cocoon offering a fantasy of autonomous self-gestation. As a cocoon housing a 'moth larva', she is also protected from her wartime surroundings: while her sense of self may be 'confused and blurred', Hermione is empowered by her state of amorphousness, remade by the thing she makes, cocooned by the very thing she cocoons. This multi-layered dynamic suggests that in H.D.'s writing the cocoon preserves a state of being that is confined neither to the inside or the outside of the self – instead, like a Möbius strip, it can be both.

Throughout *Asphodel*, Hermione's sense of self seems at its most defined while in a state of nebulous creating, thus disclosing a key aspect of the cocoon in H.D.'s writing as an exoskeletal structure that is able both to protect and recreate the self. The overlap between the active state of 'holding' and the more passive condition of being 'housed' that constitutes Hermione's 'cocoon state' is reminiscent of the linguistic concept of 'middle voice', a self-reflexive state in which the subject is both active and passive, enmeshed within and outside of the activity it describes. Adopted by Roland Barthes and others as a way of describing the intransitive style of modernist writers such as Joyce and Beckett, the concept of the middle voice has since been taken up by trauma theorists such as Dominic LaCapra, who characterises it as an '"in between" voice of undecidability' that speaks of the 'unavailability or radical ambivalence of clear-cut positions'.[47] There is a similar tone of undecidability in H.D.'s evocation of Hermione's cocoon-state: 'Herself had woven herself an aura, a net, a soft and luminous cocoon' (*A* 185). H.D.'s repetition of 'herself' creates a confusing self-reflexivity, as subject and object, proper noun and pronoun, begin to merge into a single amorphous referent while also resembling a network of discrete selves acting on and acted on by one another.

Susan McCabe has identified a 'resistance to a finely demarcated bodily ego' in H.D.'s writing, observing how 'bodily identities can merge and potentially reclaim new outlines'.[48] The word 'potentially' is key: throughout *Asphodel*, Hermione's attempts at self-recreation are continually deferred while also held in mind as a future state of determination – a pregnant possibility, if you will. With recourse to the developmental stages of insect life, the text seeks to distinguish between various permutations of trauma, establishing an important contrast between Hermione's 'cocoon state' and the 'uncanny and evil metamorphosis' that her husband Jerrold Darrington undergoes as he transforms into a shell-shocked soldier. Based on Richard Aldington, who suffered from symptoms of post-traumatic stress disorder after returning from the front line, Darrington is a volatile and oversexed figure whose kisses breathe poison gas from the battlefield into Hermione's lungs. H.D. describes how his body 'loom[s]' over Hermione's in bed like 'a bloated great zeppelin'; even his teeth summon images in her mind of 'rows and rows of livid dead'. Emerging from his soldier uniform towards the end of the text, Hermione describes how he 'crept out of the brown lean khaki, like a great moth, elegant in shape, still a little foreign in his bronze but all different' (*A* 198, 145, 192). Now resembling a perfect instrument of war, Darrington has metamorphosed into an imago of destruction.

Darrington's warlike transformation into a 'great moth' recalls Hermione's encounter with another of industrial modernity's hideous progeny, Walter Dowell. Based on H.D.'s brief acquaintance with Walter Morse Rummel, whose grandfather invented the telegraph, Dowell is a consummate pianist who is technically gifted but ultimately indifferent to art. Despite being lauded for his interpretations of Debussy, Dowell '[d]oesn't really care' about the music that he performs, conceiving of it merely as a variation of the Morse code signal invented by his family. Hermione observes that 'Walter had reached perfection of a technical order. Therefore he must reach beyond it, destroy in a gesture his exquisite technique.' That Dowell's state of technical perfection is associated with the final, perfect stage of insect life is also suggested when, finding herself disturbed by his cold logic, Hermione likens him to 'a sort of moth that has frozen, frozen – it's all very inexact – a sort of moth whose feathers are snow crystals', with the narrator adding: 'She had hardly formulated it. But there was something of a butterfly rimed with frost between them.' As well as demonstrating how Hermione's 'inexact' form of expression appears designed to counter the rigid finality of her crystallised contemporary, the image of the frostbitten moth recurs during Hermione's description of Darrington's 'moth's breath' that threatens to freeze 'the tender feelers of her being' (*A* 34–7, 148).

Perfect insects tend to be associated with harmful, usually male figures in H.D.'s writing. In her inter-war novella *Nights* (1935), Natalia's domineering husband Neil resembles a 'butterfly with platinum-lined intention', while in *Her*, George Lowndes (based on Ezra Pound) is likened to a 'giant mosquito' bearing down on Hermione: 'She felt the weight of his weighted heavy gauze wings' (*H* 85).[49] In *Asphodel*, the moth-like figure of Darrington appears to correspond to an absolute state of trauma in that his direct exposure to the industrial machine of warfare has resulted in the development of a deadening numbness that leaves him capable only of harming those around him. To emerge from one's cocoon, H.D.'s writing suggests, is to be arrested in a state of insensitivity that precludes the possibility of psychic recovery. In *Asphodel*, the author appears to be asking how it might be possible to resist this troubling development, with the formal inconclusiveness of the text seemingly part of an attempt to prevent subject and text from succumbing to the more destructive effects of 'Shell shock' (*A* 202).

By repeatedly modifying the import of Hermione's 'cocoon state', dissolving its significance and inverting its function, the text seeks to prevent its protagonist's psychically wounded state from either hardening into an 'absolute formula' or from being cured of an experience of trauma that H.D. suggests is not only irrevocable, but also of significant creative value. While 'holding herself in so many layers' Hermione exhibits a form of mental acuity denied to those caught up in the pervasive 'fog' of war. At one point, she reflects back on her own passing reference to life 'since the – war', asking herself: 'What is the war? There is a thing you mean when you say "since" and "the"' (*A* 138, 149–50). The reflexivity of this passage is reminiscent of the function of the middle voice, in which the self is both the subject and the object of the action, shifting between personal and impersonal states. By addressing herself in the second person, Hermione is able to interrogate the terms of the conflict; in its disorganised state, her mind is able to apprehend the ways in which war has been 'formulated' and thus normalised through language. H.D. contrasts her protagonist's mental state with those caught up in the midst of events, who 'didn't seem to understand death, didn't know it when it faced them' (*A* 150). Physically insulated from the conflict, Hermione appears psychically exposed to its true nature, in contrast to figures such as Darrington, who are directly exposed to war and yet seem troublingly insensitive to its effects.

Hermione likens her perceptiveness to '[b]utterfly antennae', a set of 'tender feelers' capable of sensing the danger posed by her soldier husband. 'I felt with senses that you don't know', she informs him at one point (*A* 147–50).[50] These antennal analogies recall Freud's account of the receptive outer layer surrounding the psyche, which, in addition to protecting the psyche from the 'enormous energies at work in the external world', takes '*samples* of the external world' such that it may be compared with 'feelers which are all the time making tentative advances towards the external world and then drawing back from it'.[51] In its ability to sense the threat of further destruction, Hermione's 'web of gauze' resembles an additional layer of nerve fibres surrounding her psyche – a network of feelers capable of registering the faintest external tremor. Clearly, the 'delicate fibre' of this shell is vulnerable in the way that the insect exoskeleton is not, and yet its success as a form of self-protection lies in its ability to register the possibility of an attack and to transmit this possibility to the cocooned subject well in advance of the expected blow.

What Robert Spoo characterises as 'the busy microlevel' of H.D.'s prose, rich with 'molten mutating accidentals' is consistent with my sense of the way in which *Asphodel*, in particular, seeks to stave off the deadening effects of trauma by registering even the slightest sensation on its quivering surface.[52] Flitting without warning from a formal to an informal register, as well as between free indirect speech, second-person address and a first-person stream of consciousness, the narrative is formed of a disconcerting array of nervous ticks and tremulous expressions. Interweaving dense cross-currents of inner and outer voices, the text envelops its reader in a tangle of confused thought processes, oblique conversations and 'half formulated' ideas. Moments after asserting: 'She was stronger than men', the narrator interjects: 'But was she? "I can't stand it." She didn't know what she couldn't stand' (*A* 163). Statement is followed by counter-statement, as assertions frequently give way to self-questioning. Throughout the novel, the possibility of finality is frequently undercut by a tone of ambivalence that seems designed to forestall the dangerous air of complacency exhibited by figures such as Darrington.

H.D.'s formal strategies may be situated in relation to a wider tendency seen in aesthetic responses to modernity. In 'The Painter of Modern Life' (1863), Charles Baudelaire describes an artistic sensibility that has adapted to the sensory onslaught of urban existence, 'mov[ing] into the crowd as though into an enormous reservoir of electricity'.[53] The essay outlines a new mode of sensory experience arising from the shocks and jolts of modernity, in which the modern artist is able to convert the powerful energies at work in the metropolis into a creative force. Returning to Baudelaire's writing in 1939, Walter Benjamin posits that Baudelaire not only 'placed shock experience [*Chockerfahrung*] at the center of his art', but that he also recognised the value of this state of anxious excitation.[54] Drawing on Freud's account of trauma in *Beyond the Pleasure Principle* as an excess of stimulation that breaks through the protective shield against stimuli, Benjamin outlines an aesthetic tendency that is discernible throughout much of the writing examined by this study; namely, that by positioning oneself in the midst of the 'enormous energies' of the outer world it becomes possible to channel this sensory onslaught into a form of countercharge.[55] We see this in Lewis's strategic exposure of his writing to various perceived threats in his cultural and political surroundings, as well as in Lawrence's baring of his body of work to the swarming energies of social life. In the case of H.D., this process involves the repeated re-exposure of her writing to her initial 'war shock', in turn transforming its disruptive force into a source of 'inspiration' (*TF* 93).

Towards the end of *Asphodel*, while walking through Richmond Park surveying the soldiers in hospital gowns sitting on benches labelled 'for the wounded', Hermione experiences a sudden paradigm shift:

> The whole world had melted ... and Hermione thanked ... someone (she couldn't remember who ...) for having injured her, wounded her so that she, like the soldiers on a bench perceived a world outside or inside the world, part of the world ... and yet not part of the world. (*A* 182–3)

The rhythms of undecidability that characterise the middle voice of trauma – from Hermione's vague sense of her position 'outside or inside' to her hesitant grasp of diction in the tautologous 'injured her, wounded her' – are suggestive of an understanding of the self that remains wilfully undetermined. By aligning her protagonist with these frail figures, H.D. hints at the idea that by submitting to a state of psychic woundedness it might be possible to experience the world in newly sensitised ways: 'we (Hermione, soldiers on a bench) were permitted to see the odd penumbra, the light that the earth ... gives out. It was our so great privilege' (*A* 183). Cocooned in parenthesis, the perspective of Hermione and the wounded soldiers is not only brought together, but also set apart from the unwounded, the unprivileged. Paul Sheehan argues that the 'moment of epiphany' in modernist writing constitutes 'a kind of counter-trauma' that moves 'beyond shock to realization and insight'.[56] Rather than moving 'beyond shock', however, H.D.'s war writing invites us to consider whether remaining psychically 'wounded' may be instrumental to such moments of revelatory, supraliminal consciousness in the modernist text, in which to embrace the disintegrative effects of trauma at the level of language and literary form is to hold together in ways denied to those who have sought to remain intact.

Suspended Life

In her 1920s prose, H.D. asks what it might mean not to emerge from a state of trauma and instead to remain held by, while also gaining a hold over, its affective charge. By the mid-1930s, however, H.D.'s efforts to work through her initial 'war shock' were increasingly overshadowed by the threat of a new outbreak of military violence. In 1933, the author travelled to Vienna to undergo analysis with Freud, where she was confronted with daily 'signs and symbols of the approaching ordeal', including swastikas chalked on buildings, barbed wire on roadsides, and guns stacked up on street corners. Recognising the need to 'fortify and equip' herself to 'face war when it came', the author's writing from this period sees her delving deep into her psychic history, revisiting past traumas in order to prepare for future ones (*TF* 93).

Early on in 'Advent', a series of fragmentary journal entries detailing her sessions with Freud, H.D. finds herself haunted by a half-remembered entomological incident from her childhood. For several nights before she goes to sleep the author's mind is drawn back to the caterpillar that hatched into an enormous moth in her father's study. On the first night, H.D. remembers discovering a cocoon in her garden and placing it for safekeeping in the study on a high shelf, before recalling that it was a 'giant worm' rather than a cocoon that she had put in a cardboard box on the shelf. The author's imperfect recollection serves to heighten her interest in the sequence of events, as she embarks on a process of anxious self-interrogation: 'Did I hear him scratching? Did he flutter and beat his wings against the box?' The next night, having failed to resolve this 'half finished image', H.D. realises that the creature would have 'woven its shell' before reaching its winged stage: 'But how long did it take a caterpillar to weave its elaborate vestment? Why did I forget the caterpillar? Why did I remember it?' (*TF* 126, 128, 132).

Located on the threshold, as Huyssen puts it, 'between remembering and forgetting', the caterpillar exerts a powerful hold over the author's thought processes. Unable to face this shadowy memory in the light of day, and withholding it from her sessions with Freud, H.D. uses her notebook to work through her growing sense of dread regarding the fate of her 'cocoonless' creature. After several nights, the author has a sudden breakthrough, recalling another early memory in which she witnessed a group of boys torturing a caterpillar:

> I could see it writhing . . . It is not a thing that the mind could possibly assimilate. They are putting salt on the caterpillar and it writhes, huge like an object seen under a microscope, or looming up it is a later

film-abstraction. No, how can I talk about the crucified Worm? I have been leafing over pages in the café, there are fresh atrocity stories. I cannot talk about the thing that actually concerns me, I cannot talk to Sigmund Freud in Vienna, 1933, about Jewish atrocities in Berlin. (*TF* 134–5)

The 'crucified Worm' incident is made available to the author retrospectively through the medium of film, with her experiences of watching 'gargantuan night-moths' at the movie theatre helping to bring this suppressed childhood memory back into view. Consequently, just as Ermy's 'half formulated' tale brings Raymonde's suppressed wartime experiences into focus in *Palimpsest*, H.D.'s overlaying of the two memories resembles a form of double exposure, in which the second incident serves to clarify aspects of the first.

By connecting the 'recent Jewish atrocities' to this early memory, H.D. suffuses the incident with a premonitory awareness, removing the element of surprise that gives shock its puncturing force. Linking the second caterpillar back to the first also enables the author to gain a retrospective hold over a traumatic experience that it wasn't possible to assimilate at the time, recognising in the boys' act of violence an incipient form of a much more widespread human cruelty. Once this connection is made, the page ceases to writhe with questions; in the next entry H.D.'s thoughts have moved on to more consoling memories of her mother's jewellery box. A clue as to what is occurring between these two passages is contained in the verb 'leafing', which recalls the author's account of placing the caterpillar in a cardboard box for safekeeping: 'In the box, among the fresh green tobacco leaves . . . he wove his huge cocoon' (*TF* 128). Once wrapped in the pages of 'fresh atrocity stories' the 'crucified Worm' appears to be held in check, cocooned within the author's psyche.

Originally a seafaring term, the verb 'to loom' means to 'appear indistinctly in an enlarged and indefinite form'. H.D.'s use of the word to describe the caterpillar harks back to her description of Darrington in *Asphodel*, who 'looms over' Hermione in bed, as well as the 'odd looming creatures' that lurk in the fog of wartime London (*A* 139). Significantly, moreover, the word 'loom' also refers to the apparatus used to weave fabric by crossing threads over one another, as well as the web formations of caterpillars and spiders.[57] Although H.D. is clearly using the term in the former sense to describe the indistinct appearance of this larval figure, it follows on from her image of the worm 'weav[ing] its elaborate vestment' (*TF* 132), just as her reference to a 'later film-abstraction' conjures up the image of caterpillars spinning their silken shells in 'Secrets of Nature'. The double meaning of the term loom, then, provides a way of thinking through H.D.'s efforts to construct a form of expression that is capable of articulating 'enlarged and indefinite' experiences, while also containing their traumatic force using the woven threads of narrative. In connecting up old and new fears, personal memories and wider political events, the text seeks to harness these 'looming' threats to the author's psyche.

Like Lewis and Lawrence's entomological wordplay, H.D.'s insect imagery is able to house multiple, at times conflicting, associations, allowing meanings to coexist 'in so many layers'. The author's pupal symbolism, in particular, gives rise to a host of linguistic interpretations, functioning in a manner akin to Claude Lévi-Strauss's notion of the 'floating signifier', a word that is able to denote 'force and action; quality and state; substantive, adjective and verb all at once' remaining 'abstract and concrete; omnipresent and localised'. The floating signifier, Lévi-Strauss argues, may be understood as 'the conscious expression of a semantic function, whose role is to enable symbolic thinking to operate'. In its refusal to take on a coherent outline the cocoon also enables a certain kind of thinking to operate in H.D.'s writing – one that eschews conclusive outcomes in favour of ongoing possibilities. Lévi-Strauss describes how this kind of 'magical thinking offers other, different methods of channelling and containment'.[58] These remarks can help to make sense of the dual function of the cocoon in H.D.'s writing, which serves not only as a kind of medium for this kind of imaginative thinking, but also as an outer limit or container for thought.

Psychoanalysis appears to have held a similar significance for the author. In *Tribute to Freud*, H.D. writes favourably of Freud's belief that 'there are always a number of explanations for every finding, two or a multiple . . . No answer was final. The very answer held something of death, finality.' During her time with Freud, the author discovered a form of 'healing implicit' in the 'unravelling of the tangled skeins of the unconscious mind' (*TF* 144, 30, 16). H.D.'s use of the term 'unravelling', which is often used figuratively to describe states of decline, unfulfilment or psychic breakdown, suggests that she understands the process of psychic repair to involve coming undone. The author's remarks also hark back to her description of the 'healing in the blur of half tones and hypnotic vibrant darkness' offered by silent cinema, suggesting that, like the movie theatre, the consulting room functioned as a space of creative possibility. Laura Marcus notes that, for H.D., 'psychoanalysis . . . was a cinematographic arena, with both analyst and analysand facing towards a surface – wall or screen – onto which memories and imaginings could be projected.'[59] In Freud's consulting room, H.D. also discovered another kind of double vision, in which both analyst and analysand were able to 'add imagination' to a 'half finished' image or symbol brought up from the depths of the unconscious mind.

As we have already seen, Freud's perspective did not always align with H.D.'s. In her writing from this period, the author admits that she found some of his interpretations 'too illuminating' – too close to the kind of technical perfection that she associated with the Movietone. H.D. would even go as far as defining her own way of perceiving in opposition to Freud's:

I was swifter in some intuitive instances, and sometimes a small tendril of a root from that great common Tree of Knowledge went deeper into the sub-soil. His were the great giant roots of that tree, but mine, with hair-like almost invisible feelers, sometimes quivered a warning or resolved a problem. (*TF* 30, 98)

Against Freud's systematic, rational understanding of the world, H.D. advocates a more nascent and intuitive mode of perceiving – 'small tendril[s]' as opposed to 'great giant roots'. The author's account of her 'almost invisible feelers' recalls Hermione's 'tender feelers' capable of tuning into scarcely perceptible dangers. Here and elsewhere in her writing, H.D. highlights the importance of protective sensitivity – an alertness that shields the self from danger. That said, the above passage also indicates that the author's method of understanding derives from the same 'great common Tree of Knowledge' as Freud's. In psychoanalysis, H.D. discovered a corollary to her efforts to work through without seeking to resolve her war trauma. 'My discoveries are not primarily a heal-all', Freud informs her at one point, adding: 'There are very few who understand this.' As is suggested by the author's use of the present participle 'healing' to describe the effects of psychoanalysis and silent cinema on the psyche, H.D. shared with Freud an understanding of the importance of working through past experiences as part of an ongoing and necessarily incomplete sequence of recovery. The author's interest in the consulting room as a space of suspended outcomes is hinted at in her journal, in which she reflects after a particularly fruitful session: 'I have been caterpillar, worm, snug in the chrysalis' (*TF* 18, 177).

At the time that the author embarked on her analysis with Freud, images of cocoons had begun to surface not only from the depths of her unconscious mind but also from the ancient past. In a letter to her partner Bryher written in March 1933, H.D. asks: 'Can you find . . . that brochure of Sir Arthur Evans, on the last analysis of some coins he found, on a ring, butterfly, and chrysalis? Freud had not seen it . . . He was so excited. He has all Evans on his shelf'.[60] In the study to which H.D. is referring, *The Earlier Religion of Greece in the Light of Cretan Discoveries* (1931), the archaeologist Arthur Evans reports on the recent discovery of objects representing the pupal stage in Minoan depictions of the underworld:

> The popular belief that departed spirits could take the form of butterflies is of course of world-wide occurrence . . . But the chrysalis, as representing the intermediate stage of suspended life, seems to be new to religious symbolism.[61]

The symbolism of the Minoan chrysalis resonates with H.D.'s interest in the 'intermediate stage of suspended life' represented by the cocoon as opposed to the more familiar form of the butterfly. In an observation that recalls Lévi-Strauss's account of the floating signifier, Evans adds that the image of the cocoon does not replace or merge with the butterfly but rather hovers alongside or above it. Like the ghostly underlay of the palimpsest, the addition of the chrysalis to this all too familiar symbol of rebirth creates what Evans refers to as a 'double emblem'.[62]

When H.D. and Freud discuss 'Arthur Evans and his work', he remarks that 'his little statues and images helped stabilise the evanescent idea'. In a similar vein, Evans's account of the chrysalis helps to firm up ideas that are already present, albeit in a nascent form, in H.D.'s 1920s writing – from the 'post-war Limbo' of 'Murex', to the multiple layers of self that comprise Hermione's 'cocoon state'. Evans's ancient 'new' emblem also surfaces as a timely symbol of the suspenseful atmosphere enveloping inter-war Europe during in the mid 1930s – a period, as H.D. puts it, 'overshadowed with the black wing of man's growing power of destruction and threat of racial separateness' (*TF* 175, 82). In his study of inter-war modernism, Paul Saint-Amour identifies a pervasive strain of apprehensiveness in the writing from this period, 'an uncanny condition in which some still-forming thing appears to take hold of us, as if from a future that has itself become prehensile'. Saint-Amour's sense is that this state of suspense is detrimental to the psyche, afflicting the sufferer with a kind of '*pre*-traumatic stress disorder'.[63] H.D.'s inter-war writing, however, appears to suggest that in allowing oneself to be taken hold of by 'some still-forming thing', it may be possible to gain a grip on these nascent terrors. In *Beyond the Pleasure Principle*, Freud proposes that

> preparedness for anxiety and the hypercathexis [overcharging] of the receptive systems, represents the last line of defence against stimuli. In the case of quite a number of traumas, the difference between systems that are unprepared and systems that are well prepared through being hypercathected [overcharged] may be a decisive factor in determining the outcome . . . of a trauma.[64]

For Freud, apprehensiveness can serve to mitigate the effects of trauma, with nervous expectancy functioning as a kind of binding counterforce. With these remarks in mind, we might consider suspense to function in H.D.'s writing as a sign not of '*pre*-traumatic' disorder but rather as a form of proleptic awareness that serves to hold its symptoms in abeyance.

In addition to other meanings, suspense (from the Latin *suspendĕre*, to hang') describes a state of uncertainty and delay, in which the subject is kept in a state of nervous expectancy.[65] Suspense can often be paralysing: in 'Thoughts on Peace in an Air Raid' (1940), Woolf describes how, while waiting for a bomb to fall, 'during those seconds of suspense all thinking stopped . . . A nail fixed the whole being to one hard board.'⁶⁶ For Woolf, such apprehensiveness is inimical to thought, reducing the self to a state of helpless entomological fixity akin to Eliot's Prufrock, 'formulated, sprawling on a pin'.⁶⁷ In H.D.'s Blitz poem *The Walls Do Not Fall* (1944), by contrast, the subject's thought processes are fuelled by this suspenseful atmosphere:

> In me (the worm) clearly
> is no righteousness, but this –
>
> persistence; I escaped the spider-snare,
> bird-claw, scavenger bird-beak,
>
> clung to grass-blade,
> the back of a leaf
>
> . . . I profit
> by every calamity;
>
> I eat my way out of it
> (*WDNF* 11–12)

The caterpillar's artful strategy suggests a fresh optimism on the part of H.D. regarding the notion of persisting in a state of vulnerable exposure. Rather than fleeing from danger, it suspends itself in the midst of danger, building a home in the firing line. The status of '(the worm)', dangling in parentheses in the midst of the line, is reflected in the material circumstances surrounding the poem's composition. Ensconced in a small ground-floor room near Hyde Park that doubled as a 'snug . . . little dug-out' during air raids, H.D. was acutely aware as she sat at her typewriter that the walls might cave in at any moment.⁶⁸

That being exposed to danger may have an invigorating effect on subject and text alike is a recurring theme of the modernist writing under consideration. In the image of the worm clinging to the back of a leaf we may recall the defiant figure of Cantleman, who 'gazes bravely, like a minute insect, up at the immense and melancholy night' (*CSM* 13), or the swarming hypertrophy of 'Bits', which derives its formal dynamism from the endangering forces of social and political collectivism. If the fate of the modern subject is to be constantly imperilled – left clinging, like Woolf's tremulous insect, to a blade of grass – then like her fellow modernists, H.D. asks what it might mean to embrace this state of precariousness. The speaker's sense of being able to 'profit | by every calamity' provides the clearest indication yet of H.D.'s efforts to convert the horrors of war into an energy source in her work:

> ... I,
>
> the industrious worm,
> spin my own shroud.
>
> (*WDNF* 12)

What we are witnessing here is not only a process of cocoon spinning, but also an attempt, discernible in much of the author's war writing, to put a positive spin on things, reframing perceptions of psychic trauma and transforming calamity into a form of creative sustenance. The process may involve a degree of fabrication, so to speak, and the term spin has since acquired negative connotations due to its association with commercial bias and political deception.[69] My sense, however, is that H.D.'s spin tactics are consistent with her attempts not to falsify past experiences, but rather to rework them into something more palatable. In a letter written during the mid-1930s, the author confessed of her need 'to go on and go on spinning' her prose narratives, explaining: 'the spinning is a sort of necessity to me'.[70]

Suspense is a generative condition in *The Walls Do Not Fall*. Held in the grip of uncertainty, the mind becomes alert to buried meanings and obscured resonances:

> I know, I feel
> the meaning that words hide;
>
> they are anagrams, cryptograms,
> little boxes, conditioned
>
> to hatch butterflies ...
>
> (*WDNF* 53)

The word 'cryptogram' calls to mind Evans's discovery of chrysalises in ancient tombs – boxes within boxes – a matryoshka of meaning. It also recalls the author's early encounter with half-formed insects, in which she realises for the first time that 'there were things under things as well as inside things'. Throughout H.D.'s war writing, the cocoon functions as a cryptic textual sign that keeps something hidden beneath itself, something shrouded in mystery. And yet, as is indicated by the futurity of the phrase 'to hatch', it also contains a promise of something still to come. Jason M. Coats writes that 'the butterfly never bursts out from its chrysalis' in *The Walls Do Not Fall*; rather, 'the poem purposefully staves off the transformation it so clearly depicts'.[71] The text positions itself on the brink of change that is yet to occur: 'possibly we will reach haven | heaven', ventures the speaker in the final lines (*WDNF* 59). In its attempts to foreclose outcomes, refusing even to settle on a final destination for itself (haven? heaven?), the poem suggests that it may be possible to live, and even thrive, in a state of perpetual suspense.

Butterfly in Cocoon

H.D. would later reflect that her analysis with Freud was intended not only 'to fortify' her 'to face war when it came' for the future', but also to enable her 'to help in some subsidiary way with war-shocked and war-shattered people' (*TF* 93). Completed in 1949 and published in 1960, H.D.'s final war novel, *Bid Me to Live: A Madrigal*, seeks to prepare its readers for the potential return of war, revisiting the ghostly spectre of past conflict in order to face the potential threat of nuclear destruction. The narrative replays the events of *Asphodel*, detailing the traumatic aftermath of protagonist Julia Ashton's stillbirth part way midway through the First World War, followed by the deterioration of her marriage to her soldier husband Rafe Ashton. This time, however, Julia exhibits an awareness of the future that is lacking in Hermione Gart, with her present-day self communicating to her past self what it cannot yet know.

Following Rafe's conscription, Julia becomes increasingly alert to his destructive impact on her psyche. As the couple sit together in her cramped London lodgings during one of his return visits, her retrospective narrative voice warns: 'this was the terrible moment when something was about to happen.' By living 'a world ahead', Julia is able to 'pull away from the endangering emotional paralysis' in advance of its occurrence. H.D. envelops the text with an atmosphere of proleptic awareness, describing how Julia remains 'unconsciously . . . alert' while Rafe is home on leave: 'she was waiting for the sound of the warning, of the air-raid warning' (*BL* 7–8, 41). By delaying the explanation of this 'warning' as one that relates specifically to the air raid, H.D. hints that her protagonist may be tuning into more distant portents of destruction, as she finds herself 'listening, as one listening far, far off, to an echo . . . in a shell'. Julia is capable of 'resounding' to events, hearing them 'refracted back' before they actually occur, with the text developing the nervous threads of Hermione's 'web of gauze' into an amplifying 'shell' capable not only of registering, but also transmitting early signs of danger (*BL* 6, 25).

Like her author, Julia begins to experiment with prose during the war, and through this new medium she is able to apprehend events prior to their actual unfolding: 'To-day she would relate to yesterday and by a subtle and valiant trick of *léger-de-main*, to to-morrow'. As well as recalling H.D.'s linking of her caterpillar memory to the threat of Nazi violence in *Tribute to Freud*, Julia's sleight of hand recalls the spin tactics of the worm in *The Walls Do Not Fall*. Rather than changing the course of events, H.D. alters their position in relation to the protagonist, so that when her traumatic experiences do recur it is with an air of weary inevitability: 'He was going to say it. He did say it.' When Rafe informs Julia of his affair with young art student Bella, Julia responds with a 'familiar gesture' to the 'familiar creature' before her: '"Well, you and Bella must work that out between you"' (*BL* 23, 10, 27). In this way, the text insulates its protagonist from the shock of her initial experiences, granting her the foresight to deal with circumstances that were unassimilable at the time that they occurred. The narrative recovers lost thought processes, describing how Julia 'would think (not thinking in these words) now for this moment, it's perfect' or: 'There were three doors; they opened out into other rooms, other vistas. She did not think this' (*BL* 6, 11). The result is a layering of perspectives that corresponds to the subtitle of the text: a madrigal is a song that consists of multiple overlapping parts, resulting in a composite vocal structure. The term also evokes H.D.'s previous iterations of her wartime experiences in 'Murex' and *Asphodel*, with the author describing her tendency to 'begin again and again a fresh outline of the "novel"' detailing these events, adding: 'It must be Penelope's web that I am weaving' (*TF* 153).

What Susan Stanford Friedman characterises as the 'double weave' of H.D.'s prose is also a process of unweaving, in which past experiences are continually revised, so that what may seem fixed and irrevocable in the author's own history appears suddenly nascent and potential.[72] Early on in the text, when Rafe insists to Julia as he departs for the front line: '"Remember if I don't come back . . . remember this was this, and this is always"', her narrative voice undercuts his logic of permanence, remarking sardonically: 'Always? It was a long time.' The text likens Julia's retrospective narrative agency to 'a frail-spider-web of a silver cord' that weaves its way through her psyche, connecting up isolated cells in her memory:

> Like a tightrope walker, she must move tip-toe across an infinitely narrow thread . . . the silver cord that bound them to that past . . . The thread binding past and present was not broken, would not yet break. She was living along a thin wire, or thin living web. (*BL* 10–12, 23)

As well as 'binding' the wound in her psychic armour, these threads are capable of registering sensations that were subsumed beneath her initial trauma. Like the 'web of gauze' that comprises Hermione's 'cocoon state' in *Asphodel*, Julia's 'thin living web' functions as a sensory apparatus – a network of feelers capable of tuning into her surroundings.[73] That H.D. discerns structural similarities between these two kinds of web is suggested by her late poem *Helen in Egypt* (1961), which likens 'a woman's wiles' to a net:

> what unexpected treasure . . .
> may the net find?
> frailer than spider spins
> or a worm for its bier.[74]

In her novel *Hedylus* (1928), H.D. also describes the 'threads of silver' of a nearby spider's web glistening in the sunlight, before remarking of the eponymous protagonist: 'The web to catch his thoughts was just of such a spinning.'[75] In an image that recalls the author's description of her 'almost invisible feelers' which 'sometimes quivered a warning or resolved a problem', the web serves in H.D.'s writing not only as a form of protection for the subject caught within its confines, but also as a structure capable of mining 'unexpected treasure' from the ruins of the past.

Bid Me to Live casts its net forwards in time as well as backwards. After the Second World War, H.D. experienced a series of psychic premonitions regarding the 'coming of the atom bomb', later recalling how she had been contacted during a séance by a series of RAF pilots killed in the Battle of Britain who warned her of the threat of nuclear war.[76] By returning to the events of the First World War in *Bid Me to Live*, the author appears to be preparing her readers to face the looming prospect of a future war. In the midst of the conflict, Julia visits a cinema packed with troops in Leicester Square and finds herself caught up in an action scene in which a car veers 'to destruction along the edge of a narrow cliff'. As the scene unfolds, Julia's attention shifts to the audience, 'her eyes were adjusting, focussing to this scene of danger without . . . here, a thousand doomed, the dead were watching destruction.' As though tuning into distant threats, Julia's gaze sweeps around the room, building up a wider perspective of the surrounding threat. Realising that she, along with the soldiers around her, have been caught up in a 'narcotic dope of forgetfulness', Julia forces herself to confront the 'far ghosts' of the past and the future, envisioning 'men who might be ghosts to-morrow, the latest vintage (1917) grapes to be crushed' (*BL* 72–5). H.D.'s parenthetical reference to the year is more than a playful homage to the custom of the winemaker, but rather a reminder that years, wars and lives are in danger of bleeding together in the ferment of history. By overlaying these ghostly figures onto the cinema screen, the text encourages its readers to detect an uncanny echo of the past in the present.

In returning once more to the events of the First World War, *Bid Me to Live* also registers the birth of a more constructive force during this period. In a narrative thread that is absent from *Asphodel*, the text details Julia's relationship with fellow writer Rico, based on D. H. Lawrence, with whom H.D. shared a friendship during the war. Inspired by Rico's 'luminous phrases', Julia identifies 'a trail, a communication between them', finding herself drawn inexorably to his 'spider feelers' (*BL* 109, 47, 100). Recalling how Rico had encouraged her to abandon the 'frozen altars' of her verse in order to embark on a process of 'preliminary scribbling', Julia describes him as 'a medium' for a nascent form of artistic energy known as 'the *gloire*':

> The child is the *gloire* before it is born. The circle of the candle on my notebook is the *gloire*, the story isn't born yet.
> While I live in the unborn story, I am in the *gloire*. I must keep it alive, myself living within it. (*BL* 30–1, 107)

The 'unborn story' is here presented as a mutually sustaining space in which, like the cocoon, the self is remade by what it makes, contained by what it contains. The term *gloire*, moreover, derives from a conversation between Julia and Rico about the chromatic indeterminacy of *gloire de Dijon* roses, which he explains are neither white nor red, but a pale gold shade that lies between. By tracing the term back to Lawrence, who describes this indeterminate 'golden' hue in his poem 'Gloire de Dijon' (1917), H.D. uncovers a 'trail, a communication' between their writing, identifying a shared investment in the literary text as a medium capable of preserving a form of incipient being – what Lawrence refers to as the 'vital, potential self' (*STH* 20).[77]

In contrast to Lawrence, however, H.D.'s writing asks what it might mean to remain in a state of radical indeterminacy, not casting off one form of being in favour of another but rather exploring what it means to remain in between forms – defining oneself, in terms that the author uses to describe the *gloire*, as 'both and neither'. Early on in *Bid Me to Live*, H.D. reaffirms the value of remaining 'in the middle of something':

> The greater the gap in consciousness . . . the more unformed the black nebula, by reasoning, the more brilliant would be the opening up into clear defined space, or the more brilliant a star-cluster would emerge. (*BL* 107, 3, 5)

H.D.'s emphasis is on that which has yet to 'emerge' from the blurry nebulousness of a form 'not yet concentrated out into clear thought' (*BL* 4). Her use of comparative constructions – 'The greater . . . the more brilliant' – establishes a direct correlation between the negative impact of Julia's war shock and the positive experiences that may yet emerge from it: rather than simply attempting to live with her trauma, she recognises its potential to produce a 'more brilliant' (illustrious, brightly shining) state of consciousness than that which preceded it. Rachel Blau DuPlessis argues that H.D.'s constant revision of her wartime experiences in her prose narratives is motivated by a desire to 'de-story the old story, lift the weight of the accustomed tale'.[78] In repeatedly de-storying (or rather destroying) and recreating her wartime experiences through her prose,

H.D. demonstrates that her writing has more to gain from working with the force of trauma than, to paraphrase Djuna Barnes's account of the silkworm, by attempting to purge her body of work of its theme.

In the final part of *Bid Me to Live*, Julia retreats from wartime London to the remote reaches of Cornwall in search of a 'reprieve' from 'the war-years' wear and tear'. The conflict continues to reverberate through her mind as she wanders through empty fields: 'The sound of shrapnel. The noises . . . off. The tin-trumpet of the boy scout in the Square after the raid.' This episode encapsulates the text as a whole, which tunes into the war from a distance, simultaneously channelling and containing its noisy energies. Registering these sounds helps Julia to make peace with the ongoing conflict: 'Her perception was sharpened, yet she was not thinking. The tick-tick of her brain had been stilled, that pulse of fever in her, quieted.' H.D.'s use of the verb 'stilled' allows us detect a new tone of stillness in her late writing – both a state of calm and a sense of dogged persistence: a still-ness. As she listens to the distant reverberations of war, H.D. describes how her protagonist, who is at this point shrouded in the 'cold, healing mist' of the Cornish coastline, 'hugged her old coat tight, hugging herself tight, rejoicing in herself, butterfly in cocoon' (*BL* 96, 92, 88). The shift from the past tense to the present continuous that occurs in this passage is suggestive of the author's efforts to shift past events into an ongoing sequence of recovery – 'working through . . . a tangle', rather than seeking to emerge from it.

In her experimental autobiography, *The Gift* (1941–3; pub. 1982), H.D. reflects that following a traumatic event 'parts of the mind can be broken; shock can scatter the contents of this strange camera obscura'. She then adds that shock 'can also, like an earthquake or an avalanche, uncover buried treasure', adding that there is no 'formula yet discovered' for this curious state of affairs.[79] In the cocoon, the author discovered not a formula but rather something 'half formulated' with which to express the revelatory potential of traumatised subjectivity. Throughout H.D.'s war writing, the contents of the mind are disordered by shock, but also reconfigured – broken apart, yet also opened up to new ways of thinking and perceiving. Marina Warner notes that insect metamorphosis is often representative of 'the settled idea of development . . . as the psyche moves towards epiphany, fulfilment, and closure (the butterfly as *telos*, or finality)'.[80] Significantly, however, H.D.'s writing resists this movement towards a state of psychic and formal 'closure', finding something more constructive in the idea of returning to a more undeveloped stage of being: 'my butterfly | my Psyche', she writes in *Helen of Egypt*, 'disappear into the web, | the shell, re-integrate'.[81] H.D. is not alone in recognising the aesthetic possibilities of a kind of metamorphosis in reverse. The next chapter will explore Beckett's struggle in his post-war writing to return subject and text alike to a 'larval' stage of development, a mode of incipient, pre-conscious being that is lost as soon as language intervenes.

Notes

1. Barker, *Regeneration*, 184.
2. Aristotle, *Historia Animalium*, 551^{a}13.
3. Sleigh, *Six Legs Better*, 72.
4. Rivers, *Instinct and the Unconscious*, 69.
5. The manuscript of *Asphodel* is dated 1921–2, but in a 1949 letter H.D. writes that both *Her* and *Asphodel* 'were written in London, 1926–1927', Spoo, 'H.D.'s Dating of *Asphodel*', 31–40.
6. See Wigglesworth, *Insect Physiology*, 91–4.
7. 'imaginal, *adj.*', OED.
8. Huyssen, *Present Pasts*, 8.
9. H.D., 'Art and Ardor', 148.
10. See Randall, 'War-Days', 124–55; Henke, *Shattered Subjects*, 25–54.
11. Quoted in Zilboorg, *Aldington and H.D.*, 78.
12. 'H.D. by Delia Alton', 184. H.D. was first described as the 'perfect Imagist' by Harriet Monroe in a 1916 review in *Poetry: A Magazine of Verse*, 258. The epithet stuck, as did the adjective 'crystalline'. In a letter to her partner Bryher written in the late 1920s, H.D. complained: 'You might think that they cost me no sweating, so perfect is the crystalline finish', quoted in Collecott, *H.D. and Sapphic Modernism*, 135. In 1949, the author remarked: 'I grew tired of hearing these [early] poems referred to, as crystalline', 'H.D. by Delia Alton', 184.
13. 'perfect, *adj.*, *n.*, and *adv.*', OED.
14. H.D., 'Marianne Moore', 118.
15. Quoted in Friedman, *Penelope's Web*, 38.
16. Lowell, 'Preface', *Some Imagist Poets*, vi.
17. Bachelard, *The Poetics of Space*, 85.
18. In another film essay from the same period, H.D. alludes to the techniques of 'Secrets of Nature' while describing cinema as 'the medium par excellence of movement – of trees, of people, of bird wings. Flowers open by magic and magic spreads cloud forms.' 'Restraint', 113.
19. Few of these short films have survived intact, but their contents were summarised in the film journal *Bioscope* after they aired. 'The Emperor Moth' (1926), for instance, features footage of 'a young caterpillar feeding alone; close-up, with details of bristles; later stages, feeding, with head in close-up; it weaves a cocoon; section showing how cocoon works; section showing caterpillar inside; it casts its old skin; the moth emerges; its wings unfold'. *National Film Archive Catalogue*, 88.
20. Carter, *The New Spirit in the Cinema*, 278; Marcus, *The Tenth Muse*, 4.
21. Adorno, *Minima Moralia*, 55.
22. Hovanec, *Zoological Modernism*, 146–7.
23. *Skilled Insect Artisans*, 1.44.
24. Imms, *Insect Natural History*, 22.
25. H.D., *Mira-Mare*, 87.
26. Francis Wolle's publications include *Desmids of the United States and List of American Pediastrums* (1884) and *Fresh-Water Algae of the United States* (1887).
27. Quoted in Zilboorg, *Aldington and H.D.*, 76–7.

28. Morris, 'Science and the Mythopoeic Mind', 195.
29. Woolf, 'The Cinema', 172, 175. The shadow was most likely a cue mark on the top right-hand corner of the frame. Cue marks, which resemble a dark circle or blob, were added to the film strip to alert the projectionist when it was time to change the film over to the next reel.
30. 'The Cinema', 174.
31. See 'The Film Society 1925–1939, A Guide to the Collections', 5–7, <https://www.bfi.org.uk/sites/bfi.org.uk/files/downloads/bfi-the-film-society-1925-1939-a-guide-to-collections.pdf> (last accessed 10 December 2018); Kime Scott, *In the Hollow of the Wave*, 44.
32. 'parchment, *n.*', OED.
33. H.D., 'Notes on Thought and Vision', 18.
34. Freud, *Beyond the Pleasure Principle*, 303.
35. Freud, 'Project for a Scientific Psychology', 356.
36. Caruth, *Unclaimed Experience*, 7, 17.
37. Sontag, 'Notes on "Camp"', 283.
38. Land, 'Giotto's Fly', 14–15.
39. See Burnett, 'A Poetics Out of War', 57.
40. Dillon, 'Palimpsesting', 31; Friedman, *Penelope's Web*, 244.
41. Kloepfer, 'Fishing the Murex Up', 185; Aiken, quoted in Friedman, *Penelope's Web*, 28.
42. 'H.D. by Delia Alton', 218.
43. 'involution, *n.*', OED.
44. H.D., *Magic Mirror*, 29.
45. 'H.D. by Delia Alton', 218.
46. Spoo, 'H.D.'s Dating of *Asphodel*', 31–40.
47. LaCapra, *Writing Trauma*, 20; Barthes, *The Rustle of Language*, 11–21.
48. McCabe, 'H.D.'s Borderline Bodies', 153.
49. H.D., *Nights*, 35–6.
50. These feelers recall those of another invertebrate in H.D.'s writing. In 'Notes on Thought and Vision' (1919), H.D. likens her creative mind to a jellyfish equipped with a 'set of super-feelings' that 'extend out and about us; as the long floating tentacles of the jelly-fish reach out and about him', 18–19.
51. *Beyond the Pleasure Principle*, 299; original emphasis.
52. Spoo, 'H.D. Prosed', 213.
53. Baudelaire, *Selected Writings*, 400.
54. Benjamin, 'On Some Motifs in Baudelaire', 319.
55. *Beyond the Pleasure Principle*, 299.
56. Sheehan, *Modernism and the Aesthetics of Violence*, 172.
57. 'loom, $v.^2$, $n.^1$', OED.
58. Lévi-Strauss, *Introduction to the Work of Marcel Mauss*, 63–4.
59. Marcus, *The Tenth Muse*, 367.
60. H.D., *Analyzing Freud*, 127.
61. Evans, *The Earlier Religion of Greece*, 28.
62. *The Earlier Religion of Greece*, 30.

63. Saint-Amour, *Tense Future*, 93, 8; original emphasis.
64. *Beyond the Pleasure Principle*, 303.
65. 'suspense, *n.*', OED.
66. Woolf, *The Death of a Moth*, 211.
67. Eliot, *Complete Poems and Plays*, 14.
68. H.D., *Within the Walls*, 22.
69. The first OED citation of the word spin to mean 'bias or slant on information, intended to create a favourable impression when it is presented to the public' is from 1977, 'spin, *n.*¹', OED.
70. *Analyzing Freud*, 426.
71. Coats, 'H.D. and the Hermetic Impulse', 96.
72. Friedman, *Penelope's Web*, 1–6.
73. In Woolf's novel *The Years* (1937), a spider's web is also used to register the more subtle reverberations of the First World War. The 1917 section of the text describes how while sheltering below ground during an air raid, Eleanor 'noticed a spider's web in the corner . . . There was a violent crack of sound, like the split of lightning in the sky. The spider's web oscillated . . . One, two, three, four, Eleanor counted. The spider's web was swaying', 254.
74. H.D., *Helen in Egypt*, 93.
75. H.D., *Hedylus*, 58.
76. H.D., *The Sword Went Out to Sea*, 35.
77. Lawrence, *Poems*, Vol. 1, 176.
78. DuPlessis, *The Pink Guitar*, 24.
79. H.D., *The Gift*, 50.
80. Warner, *Fantastic Metamorphoses*, 83.
81. *Helen in Egypt*, 170.

4

LARVAL FORMS: SAMUEL BECKETT

> Être un ver, quelle force! [To be a worm, what strength!]
> Victor Hugo, *L'Homme qui rit* [*The Man Who Laughs*], 1869[1]

> Tell me about the worms!
> Beckett, *Waiting for Godot*, 1953

On 12 August 1948, Samuel Beckett wrote to his friend, the art critic Georges Duthuit, wondering where he might find 'the terms, the rhythms' necessary to go on writing. Beckett informs Duthuit that while out walking that evening 'among the dripping bracken' he had decided

> we need a motive to blow up all this dismal mixture. It is surely to be sought where everything must be sought now, in the eternally larval, no, something else, in the courage of the imperfection of non-being too, in which we are intermittently assailed by the temptation still to be, a little, and the glory of having been a little, beneath an unforgettable sky. Yes, to be sought in the impossibility of ever being wrong enough, of ever being ridiculous and defenceless enough.[2]

These somewhat cryptic remarks occur in the context of a discussion between Beckett and Duthuit about the state of contemporary art, which developed into a sequence of published conversations entitled *Three Dialogues* (1949). In it, Beckett speaks of an art that has turned away from existing forms of expression in order to confront its overwhelming sense of helplessness and failure – an art that is 'weary of pretending to be able, of being able . . . of going a little further along a dreary road' (*PTD* 103). Here too, the emphasis is on 'the impossibility of ever being wrong enough' or 'defenceless enough', and yet there is also something faintly hopeful in the author's account of a post-war subject who, having been reduced to a frail and shell-less creature, senses some small prospect of new life stirring beneath 'an unforgettable sky'. Creative expression, Beckett seems to be suggesting, is now to be sought on the threshold of being – between the 'glory of having been a little', and 'the temptation still to be, a little' – where life, having reached the verge of extinction, seems somehow to persist at this low level.

In his reading of *Endgame* (1957), Adorno likens Beckett's 'figures' (he hesitates to call them characters) to 'flies that twitch after the swatter has half smashed them', arguing that the text exemplifies the sense of collapse exhibited by post-Holocaust art:

> After the Second War, everything is destroyed, even resurrected culture, without knowing it; humanity vegetates along, crawling, after events which even the survivors cannot really survive, on a pile of ruins which even renders futile self-reflection of one's own battered state.[3]

This account of post-war life, in which the subject is reduced to a crawling creature, recalls Beckett's direct confrontation with the shattered remnants of human civilisation when he worked as an Irish Red Cross volunteer in Saint-Lô in the autumn of 1945. In his correspondence from the time, Beckett, along with his French countrymen, refers to the heavily bombed city of Saint-Lô as 'the capital of the ruins' formed of a 'sea of mud'.[4] In an eyewitness account published in the *Irish Times*, however, the author reflected that the city had revealed to him 'a vision and sense of a time-honoured conception of humanity in ruins, and perhaps even an inkling of the terms in which our condition is to be thought again' (*CSP* 278). There is thus an important distinction to be made between these accounts of post-war destruction: while for Adorno there appears to be little chance of recovery, Beckett's sense is that this state of collapse may offer an opportunity to rethink the human condition.

Beckett's use of the word 'inkling', which denotes a 'a faint or slight mention', evokes the muted energy of his post-war writing, which often intimates itself to the reader in a low murmur or undertone.[5] It is also reminiscent of one of the 'terms' in his letter to Duthuit: although he quickly retracts the phrase, Beckett posits that artistic inspiration is to be sought in the 'eternally larval'. Describing the initial stage of an insect's development when it resembles a wormlike entity, the word 'larval' is consistent with Beckett's impression of the human subject and its forms of expression as something that has yet to fully materialise after the war, and is instead 'to be thought again', 'to be sought' and ultimately 'still to be'. The term resurfaces on a number of occasions in the author's *oeuvre*: C. J. Ackerley and S. E. Gontarski have traced a series of references to the 'larval stage' in Beckett's writing – from his first published novel *Murphy* (1938) to his final extended work of prose, *How It Is* (1964).[6] This chapter understands the 'larval' to be one of 'the terms, the rhythms' with which the human is 'thought again' in Beckett's writing, arguing that the author experiments with a form of representation that remains in an eternal state of beginning.

Beckett's writing displays more than a passing interest in invertebrate life forms. Angela Moorjani detects an echo of Maurice Maeterlinck's lyrical study of apiculture, *The Life of the Bee* (1901), in Moran's rapturous response to his dancing bees in *Molloy* (1955): 'Here is something I can study all my life, and never understand' (*TN* 163). James Carney concurs with Moorjani that Beckett may also have been alluding to the work of the German ethologist Karl von Frisch in the 1940s on the waggle dance of the honeybee, arguing that 'Beckett's work is informed, at least partially, by a remarkably prescient awareness of developments in contemporary entomology'. Responding to a direct prompt from the author that some of the flies in his writing 'might be made to mean something', Steven Connor uncovers a dizzying array of references to diptera in Beckett's *ouevre*, while Dirk Van Hulle and Mark Nixon have outlined the author's reading of biological texts, transcribing a reference in his notebooks to 'Darwin poring over the aphids'.[7] Beckett alludes to a number of *fin-de-siècle* works of evolutionary biology in his writing, including Darwin's *Origin of Species* (1859), Ernst Haeckel's *The Riddle of the Universe* (1901) and Henri Bergson's *Creative Evolution* (1911). As we shall see, the author was drawn to the parts of these texts that focus on the developmental stages of insect life, particularly what Darwin characterises as 'the first condition of an insect at its issuing from the egg when it is usually in the form of a grub, caterpillar, or maggot'.[8]

In addition to reading scientific texts, Beckett engaged in acts of observational fieldwork, detailing his 'deductions of nature, based on observation' in his correspondence from the late 1940s and early 1950s. As well as marvelling at mayflies and beetles, Beckett wrote of his curious fascination for caterpillars and earthworms, remarking in a July 1951 letter to Duthuit: 'Never seen so many butterflies in such worm-state, this little central cylinder, the only flesh, is the worm.'[9] With recourse to the prose experiments that Beckett conducted alongside his observations of nature, this chapter proposes that the vermicular rhythms of his post-war writing were inspired by the notion of resisting the exigencies of development in order to remain in the longed for 'worm-state'. Tracing this aesthetic tendency back to the author's first published novel *Murphy*, before moving through *The Unnamable* (1958) to *How It Is*, I argue that these lowly creatures take on an increasingly central role in the author's thinking after the Second World War, helping him to contemplate the possibility, as well as the practical impossibility, of an 'eternally larval' form of literary expression.

The Worn-Out Shell

Before examining Beckett's fascination with the larval stage in further detail, it is necessary to consider what remains of the exoskeleton as a structural principle in the author's writing. In *Fables of Aggression*, Fredric Jameson argues that 'the various modernisms' all involve 'the exploration of a new Utopian and libidinal experience of the various sealed realms of the psychic compartments to which they are condemned, but which they also reinvent'.[10] Jameson's reading is consistent with my understanding of the exoskeleton as an aesthetic response to a psychic necessity: if the subject of modernity is 'condemned' to be enshelled within the 'sealed realm' of the psyche, then the modernist text strives to 'reinvent' this outer casing – from Lewis's surface modifications to H.D.'s cocoon states. In Beckett's early writing, however, there are signs that this protective apparatus has begun to exhaust its energy supply, and yet in the absence of an alternative the subject continues to cling to these exoskeletal defences.

Set in London in 1935, Beckett's first published novel *Murphy* opens in the eponymous Irishman's West Brompton lodgings, a 'condemned' dwelling 'curtained off from the sun'. Lying naked in a rocking chair, to which he has bound himself using seven scarves, Murphy attempts to retreat into the inner recesses of his mind, which he pictures as a 'large hollow sphere hermetically sealed from the universe without' (*M* 5, 63). The efforts of this 'seedy solipsist' to seal himself off from his surroundings are soon thwarted by his lover Celia, who calls to remind him of his economic instability before sending him out onto the streets in search of work (she herself is a street-walker). Before heading out into the metropolitan sprawl, Murphy attempts to arm himself against the 'various threats to his . . . person' by clothing himself in an 'aeruginous suit' coated with a 'livid gloss':

> No less than the colour the cut was striking. The jacket, a tube in its own right, descended clear of the body as far as mid-thigh, where the skirts were slightly reflexed like the mouth of a bell . . . The trousers in their heyday had exhibited the same proud and inflexible autonomy of hang. But now, broken by miles of bitter stair till they were obliged to cling here and there for support to the legs within, a corkscrew effect betrayed their fatigue. (*M* 50, 44–6)

The clinging effect of Murphy's trousers is suggestive of his continued reliance on some sort of external support structure. As John Keller notes, Murphy's sartorial shield resembles 'an exoskeleton' that equips him to face 'the world armoured, protected within its concrete-like rigidity . . . forestalling any genuine contact by acting as a hard shell/autistic barrier that only allows detached experience'.[11] Significantly, however, Beckett establishes that while 'the bold claim was advanced by the makers that it was holeproof', the suit has passed its 'heyday', resembling merely the 'remains of a decent outfit' (M 45).

In accordance with the deterioration of his protective suit, Murphy finds himself unable to exclude the onslaught of sensations that beset him on his path through the city. Desperate to find somewhere to lie down and close his eyes, he soon realises that there is no space for him to do so that hasn't been 'buried under . . . malignant proliferations of urban tissue'. The text presents these 'residential cancers' as a form of invasive growth capable of breaking through the psychic barrier that Murphy has erected between himself and his environment, leaving him an exhausted and 'defenceless' creature (M 47–8). Patrick Bixby has suggested that by walking through the city at leisure and 'abstaining from participation in the capitalist enterprise', Beckett's protagonist seeks to emulate the spirit of the *flâneur*.[12] My sense, however, is that Murphy's efforts to navigate an increasingly pervasive social reality in which psychic inurement is no longer possible reduces him to a parody of the modernist *flânerie* depicted in Joyce's *Ulysses* (1922) or Woolf's *Mrs Dalloway* (1925). Consider the contrast, for instance, between Clarissa Dalloway's impression of herself as the architect of her urban surroundings: 'For Heaven only knows why one loves [London] so, how one sees it so, making it up, building it round one, tumbling it, creating it every moment afresh', and Murphy's inability to carve out a space for himself amid the swelling of the 'service flats' (M 48).[13] Over the course of the text, Murphy seeks to shelter from the chaos of the outer world in a number of 'closed system[s]' – surrogate exoskeletons which include horoscopes and chess, as well as the 'oyster-grey' padded cells of the Magdalen Mental Mercyseat asylum where he accepts a job as an orderly. Yet his efforts to reinforce himself are continually foiled, as is suggested by the text's description of his final, dissolute state following his untimely death, in which his ashes are 'freely distributed' across a pub floor before being 'swept away with the sand, the beer, the butts, the glass, the matches, the spits, the vomit' (M 60, 103, 154).

Before stepping out on the job hunt, Murphy asks Celia to tuck his suit in so as to exclude a draught: 'She made a long dent in the waist of the coat. In vain, it filled out again immediately, as a punctured ball will not retain an impression' (M 82). Beckett's description of Murphy's suit as a 'punctured ball' that 'will not retain an impression' is suggestive of an unreceptive textual surface: not only does his psychic armour fail to protect him from the outer world, but the text as a whole appears to be suggesting that literary form is no longer able to convert what Freud refers to as the 'enormous energies at work in the external world' into a creative countercharge.[14] The author's foregrounding of the flimsy remnants of Murphy's outer defences may therefore be linked to the waning significance of the formal structures by which, as Adorno argues, modernist writers sought to protect the artwork from destructive social and political surroundings by withdrawing 'into the zones of subjective experience'.[15] Although, as this study has sought to demonstrate, the so-called insularity of the modernist text is not borne out in the writing under consideration, during the period in which *Murphy* was written there was an 'overarching opposition' in contemporary cultural circles, as David Weisberg puts it, between 'socially indifferent formalism and socially responsible writing'. Marina MacKay notes that by the late inter-war period, modernism 'had ossified into a self-contained literary period'.[16] Murphy's suit, with its 'inflexible autonomy of hang', may therefore be understood not as a reaction against the formal procedures associated with high modernism per se, but rather its growing rigidity as a cultural product.

Another 'closed system' that Beckett might have had in mind when he wrote *Murphy* was James Joyce's schemata to *Ulysses*. Produced by the author to help readers understand the text's complex structure, the Gorman-Gilbert and Linati schemas offer diagrammatic representations of each section of the novel, resembling what Joyce referred to as a 'skeleton-schema'.[17] During a conversation with Richard Ellmann in 1953, Beckett recounted Joyce's admission that he 'may have oversystematised *Ulysses*' approvingly, indicating that he shared this view.[18] In a fitting metaphor, Maud Ellmann posits that Joyce's imposition of the schemata onto *Ulysses* 'create[s] an exoskeleton, a carapace, a defensive second skin imposed upon a writing forever threatening to overflow its bounds'.[19] Ellmann's observation indicates that as well as imposing a degree of order upon its material, the exoskeleton may create the necessary conditions for modernism's aesthetic of 'overflow' – a formal excessiveness discernible in Lewis's aesthetic outbursts, Lawrence's 'swarm poesis', as well as in H.D.'s 'fluid, inchoate' style (*A* 158). Although he freely acknowledged Joyce's influence on his early writing, Beckett argued that in contrast to Joyce's stylistic superfluity: 'my own way was in impoverishment . . . in taking away, in subtracting rather than in adding'.[20] As well as highlighting an important distinction between the two writers, these remarks help to distinguish the addition of exoskeletal devices in the writing of Lewis, Lawrence and H.D. from Beckett's aesthetics of subtraction – a term which not only implies the removal of material, but also the withdrawal of something useful or beneficial. Just as Murphy attempts to retreat into various psychic compartments, Beckett's 'defenceless' post-war subjects often hark back to the safety of various shell-like enclosures which, though eagerly sought, no longer appear to be available.

Tyrus Miller argues that Beckett's late modernist writing offers what Walter Benjamin, in his *Origin of German Tragic Drama* (1928), identifies as a retrospective optic with which to view the aesthetics of high modernism.[21] This 'backward-turned glance' is able to intuit meaning from the remnants of an artwork or cultural movement:

> The false appearance of totality is extinguished. For the *eidos* disappears, the simile ceases to exist, and the cosmos it contained shrivels up. The dry rebuses which remain contain an insight, which is still available to the confused investigator.[22]

Benjamin's choice of imagery is reminiscent of Murphy's shrivelled suit, broken 'by miles of bitter stair', as well as the exuvia (or discarded exoskeleton) of a recently moulted insect. While remaining mindful of what Beckett, in his critical work on Joyce, terms 'the neatness of identifications', I want to suggest that from his 1930s writing onwards, Beckett provides an insight into the exoskeletal defences associated with high modernism – the psyche as an armoured structure, the text as a protective and connective barrier – defences which appear in an impoverished form in his writing, shrivelled to 'dry rebuses'.[23] In *Molloy*, Moran evokes the breakdown of something akin to an exoskeletal defence while reflecting on his gradual self-dispossession: 'I seemed to see myself ageing as swiftly as a day-fly . . . And what I saw was more like a crumbling, a frenzied collapsing of all that had always protected me from all I was condemned to be' (*TN* 142–3). In *The Unnamable*, the anonymous speaker struggles to locate the boundary separating self from world:

> an outside and an inside and me in the middle, perhaps that's what I am, the thing that divides the world in two, on the one side the outside, on the other the inside, that can be as thin as foil, I'm neither one side nor the other, I'm in the middle, I'm the partition, I've two surfaces and no thickness, perhaps that's what I feel. (*TN* 376)

Here the division separating inside from outside has thinned to a membrane 'thin as foil' with 'no thickness'; while there is still an intervening layer of some sort, the speaker is 'neither one side nor the other'. Although it doesn't disappear entirely, the exoskeleton is in the process of dissolving in Beckett's writing, evoking a state of being that lacks clear borders and separations, in which it is no longer possible to determine what is and isn't a part of the self: 'perhaps that's what I am', 'perhaps that's what I feel'. While alarming, these 'frenzied collapsing[s]' also have the potential to be liberating. As early as *Murphy*, there are hints as to what might emerge from the breakdown of these exoskeletal defences.

Larval Origins

Murphy's rocking chair reverie is presented as an attempt to return to a 'larval and dark' stage of consciousness that he associates with the 'embryonal repose' of his prenatal existence (*M* 104, 48). Outlining the zones of Murphy's mind, 'light, half-light, dark, the narrator describes this longed-for state as follows:

> a flux of forms, a perpetual coming together and falling asunder of forms . . . becoming and crumbling into the fragments of a new becoming . . . Here he was not free, but a mote in the dark of absolute freedom. He did not move, he was a point in the ceaseless unconditioned generation and passing away of line. (*M* 65–6)

There is something akin to H.D.'s account of the cocoon-like space of silent cinema in Murphy's dark zone, which combines energetic activity ('a flux of forms') and total stillness ('He did not move'). Rather than presenting the mind with a 'half finished image', though, these 'fragments of a new becoming' are suggestive of a form of representation that has yet to take shape. Here, the subject fantasises about returning to an undifferentiated state prior to the formation of stable categories, a borderless realm of perpetual beginnings and endings in which the line of narrative and of self-development dissolves as soon as it is created.

Given that Beckett first deploys the term larval in *Murphy*, it seems necessary to investigate the provenance of the term in his thinking. Ackerley and Gontarski wonder whether Murphy's 'larval and dark' zone may have been inspired by a passage from Dante's *Purgatorio*:

> Do ye not perceive that we are worms
> Born to form the angelic butterfly? . . .
> You are like defective insects
> Like the worm in whom formation is lacking![24]

This claim is corroborated by Daniela Caselli's discovery that the manuscripts of *Murphy* are densely interspersed with Beckett's reading notes of the *Purgatorio*.[25] Ackerley and Gontarski also cite the work of Denis Diderot, who Beckett read during the early 1930s, as a possible source of his interest in the larval stage. In his dialogue *Le Rêve de d'Alembert* [*D'Alembert's Dream*], Diderot's speaker Bordeu harks back to the embryonic stage of human life, 'when you were simply a soft substance, fibrous, shapeless, vermicular substance'.[26] A similar image appears in Beckett's late play *That Time* (1975) when the decrepit speaker harks back to the intrauterine state: 'that time curled up worm in slime when they lugged you out and wiped you off and straightened you up' (*CDW* 390).

Beckett's interest in the larval stage can also be traced back to his reading of evolutionary biology. After Murphy's former lover Miss Counihan pipes up with a series of unwelcome pronouncements on Cartesian dualism, a group of his followers attempt to shout her down, and when she pauses briefly to regain her composure one of them quips: 'She quite forgets how it goes on . . . She will have to go right back to the beginning, like Darwin's caterpillar' (*M* 122). Beckett is alluding to the experiments of Darwin's fellow naturalist, Pierre Huber, with the larva of the apple leaf miner moth, which are detailed in the *Origin of Species*. In his chapter on 'Instinct', Darwin argues that if a person is interrupted while recounting a well-known song then he or she is 'generally forced to go back to recover the habitual train of thought':

> So P[ierre] Huber found it was with a caterpillar, which makes a very complicated hammock; for if he took a caterpillar which had completed its hammock up to, say, the sixth stage of construction, and put it into a hammock completed up only to the third stage, the caterpillar simply re-performed the fourth, fifth, and sixth stages of construction. If, however, a caterpillar were taken out of a hammock made up, for instance, to the third stage, and were put into one finished up to the sixth stage, so that much of its work was already done for it, far from deriving any benefit from this, it was much embarrassed, and, in order to complete its hammock, seemed forced to start from the third stage, where it had left off, and thus tried to complete the already finished work.[27]

Darwin's work is renowned for its anthropomorphism, but rather than denoting abashedness his description of the 'much embarrassed' caterpillar appears to correspond to an older definition of embarrassment to mean 'affected or characterized by obstacles or difficulties; hampered, impeded, hindered'.[28] Beckett circles back to this larval anecdote on a number of occasions in his writing to evoke instances where thoughts have been held up or hampered in their development. In an early short story, 'Echo's Bones' (1933), Belacqua asserts that his memory has gone to hell and 'if you can't give me a better cue I'll have to be like the embarrassed caterpillar and go back to my origins'. This sentiment is echoed in *Watt* (1953) after Mr O'Meldon is interrupted mid-flow and Mr Magershon instructs him: 'Go on from where you left off . . . Or are you like Darwin's caterpillar?'[29]

The resurfacing of the caterpillar analogy in *Watt*, which was written more than a decade after 'Echo's Bones', suggests that Huber's observation captured the author's imagination for a significant stretch of his writing career.[30] Echoing the instinct of the caterpillar, Beckett evidently went back to his *Origin* at a later stage: although he dismissed Darwin's study in 1932 as 'badly written catlap', in a 1961 letter he claimed to be re-reading it 'with much pleasure'.[31] Readers of Beckett have also circled back to the embarrassed caterpillar on several occasions: Kirsten Shepherd-Barr suggests that it signals Darwin and Beckett's shared interest in 'the force of habit'; Kathryn Chiong writes of

Beckett's 'caterpillar logic', where '"going on" finally takes priority over all ends', while Michael Beausang reads the caterpillar's movement as a comment on the tendency for Western thinkers 'to become prisoned in their own logical constructions'.[32] In a further intervention, Daniel Newman places the caterpillar's regressive loopings in a longer sequence of narrative experimentation, arguing that novelists from George Eliot to Samuel Beckett recognised in the caterpillar's 'iterative reversions to the larval stage . . . a new developmental plot'.[33]

Returning to *Murphy*, it is possible to observe marked affinities between the caterpillar's instinct to return to an earlier stage of construction and the tendency of the narrator to circle back to an earlier train of thought. Perhaps the most striking example of this is the verbatim repetition of Murphy's rocking chair stillness at the beginning of the text – 'soon his body would be quiet, soon he would be free' – to describe his death towards the end (*M* 9, 142). In an image that recalls Darwin's caterpillar, Ruby Cohn argues that in *Murphy*: 'The narrator's primary stylistic weapon is repetition, and around those repetitions, Beckett weaves those of the characters.'[34] Celia's impression of Murphy's regressive speech patterns: 'each word obliterated, before it had time to make sense, by the word that came next; so that in the end she did not know what had been said', could easily be describing the wider impulses of the text, which often appears to be attempting to disrupt its own movement towards a state of completion (*M* 27). In a reading of the novel's attack on conventional metaphors, including the narrator's description of Murphy being 'strangled into a state of respiration', H. Porter Abbott posits that these 'inversions' constitute a 'series of affronts to the novel shell in which they are contained'.[35] This exoskeletal analogy evokes the way that the text often seems to be pushing back against its status as an 'already finished work', as though attempting (like the embarrassed caterpillar) to return to an earlier stage of formal development.

At the same time, the novel's emphasis on thwarted progress exists in tension with what John Bolin refers to as its 'contrived narrative trajectory – which inevitably moves towards closure and the affirmation of a hierarchy of values'.[36] Despite his efforts to return to a state of larvality, Murphy is driven onwards by the exigencies of the plot. While walking the streets in his aeruginous suit in search of work, the narrator remarks: 'Regress in these togs was slow.' The movement of the text towards a state of finality is presented as an ineluctable fact: 'all things limp together for the only possible' the narrator intones wearily on more than one occasion (*M* 45, 131). Murphy's 'larval and dark' zone, I want to suggest, represents an incipient stage of development that the novel fantasises about but finds itself unable to express within the confines of existing narrative structures. This dilemma is most apparent in the extreme lengths that Murphy goes to over the course of the text to sink back into a state of psychic reverie, a process that leads him quite literally to a dead end. After taking a job as an orderly at the Magdalen Mental Mercyseat asylum, Murphy is drawn to a 'limpid and imperturbable' schizophrenic called Mr Endon, recognising in his catatonic state a version of his own sought-after state of 'absolute freedom' (*M* 105). It soon becomes apparent, though, that Mr Endon's psychosis represents the negation rather than the fulfilment of Murphy's longed-for larvality.

Endon's surname derives from the Greek preposition *endon* meaning into or within, from which the term entomology (from *entomon*, 'insect' and 'cut into sections') also originates. Dressed 'in a fine dressing-gown of scarlet byssus', his 'tiny body . . . perfect in every detail and extremely hairy', Endon resembles a species of lepidoptera confined to the display case of the padded cell. This likeness is further hinted at when Murphy, finding himself captivated by 'the brilliant swallow-tail of Mr Endon's arms and legs', pins him down to look closely at his eyes, the pair poised 'for a butterfly kiss'. Despite his diminutive size and apparent fragility, Endon's imperviousness is such that when Murphy looks into his eyes he sees only himself reflected back, 'horribly reduced, obscured and distorted' (*M* 105, 138–40). Beckett's choice of name also conveys a sense of finality (to end on) anticipating Murphy's horrified recognition that Mr Endon represents not the larval but rather the imago stage of consciousness, his mind encased within a solipsistic shell so thick that there is nothing beneath its rigid exterior. As Jean-Michel Rabaté observes, Murphy's recognition of Endon's internal petrification 'generates a sort of panic that causes him to run from the scene, strip off his clothes, and lie panting on the ground'.[37] Murphy's bizarre behaviour may be read as a final desperate attempt at psychic regression. Lying naked on his belly 'in a tuft of soaking tuffets', his prone position anticipates the vermicular mud-dweller, or 'l'homme la[r]vaire' [larval man], of *How It Is*.[38] Murphy dies shortly afterwards, his mind having evacuated its contents: 'Scraps of bodies, of landscapes, eyes, lines and colours evoking nothing, rose and climbed out of sight before him' (*M* 141).

When Murphy's lover Celia replaces him in the rocking chair, she struggles with two lines of thought that lead back to her errant partner: 'the one from a larval experience to a person of fantasy, the other from a complete experience to a person of fact'. Celia's two lines of development reflect a wider opposition in *Murphy*, as well as in Beckett's writing more generally, between a fantasy of incipient being, in which the self exists in a formless state of becoming, and the immutable facts of reality. Yet although this 'larval experience' remains confined to the realm of reverie, its nascent energy surfaces in other forms. Describing the disruptive influence of the absent Murphy on their thought processes, his followers liken him to 'vermin'; he is 'so importunate', complains Neary, 'so pushing', adds Miss Counihan, 'so thrusting'. Wylie concludes that Murphy is a 'creepy thing that creepeth of the Law. Yet I pursue him' (*M* 42, 121).[39] As a person of fantasy, Murphy is capable of infiltrating the minds of his contemporaries while also thwarting (or rather embarrassing) their efforts to pin him down. Murphy's 'thrusting' energy even resurfaces posthumously in the image of Mr Kelly's kite during the closing chapter as it reaches 'the end of the line': 'The cord wormed slowly off the winch – out, back a little, stop; out, back a little, stop'. It may also be detected in the 'vermigrade wane' force that intrudes upon Celia's gloomy reverie as she waits for her absent lover in his rocking chair, a 'peristalsis of light, worming its way into the dark' (*M* 157, 78, 42).[40]

According to the *OED*, the word 'vermigrade', which describes the act of 'proceeding in a worm-like manner', is Beckett's own coinage, signalling his playful awareness of the plasticity of both worms and words. The author's use of the verb 'worming', moreover, evokes the action of making one's way 'insidiously like a worm *into* (a person's confidence, secret affairs, etc.); to burrow *in* so as to hurt or destroy. Also, to wriggle *out of* (a difficulty)'.[41] In his oft-quoted 'German letter' to Axel Kaun, which he wrote while he was struggling to find a publisher for *Murphy* in 1937, Beckett evokes a similar movement while detailing his efforts to overcome the 'terrible materiality' of language:

> More and more my own language appears to me like a veil that must be torn apart in order to get at the things (or the Nothingness) behind it . . . As we cannot eliminate language all at once, we should at least leave nothing undone that might contribute to its falling into disrepute. To bore one hole after another into it, until what lurks behind it – be it something or nothing – begins to seep through; I cannot imagine a higher goal for a writer today.[42]

Beckett's interest in what 'lurks behind' the shell of language is consistent with his attempts to access a more incipient form of expression – a 'literature of the unword'.[43] The figure of the worm, I want to suggest, is instrumental to this endeavour, functioning as a force of undoing in the author's writing that bores holes (like a bookworm) into the surface of the text, interrupting its development to a state of completion. In the image of worming, Beckett discerns a force capable of breaking down the boundary between nascent thoughts and bounded expressions, formless yearnings and formulated outcomes.

In her essay 'Conversation and Subconversation', Nathalie Sarraute describes a similar tension between the formal dimension of language and that which 'lurks behind' the surface of codified speech. In the work of modernist writers such as Joyce and Proust, she argues, it is possible to detect

> little larval actions that no inner language can convey, that jostle one another on the threshold of consciousness, gather together in compact groups and loom up all of a sudden, then immediately fall apart, combine otherwise and reappear in new forms.[44]

In a similar observation, Beckett writes of a 'number of tentative and abortive experiences' in Proust's writing, 'fugitive precursors' and 'shadowy, incomplete evocations' that are 'interrupted' before they have begun to take shape (*PTD* 30). For Sarraute, as for Beckett, the 'larval' appears representative of a form of expression that cannot be contained by language, surfacing instead in an 'apparently insignificant word, a mere intonation or a glance'. Sarraute suggests that modernist writing can accommodate these nascent elements in ways that the nineteenth-century novel, with its 'strong, coherent system of conventions', cannot.[45] But as we saw in Lewis's disdain towards Joyce's 'wormeaten wordies' or in H.D.'s 'looming' caterpillar memory, although it seeks to register a host of minor sensations and 'incomplete evocations', the writing examined by this study also seeks to contain the threat of formlessness posed by the larval. There is thus an important distinction to be drawn between Beckett's writing and the work of earlier modernists. Rather than seeking to reinforce the text against a state of overflow and collapse, the author's post-war prose suggests that the breakdown of language as a coherent system is not only inevitable, but that it may also present an opportunity for words to 'combine otherwise and appear in new forms'.

INFINITELY PLASTIC FORMS

Written between 1947 and 1950 in what the author referred to as a 'frenzy of writing', Beckett's *Three Novels: Molloy, Malone Dies, The Unnamable* encapsulate what S. E. Gontarski identifies over the course of the author's prose as 'something of a reverse Darwinism that moves from complex to simple organism'.[46] The Trilogy, which Beckett wrote in French and subsequently translated into English, begins with a man travelling through the countryside on a bicycle in search of his mother in *Molloy*, before proceeding to the bedside of a moribund subject in *Malone Dies* (1956). The final part of the sequence depicts a series of increasingly rudimentary figures, Basil, Mahood and finally Worm – a larval figure who occupies the threshold of 'non-being'. Hugh Kenner notes that *The Unnamable* 'carries the Cartesian process backwards, beginning with the bodily *je suis* and ending with a bare *cogito*', while Julia Kristeva argues that Beckett's post-war prose 'refines a syntax that marks time or moves ahead by fits and starts, warding off the narrative's flight forward'.[47] In accordance with the physical and psychological deterioration of the human subject, Beckett strips away all but the bare features of novelistic form, with *The Unnamable* moving towards a pre-narratival or larval stage of literary representation.

The embodiment of all that remains confined to the dark zone of Murphy's mind, Worm is preceded by the figure of Macmann in *Malone Dies*, who is referred to in the original version of the text, *Malone meurt* (1951), by the common French idiom 'nu comme ver' [naked as a worm].[48] A primitive creature, Macmann is

> by temperament more reptile than bird and could suffer extensive mutilation and survive, happier sitting than standing and lying down than sitting, so that he sat and lay down at the least pretext and only rose again when the *élan vital* or struggle for life began to prod him in the arse again. (*TN* 236)

Beckett is alluding to Henri Bergson's *Creative Evolution,* which coins the phrase to describe the life force inherent in all living organisms that propels them towards new forms of being. As Laura Salisbury notes, Beckett's reference to Bergson appears 'parodic rather than synchronous'; the prostrate Macmann is hardly embracing the spirit of the *élan vital*.[49] Instead, his 'struggle for life' is more in keeping with Schopenhauer's concept of the Will, an irrepressible striving for life that exists in all organisms and is the cause of much human suffering.[50] By referring back to *Creative Evolution*, however, Beckett enables us to discern an important link between Bergson's alternative theory of evolution and the backward trajectory from vertebrate to invertebrate – from Molloy to Worm – that takes place over the course of the Trilogy. In an observation that recalls the regressive instincts of the embarrassed caterpillar, Bergson proposes that the evolution of many organisms 'is not only a movement forward; in many cases we observe a marking time, and still more often a deviation or a turning back'.[51]

For Bergson, the view that life advances forward in a straight line, a simplified Darwinian notion that he attributes to the work of Herbert Spencer, omits all that undermines its neat linear trajectory. It also introduces a peculiar notion of temporality, raising questions about the continued presence of elementary life forms in a system that supposedly evolves towards a state of greater complexity. Turning his attention to the 'crowd of minor paths in which, on the contrary, deviations, arrests and set-backs are multiplied', Bergson focuses on organisms that have diverged from the conventional path of development.[52] Beckett's mutual fascination with moments of evolutionary deviation is suggested by his marking out of a subsection of Darwin's *Origin* entitled 'Rudimentary, Atrophied, and Aborted Organs', which details a series of anomalous life forms that have somehow thwarted the usual stages of growth.[53] The author also made notes on Max Nordau's account of 'coenaesthesis', a form of embryonic, pre-conscious awareness that he would later characterise in a letter to Thomas MacGreevy as 'a grey commotion of mind, with no premises or conclusions'.[54]

Beckett's interest in Bergson's alternative approach to evolution is reflected in the contents of a course on French literature that he taught during a brief stint as a lecturer at Trinity College, Dublin in 1931. The surviving lecture notes of one of his students, Rachel Burrows, contain the lines: 'interested in his [Bergson's] idea of inadequacy of the <u>word</u> to translated impressions registered by instinct'.[55] In his reading of *Creative Evolution*, Beckett would have been confronted with the idea that the development of intelligence in human beings was at the expense of a form of pre-conscious knowledge, or 'instinct', which is 'nowhere so developed as in the insect world'. Bergson surmises that while the intelligence of human beings is such that we are able to utilise objects as tools, creatures of instinct such as beetles or wasps are able to use their own bodies to achieve similar ends. Intelligence, he argues, 'treats everything mechanically', whereas instinct is 'molded on the very form of life'.[56]

Bergson's account of instinct is itself moulded on Fabre's account of the hairy sand wasp. In an article that also caught the attention of Lewis, Fabre describes how the wasp has developed an instinct to paralyse its caterpillar prey in nine separate places using its sting, before laying eggs in its body that may feed on their living host. Marvelling at the extraordinary precision of this technique, Fabre writes of his 'itching to explain' the fact that a 'paltry insect bequeathes its skill to its offspring; and a man does not!'[57] In *Creative Evolution*, Bergson echoes Fabre's assessment of humankind's inferiority to invertebrates, describing how his own account of instinct is necessarily parasitic on a mode of intelligence: 'science cannot do otherwise', he laments, but express instinct in terms of intelligence; however, 'in so doing it constructs an imitation of instinct rather than penetrates within it'.[58] Bergson's choice of language suggests that he is cognisant of his inability to be the wasp that penetrates the caterpillar at exactly the right spot; for Bergson, as for Fabre, intelligence lacks the precision of expression displayed by creatures of instinct. In his lecture on French literature, Beckett appears to be adapting Bergson's account (via Fabre) of instinct versus intelligence to distinguish between two kinds of artistic expression. By opposing the 'inadequacy of the word' to 'impressions registered by instinct', Beckett hints at a language of instinct inspired in part by the ingenuity displayed by the insect world.

In his essay on Proust, which was heavily influenced by Bergsonian thought, Beckett outlines a mode of 'instinctive perception' consisting of the 'non-logical statement of phenomena . . . before they have been distorted into intelligibility in order to be forced into a chain of cause and effect' (*PTD* 86). With these remarks in mind, I want to suggest that in *The Unnamable*, Beckett begins to experiment with a form of expression that evades the workings of intelligence, with the torturous rhythms of the text embodying the author's struggle to access a more instinctive mode of expression. This tension is reflected in the figure of Worm, who represents the origins of the Unnamable's own life in a state of pre-conscious simplicity: 'I was he, before all became confused.' The backward trajectory of Worm appears to be bound up with Beckett's resistance to 'intelligibility' coupled with his awareness of the impossibility of abandoning sequential structures entirely. After breaking off in the midst of his contemplation of Worm to consider the path of evolution, the Unnamable remarks: 'to have floundered, however briefly, however feebly in the great life torrent streaming from the earliest protozoa to the very latest humans, that I, no, parenthesis unfinished. I'll begin again' (*TN* 345, 315). This is one of several examples of aposiopesis in *The Unnamable*, with the author deploying a rhetorical figure designed to break 'the chain of cause and effect' and produce an effect of textual rupture. This example also encapsulates Beckett's attempts to transport subject and text alike back towards a more elementary stage of existence, a process that entails resisting, often unsuccessfully, the pull of 'the great life torrent' of narrative.

'The best would be not to begin' remarks the speaker early on in the text, before conceding: 'But I have to begin'. Indeed, as soon as Worm is assimilated into language the 'various stages' of his development begin – he grows an ear, a head and finally eyes, causing the speaker to remark with horror: 'he's getting humanized!' Worm's slippery ontological status seems to stem from the fact that he is designed to function less as a physical entity than as a 'peephole' to the creative instinct that lies behind the form in which he is expressed (*TN* 286, 345, 353, 350). In contrast to progressive models of evolution, Bergson argues that the *élan vital* is most prominent in the earliest living organisms, which were

> endowed with a certain freedom of action, and above all, with a shape so undecided that it could lend itself to any future determination. These animals may have resembled some of our worms, but with this difference, however, that the worms living to-day, to which they could be compared, are but the empty and fixed examples of infinitely plastic forms, pregnant with an unlimited future.[59]

Bergson makes an important distinction between worms as embryonic ancestors of all existing life forms and 'the worms living to-day', which have retained their embryonic status by refusing to evolve beyond a certain point. These two kinds of worm – the 'infinitely plastic' and the fixed – can help us to develop a clearer understanding of Worm as a figure that mediates between the potential expression of the idea 'pregnant with an unlimited future', and the inevitable rigidity of its formal manifestation. This distinction also speaks to the wider tension in Beckett's writing between the fantasy of the larval and the fact of completion. While the former may be likened to Bergson's account of early worms endowed with 'a certain freedom of action' and a 'shape so undecided', the latter might be said to resemble the 'fixed example' of worms today – the 'vermigrade' as opposed to the 'larval'.

Bergson introduces these 'infinitely plastic forms' shortly after contemplating the discrepancy between 'life in general, and the forms in which it is manifested'. This discordance, he suggests, extends from the growth of natural organisms to the evolution of language:

> Our freedom, in the very movements by which it is affirmed, creates the growing habits that will stifle it if it fails to renew itself by a constant effort . . . The most living thought becomes frigid in the formula that expresses it. The word turns against the idea.[60]

The 'constant effort' involved in the renewal of living thoughts is reminiscent of Beckett's account of boring holes in the word surface in his 'German letter', not to mention his struggle from *Murphy* onwards to reconcile the possibilities of artistic expression with the necessity of some kind of aesthetic formula. Given that Bergson goes on to discuss 'infinitely plastic' worms moments later, in the final sentence of the passage it is possible to hear the well-known proverb 'even the worm will turn', which expresses the idea that even the most placid creature will retaliate when pushed to its extreme. Despite the apparent rigidity of the well-known formula of the turning worm, this statement is suggestive of the capacity of language to behave in surprising ways when pushed to extremes; like the worm, the word may eventually turn against the idea, but its turnings may also uncover new meanings.

Throughout *The Unnamable*, the figure of Worm mediates between the text's simultaneous need for and resistance to form – a paradox expressed by the Unnamable as: 'the inability to speak, the inability to be silent'. Referred to both as 'singular' and as part of a 'multitude, one after another', Worm resists ontological fixity (*TN* 389, 354, 397). This categorical slipperiness is reflected in the various indeterminacies of the language in which he is described:

> To say he does not know what he is, where he is, what is happening, is to underestimate him. What he does not know is that there is anything to know . . . Feeling nothing, knowing nothing, he exists nevertheless. (*TN* 340)

The insistent repetition at work in this passage seems designed to thwart intelligibility – 'know' may be heard as 'no', while 'knowing nothing' and 'not know' resemble fused half-rhymes. The passage recalls the self-cancellations of Murphy's speech patterns: 'each word obliterated, before it had time to make sense, by the word that came next', and yet the shift from negation to tentative affirmation that takes place in each of these statements – 'Feeling nothing . . . he exists nevertheless' – also hints at a reversal of this process, as the sense of their being 'nothing' to begin with flickers into a kind of nascent 'knowing'.

Steven Connor posits that *The Unnamable*, 'stippled as it is with fly-speck commas, becomes more etymologically entomological (*en-tomos* = 'internally divided')' over the course of the text.⁶¹ My sense is that Beckett's frenzied use of commas bears more of a resemblance to Bergson's 'infinitely plastic forms', proliferating over the course of the text in a manner akin to the 'scissiparous . . . slime-worms' of his subsequent prose experiment *How It Is* (*HI* 98). Reading passages such as this requires a vermicular movement of the eye 'out, back a little, stop; out, back a little, stop', with the text obstructing the possibility of a linear trajectory. This forces the reader back to the start of each utterance; in order to make some sort of sense of these stubbornly amorphous statements it becomes necessary to break off and begin sentences again in a manner reminiscent of Darwin's embarrassed caterpillar. Frustrating though it may be, this regressive model of reading releases a seepage of semantic possibilities: to get a feel for the rhythm of the passage – 'what he is, where he is, what is happening' – in all of its categorical slipperiness is to gain a more instinctive awareness of what might be being expressed beneath the surface of the text.

Over the course of the Trilogy, Beckett's subjects describe a sensation of being invaded by vermin, a phenomenon that reduces human motility to a crawl while also engendering an involuntary frenzy of tics and convulsions that anticipate the 'jerks' and 'spasms' of *How It Is* (*HI* 108).⁶² At one point Mahood likens himself to a convulsive dog 'suffering from worms', at another he is devoured by flies, and elsewhere in the text he cries out: 'what to still this gnawing of termites in my Punch and Judy box'? (*TN* 315, 347, 333). The Unnamable also refers to Worm as one minute 'in the skull and the next in the belly, strange'. The mobility of this vermicular figure amid both the physical and textual corpus is consistent with his formal plasticity. In yet another futile attempt to describe Worm, the Unnamable refers to him as 'nothing but a shapeless heap' with 'no face but no doubt expressive'. Although once assimilated into language 'Worm no longer is', the progressive degeneration of narrative coherence over the course of the texts suggests that this figure is instrumental to the undoing of both the human and textual corpus, infiltrating the mind of the speaker and reducing the language of the text to little more than digestive murmurs: 'nyum, hoo, plop, psss' (*TN* 346, 350, 342, 401). In his reading of the entry on the brain in the 1911 *Encyclopedia Britannica*, Beckett may have become aware that the brain is already inhabited by a worm, namely the *vermis*, the central lobe of the butterfly-shaped cerebellum (Latin for 'little brain'), a region which coordinates movement and speech.⁶³ As though interfering with this crucial component of the human nervous system, Worm often appears to disrupt the motor function of the text, enabling the Unnamable, as well as the reader, to experience language at a more instinctive, pre-conscious level.⁶⁴

The effect is undoubtedly disconcerting for all concerned, and in the midst of this unstable atmosphere the Unnamable expresses a longing to retreat into some sort of containing structure:

> I would gladly give myself the shape, if not the consistency of an egg . . . round and hard, rather than of some irregular shape and subject to the dents and bulges incident to shock. (*TN* 299)

The image of the shell as a form of shock absorber harks back to the concept of the stimulus shield, with the speaker's assertion that he would 'gladly give' himself this 'round and hard' shape suggesting that his psychic apparatus (like Murphy's suit) is no longer able to effectively mediate the forces at work in its surroundings. In the absence of stable boundaries, the Unnamable seeks shelter in the framework of narrative, deriving comfort from 'ever murmuring my old stories'. In particular, the speaker clings to the tale of Mahood, a human figure who gradually degenerates into a limbless and immobile creature, before being '[s]tuck like a sheaf of flowers in a deep jar', a glass structure akin to a wormery (*TN* 296, 321). The story of Mahood functions in a manner akin to the jar, providing moments of containment for a narrative that remains constantly on the verge of disintegration. Elsewhere in Beckett's post-war writing, the imposition of an artificial exoskeleton to house subjects who are, in his words, 'falling to bits' is suggested by the urns that contain the subjects of *Play* (1963), the dustbins that house Nagg and Nell in *Endgame*, as well as the earth in which Willie and Winnie are buried up to their waists, and later their necks, in *Happy Days* (1961).[65]

In a review of *The Unnamable*, Maurice Blanchot proposes that Worm, rather than being a figure of formlessness, is one of the many 'masks and figures' erected by Beckett between the subject and words he no longer trusts.[66] Blanchot's analogy is reminiscent of Beckett's 'German letter', in which he characterises language as 'a mask' [*Eine Larve*].[67] Carl Linnaeus, widely considered to be the father of modern taxonomy, classified the juvenile form of the insect as a larva because it masked the adult form; to the untrained eye, a wasp or a dragonfly is indistinguishable from an ant or a butterfly during its worm-like infancy.[68] As well as being complicit in the dissolution of formal structures, Worm might therefore be said to resemble a defensive barrier constructed by Beckett against the vicissitudes of development and decline, whereby subject and text alike are arrested in a state of cryptic immaturity. Blanchot's reading of Worm helps draw attention to the way in which seemingly opposing qualities of formlessness and formal fixity can seem to merge into one another in the modernist text. As we have seen in the writing of Lewis, Lawrence and H.D., what might appear rigid and fixed is often surprisingly fluid and protean in nature, while what initially seems unprotected and vulnerable may in fact be merely another defensive mask.

If Worm functions both as an agent of undoing as well as a kind of holding structure for a subject who finds himself 'falling to bits', then this is partly because this figure appears emblematic of Beckett's struggle to reconcile the obduracies of form with the paralysing absence of formal constraint. In *Three Dialogues*, which was written in the same period as *The Unnamable*, Beckett defines contemporary art as 'a thrusting towards a more adequate expression of natural experience' (*PTD* 101). The author's use of the verb 'to thrust', which means to 'push against something' or 'to exert the force of impact upon or against (a body) so as to move it away', recalls Murphy's 'thrusting' energy, as well as the Unnamable's repeated use of the verb 'squirm' and 'squirming' (*TN* 360, 332).[69] As Arthur Rose observes, Beckett also uses the word 'squirming' in a letter to Duthuit to characterise the torturous process of composing the text.[70] Just as *Murphy* pushes back against the force of its own preordained ending, the spasmodic rhythms of *The Unnamable* appear to derive from the act of pushing against the rigidity of the form in which it is contained.

Another way of understanding the convulsive movements of the text towards and away from a state of ontological fixity can be found in Freud's *Beyond the Pleasure Principle*, a text with which Beckett was familiar.[71] After exploring the function of the protective shield surrounding the psyche, Freud turns his attention to the instincts of elementary organisms 'that survive the . . . individual being'. Identifying a tension between the sex-instinct (the will to live; the survival instinct) and the ego-instinct (the death-drive; the instinct to regress), Freud posits that there is 'an oscillating rhythm in the life of organisms':

> One group of instincts rushes forward so as to reach the final aim of life as swiftly as possible . . . the other group jerks back to a certain point to make a fresh start and so prolong the journey.[72]

There is something wormlike about this back and forth motion that anticipates the wavering self-cancellation of the Unnamable's final gasps: 'I can't go on, I'll go on' (*TN* 407). Freud's account resonates with Beckett's emphasis on recurrent beginnings – his repeated suggestion that subject and text alike can only move forwards by starting over. In his study of the influence of *Beyond the Pleasure Principle* on Beckett's writing, Phil Baker argues that the Beckettian subject gravitates 'towards the mineral state before and after life'.[73] Yet as is apparent from Murphy's pursuit of a 'larval and dark' stage of consciousness, or in the pre-conscious figure of Worm, Beckett appears to be preoccupied less with the petrification of the self than with the low vitality of elementary organisms that have persisted against the odds, refusing to yield to what Freud describes as the 'external pressure which provokes a constantly increasing extent of development'.[74]

At one point the Unnamable likens himself to a worm on a hook, remarking: 'The essential is to go on squirming forever at the end of the line.' Although in reality the subject only ever gets as far as what Malone refers to as 'well-meaning squirms that get me nowhere', it is precisely in getting nowhere that the text is able to move beyond existing forms of expression, embracing plasticity over progress – a perpetual squirming into being (*TN* 332, 218). Regardless of *The Unnamable*'s striving towards a state of elemental simplicity, however, few readers could mistake the text for anything other than a highly evolved and complex organism. One of the more striking aspects of Beckett's post-war writing is that the author's struggle to access a more incipient mode of expression necessitated ever more sophisticated formal strategies. *The Unnamable* is central to Beckett's exploration of the larval, its resistance to figuration, not to mention its persistence beneath the strictures of literary form. Yet it also marked the end of a period of intense productivity for Beckett, with critics agreeing that it functions as a kind of 'terminus' in his *oeuvre*, 'the inevitable and terrifying end', as Michael Robinson puts it, to his 'frenzy of writing' in the late 1940s.[75]

In the 1950s, the author's prose output all but ground to a halt: between 1950 and 1958, he published two short fragments – *Texts for Nothing* (1954) and 'From an Abandoned Work' (1956) – the titles of which signpost their apparent incompleteness and failure. During this period, Beckett began to channel his creative energies into other artistic media, including theatre and radio plays and later film and television. One possibility is that the black void of radio, minimalist set design, or even the 'monstrous quivering tadpole' that Virginia Woolf encountered at the cinema, provided a more apposite expression of Murphy's 'larval and dark' zone. Yet, just as the author's 'German letter' wonders whether there might be something 'paralysingly holy in the vicious nature of the word that is not found in the elements of the other arts', Beckett's inability to fully relinquish prose form, regardless of the growing struggle entailed in its usage, suggests that it remained a fitting medium with which to represent the intractability of the larval.[76]

A Ton of Worms

Having reached something of a creative dead end after completing *The Unnamable* in 1949, Beckett began to spend increasing amounts of time outdoors ground clearing and digging holes to plant trees. While working in the garden of his small cottage in the village of Ussy-sur-Marne, forty miles or so from Paris, the author embarked on a series of 'observations of nature', documenting his interest in 'the love-life of the Colorado beetle' and detailing the mating dance of 'ephemerids of a strange kind, "may-flies" I think'.[77] In the spring of 1951, around the same time that he remarked to Duthuit that he had 'never seen so many butterflies in such worm-state', Beckett wrote to his friend Maria Péron:

> Between the April showers I scratch the mud and observe the worms, an observation entirely devoid of scientific detachment. I try not to hurt them, with the spade. All the while knowing that, cut in two, they at once fashion a new head, or a new tail, whichever is the case.[78]

Beckett is describing the phenomenon of scissiparity, or the reproduction of elementary organisms by splitting into two distinct parts. The author is mistaken in his belief that the earthworms sliced by his spade could regenerate in this way – in fact, only certain types of flatworm are capable of this feat. Yet after finding himself unable to replicate the frenzy of writing that produced the Trilogy, it is perhaps understandable that Beckett's imagination was drawn to the possibility of unlaboured creative processes.

Beckett's earthworm anecdote marks the beginning of an unusual fascination that stretches into the summer months and even lingers into the following spring, when he reports back to Péron with palpable disappointment: 'Digging all day long. Fewer earthworms than last year.'[79] A sign that worms were beginning to infiltrate Beckett's thought processes during this period may

Figure 4.1 Beckett in his garden at Ussy (undated). Courtesy of Dartmouth College Library

Figure 4.2 Beckett digging holes at Ussy (undated). Beckett International Foundation/University of Reading

be found in *Waiting for Godot* (1953). In the original French version of the text, *En attendant Godot* (1949), Estragon, tiring of Vladimir's tendency to romanticise their surroundings, exclaims: 'Alors fous-moi la paix avec tes paysages! Parle-moi du sous-sol!' ['Enough of your landscapes! Tell me about the sub-soil!'].[80] When the text was performed in English in 1953, Beckett had translated these lines to: 'You and your landscapes! Tell me about the worms!' (*CDW* 57).

Before describing his outdoor observations, Beckett wonders to Péron in what was by now a familiar refrain of his letters: 'How to go on after [*The Unnamable*]? The earthworms at Ussy, I want to suggest, may have helped the author to work through this creative impasse. Shortly after his letter to Péron, Beckett likens himself to 'an invertebrate', adding: 'I shall have to try to work, go back to the wrigglings and twistings and chains of smoke.'[81] In *Texts for Nothing* (1967), a series of 'fourteen very short abortive texts' that the author wrote between digging holes, Beckett presents the weak musings of an anonymous subject who appears to be on the verge of death:

> The mind slow, slow, nearly stopped. And yet it's changing, something is changing . . . perhaps we're in a head, it's as dark as in a head before the worms get at it, ivory dungeon. The words too, slow, slow, the subject dies before it comes to the verb, words are stopping too. Better off than when life was babble? (*CSP* 106)[82]

Here, life may have 'nearly stopped' but something new is stirring. The infiltration of the mind by vermin creates room for the possibility of a kind of a textual afterlife capable of superseding the ivory shell of the mind from which it is generated – a low and persistent energy that inheres in the ooze of assonance, 'slow, slow'. The speaker's fading mind slips easily from 'worms' to 'words', forging an implicit connection between the proliferation of maggots on a dead body and the disintegration of linguistic structures. Beckett situates the text on the brink of a kind of deathly rebirth, in which the human 'subject' is succeeded by a profusion of larval entities capable of 'go[ing] on' after words stop.

The association of worms in Beckett's post-war writing with a kind of nascent afterlife is also hinted at in the Trilogy when the aged Malone lists examples to support his impression that he has not yet died, including 'my system of nutrition and elimination'. He then wonders whether this peristaltic movement is 'in reality . . . nothing but my worms' (*TN* 213). The author's interest in what might be left behind after words fail may also be linked to his contemplation of 'what little remains' of the human and its forms of expression after the Second World War (*HI* 93). Just as the spectacle of the survivors at Saint-Lô amid a 'sea of mud' prompted Beckett to consider 'the terms in which our condition is to be thought again', the proliferation of worms in the mud

Figure 4.3 Saint-Lô in June 1944

at Ussy seems to have enabled the author to contemplate the kind of life that might be able to endure amid an atmosphere of decay.

These thoughts are already beginning to stir in the Trilogy: like a worm cut in two, Macmann is able to 'suffer extensive mutilation and survive', while Worm has 'survived them all, Mahood too' (*TN* 331). Simon Critchley has argued that 'Worm is that which somehow *remains*, he is a remainder, what Blanchot calls "une survivance" outside of life and the possibility of death'.[83] In apprehending Worm as a 'remainder', or a leftover part of something, we might also consider the extent to which in Beckett's post-war writing the larval is that which succeeds as well as precedes the human subject.

In a 1948 letter to Duthuit, Beckett quipped morbidly: 'They must have great conversations, the worms with the bodies fermenting, on Joyce and Klee.'[84] This observation displays a characteristically Beckettian pessimism about the future of art, in which the carrion of creativity is all that's left. Yet it is also possible to detect a fantasy of redistribution, in which the creative spirit of the pair persists in their maggoty offspring. Much has been said about Beckett's preoccupation with decrepitude, exhaustion and death, but less attention has been paid to the curious reserve of posthumous (from the Latin *post*, after, *humus*, earth) energy that emerges from this state of dereliction. In 'From an Abandoned Work' (1957), which Beckett wrote at Ussy in the mid-1950s, an elderly speaker contemplates his demise while walking through muddy terrain:

> Just under the surface I shall be, all together at first, then separate, and drift through all the earth and perhaps in the end through a cliff into the sea, something of me. A ton of worms in an acre, that is a wonderful thought, a ton of worms, I believe it. Where did I get it, from a dream, or a book read in a nook when a boy, or a word overheard as I went along, or in me all along and kept under till it could give me joy. (*CSP* 160)

The speaker is not the first in Beckett's writing to contemplate the worms beneath his feet: in *Mercier and Camier* (1946), Camier pauses amid the turf-bogs, asking nervously: 'Do you think there are worms? . . . Shall we dig a little hole and see?'[85] Here, however, the proliferation of this 'ton of worms' is a source of 'joy' to the speaker, who begins to contemplate a kind of larval afterlife in which a remnant of the self – 'something of me' – is carried over into this multitude of elementary cells (selves). The phenomenon of scissiparity (from the Latin *scissus*, meaning to split, and *parity* to give birth) can also be observed at the level of syntax. Throughout this purportedly 'abandoned' opening to a novel, fragmentation becomes a mode of lexical reproduction as each comma splice sprouts new combinations of existing forms.

The speaker's reiteration of the phrase 'a ton of worms' is consistent with the way that the text moves forward by doubling back on itself – a trajectory reflected in the speaker's daily journey 'out, on, round, back'. This regressive movement is also evident in the repetitive rhythms of the passage, which appear to be generated in part from the echoing of sounds – 'sea' and 'me', 'book' and 'nook'. Shortly after contemplating the worms beneath his feet, the speaker remarks:

> Over, over, there is a soft place in my heart for all that is over, no, for the being over, I love the word, words have been my only loves, not many. Often all day long as I went along I have said it, and sometimes I would be saying vero, oh vero. (*CSP* 162–3)

The desire to be 'all over instead of in store' is compounded by each repetition of 'over', which expands into various applications – being spread over the earth's surface, starting 'all over' again, not to mention the desire for life to be at an end. The beginning and end of the statement demonstrates the speaker's generation of new material out of old elements – from over to vero – as the o is transported from head to tail. Beckett is treating words like the worms at Ussy, splitting them apart in order to witness them 'fashion a new head, or a new tail'. Throughout the text, scissiparity functions as an anti-teleological strategy, in which Beckett explores the prospect of going on as simply that of going on and on – persisting without progressing.

In the above passage it is possible to hear the French *ver*, or worm, as well as the Latin *vertere*, from which the word 'verse' derives, and out of which the compound 'worm-turn' may be excavated.[86] *Vero* is also the Latin word for 'truth', and this sense of the word calls to mind Russell Smith's definition of truth in Beckett's writing as 'an event that breaks into the established order of things, forcing us to consider a new way of being'.[87] By introducing a host of linguistic resonances, the meanings of which multiply in translation, the text hints that the breakdown and redistribution of individual words is able to release a host of polyglot pullulations. The figure of the worm is thus instrumental to the overturning of the notion of a singular, unified self as it is bound up in language. In presenting words as a multitude of intermingling, ruptured and renewed forms Beckett experiments with a more disparate mode of existence in his writing – one that emerges in part from the collapse of human structures.

If the 'sea of mud' at Saint-Lô allowed Beckett to contemplate 'humanity in ruins' as well as 'the terms in which our condition is to be thought again', then it makes sense that he would turn his attention to life forms capable not only of thriving in the mud but also of maintaining its vitality. Although the origins of this 'wonderful thought' are lost to the speaker, the 'book' in which the speaker encountered the 'ton of worms' statistic may well have been Darwin's *The Formation of Vegetable Mould through the Action of Worms, With Observations on Their Habits* (1881), in which he estimates with almost comic precision that there are approximately 53,767 worms per acre. In his final study Darwin revealed that worms not only maintain the fertility of the soil through their collective digestive processes, but that they also preserve human structures intact. 'Archaeologists ought to be grateful to worms', he asserts, who 'protect and preserve for an indefinitely long period every object, not liable to decay . . . burying it beneath their castings.'[88] Adam Phillips observes that, like Freud, 'Darwin is interested in how destruction conserves life; and in the kind of life destruction makes possible.'[89] These remarks are applicable to Beckett's post-war prose, as well as to all of the writing examined by this study, which turns to the insect world in order to contemplate the kind of life that might be able not only to survive, but thrive, amid an atmosphere of destruction.

Darwin's account of these 'small agencies and their accumulated effects' resonates with Beckett's presentation of survival in his post-war writing as a diminished yet surprisingly productive state of being – a faint but persistent murmur of activity.[90] Darwin's study of worms was largely overlooked until the end of the Second World War, when a number of studies of soil fertility were published with the view of increasing national food production. In his 1945 introduction to the reissue of the text, agriculturalist Sir Albert Howard explains:

In directing attention to one of Nature's chief agents for restoring and maintaining the fertility of our soils, the publication of this new edition of Darwin's book will do much to establish the truth that Nature is the supreme farmer and gardener. The study of her ways will provide us with the one thing we need – sound and reliable direction.[91]

While gardening at Ussy, Beckett may have encountered Darwin's 'ton of worms' in one of the many soil studies that were published in the mid-1940s, which highlighted the role of earthworms in maintaining the vitality of the land.[92] Regardless of the 'origin' of the speaker's 'wonderful thought', worms appear to have provided a new direction to the author's prose. In *How It Is* (1964), Beckett continues to experiment with states of radical self-division, splitting the text apart as a means of spawning new forms.

A Scissiparous Frenzy

How It Is, which was published in French in 1961 under the title *Comment c'est*, depicts a wormlike subject crawling naked through 'primeval mud impenetrable dark'. The survival of life amid this inhospitable terrain remains a constant source of surprise to the speaker ('I drag myself and drag myself astonished to be able') who, in addition to the tins of prawns and sardines that he keeps in his sack, is sustained by the mud that he ingests and excretes (*HI* 7, 11). The recirculation of waste products provides fertile terrain for the speaker's imaginative processes: encountering another, almost identical mud crawler, who he names Pim, the speaker envisages the pair as one of an infinite line of mud crawlers endlessly regenerating. There are residual traces of the earthworms at Ussy in the speaker's inability to identify Pim's extremities ('the cries tell me which end the head but I may be mistaken') as well as in his description of the procession of identical couples 'in a straight line with neither head nor tail in the dark the mud'. The speaker's inability to make head or tail of his companions is reflected in the form of the text, which confounds any clear distinction between beginnings or endings, presenting itself as 'bits and scraps in the mud' and 'old words back from the dead' (*HI* 46, 108, 14, 82).

In what some critics consider to be his final experiment with novelistic form, Beckett dispenses with the sentence altogether, generating the text out of what Hugh Kenner terms 'a few dozen expressions'. H. Porter Abbott notes that from *Texts for Nothing* onwards, 'bringing to ruin the epic of containment and radiant design Beckett concentrated attention on the wonders of origination'. In doing so, 'he trebled his capacity to surprise us with ever new and striking inventions from the same old material'.[93] Abbott's remarks capture the growing emphasis in Beckett's post-war writing on the creative possibilities of recycled material: 'the same voice the same things nothing changing but the names'.

This is particularly apparent in the final part of *How It Is* when the subject is left alone in the mud to resume his endless journey. In his isolation, the speaker envisages a scenario in which he and Pim are part of millions of identical couples 'that eternally form and form again all along this immense circuit that the millionth time that's conceivable as the conceivable first' (*HI* 99, 105). This 'eternally larval' procession stretches across the final part of the text and involves a series of protracted mathematical hypotheses:

> for take twenty consecutive numbers
> no matter which no matter which it is irrelevant
> 814326 to 814345
>
> (*HI* 104)

The notion that each spawning is as 'conceivable as the conceivable first' indicates that this process of reproduction continually refers back to a state of origination; the figures are 'irrelevant' because, as the speaker notes, 'you begin again all over more or less in the same place' (*HI* 16).

The text likens this endless procession of identical selves to a 'migration of slime-worms then or tailed latrinal scissiparous frenzy days of great gaiety' (*HI* 98). There is something akin to the 'joy' experienced by the speaker of 'From an Abandoned Work' while contemplating the 'ton of worms' beneath his feet. Here too, the imagined profusion of vermicular beings is not only a source of elation for the decrepit speaker, but it also serves a generative function in the text, fuelling its frenzied calculations. As a mode of unicellular reproduction that produces identical offspring (barring occasional mutations), scissiparity is anathema to narratives of progress, as well as to the humanist conception of the self as stable, bounded and individuated. It imposes a horrifying state of self-division upon the subject, as is apparent in Beckett's late prose fragment *The Lost Ones* (1971), in which the 'I' is replaced by hundreds of disoriented selves 'each searching for its lost one', or in *Fizzles 5* (1976), with its 'millions' of bodies 'six times smaller than life' that remain in a state of isolation: 'no two ever meet' (*CSP* 202, 232). Yet this ceaseless multiplication also confers a kind of immortality upon the subject – what the speaker of *How It Is* refers to 'some kind of being without end' (*HI* 122).

In the final part of the text, the speaker reveals that the endless spawning of identical selves has resulted not in a multitude of discrete entities but a collective entity 'glued together like a single body in the dark the mud':

> in reality we are one and all from the unthinkable first
> to the no less unthinkable last glued together in a vast imbrication of flesh without breach or fissure
>
> (*HI* 106, 122)

The process of division confers a kind of unity on the speaker, who is both 'one and all', first and last, individual and multitude. Once cut in two, the subject comes back upon itself: 'each always leaves the same always goes towards the same' (*HI* 99). The mud facilitates this repair of the 'breach' in the self, gluing these divided bodies back together.[94] At the same time, this wholeness remains a doubleness – what Seamus Perry helpfully refers to as a 'di-vision' or 'twofold vision'.[95] Beckett's splitting of the word 'imbrica-tion' serves as a subtle reminder of this overlapping state, in which the subjects are '*like* a single body' but remain separate entities: 'millions millions there are millions of us' (*HI* 99). Beckett's vision of a scissiparous self represents a kind of 'unthinkable' existence in which the subject remains apart and together, singular and multiple, bound and unbound. This divided state is suggestive of the breakdown of the self as a coherent entity, but crucially the split subject experiences ways of being denied to those that have stubbornly held together. At the end of the text, the speaker confesses that this 'vast imbrica-tion' is something that he dreamed up in his isolation: 'only me in . . . the dark . . . yes alone' (*HI* 128). The larval experience, it seems, remains confined to the realm of fantasy in Beckett's writing, gesturing towards a state of being and creating that lies beyond the bounds of human expression.

While he was writing *How It Is*, Beckett developed an editing technique akin to scissiparity that served to galvanise the compositional process. The first version of the text took eighteen months to write, and the six notebooks in which it was drafted contain fourteen separate attempts to begin the text.[96] The author characterised this torturous process in vermicular terms as 'three spasms forward and two back', confessing to a friend after deciding to take a break from the text: 'Relief to fly from this Pim hell and I won't have driven ten miles before I'll be fidgeting to get back to it.' A key breakthrough occurred after Beckett made the decision to 'break up into short units the continuum contrived with such difficulty', chopping sentences and paragraphs into unpunctuated segments.[97] In contrast to the slow pace of composition that preceded it, this process of rupture was highly productive. According to Édouard Magessa O'Reilly, who edited the genetic edition of *How It Is*, after Beckett imposed these cuts onto the text the 'revision progressed rapidly, as is indicated by the dates that punctuate it'.[98]

The cut-up appearance of *How It Is* forestalls the threat of closure; Daniella Caselli notes that the verb 'to open' is everywhere present – from the can opener to the speaker's 'opening' of Pim's body.[99] This openness extends to the text's self-imposed narrative framework: towards the beginning, the speaker states that the text will consist of three sections, 'before Pim with Pim after Pim'. Later on, however, he reflects anxiously that 'in trying to present three parts or episodes an affair which all things considered involves four one is in danger of being incomplete' (*HI* 3, 113). Evidently, it is precisely this danger that Beckett is attempting to introduce into the text in order to prevent it from taking on the appearance of something complete and unbroken. The author's efforts to maintain the text in a state of incompletion extended to his unorthodox editorial processes. As Magessa O'Reilly notes:

> Beckett took pains with the published text to clarify for readers the integrity of the individual units. For the French original, he instructed that each page end either with an incomplete line (making clear that the fragment was ending) or with a hyphen (making clear that the fragment continues over-page). For the English edition he eschewed altogether the page-breaking of fragments, preferring to vary the amount of space between fragments so as to avoid any overflow onto the next page – while still requiring that the last line of each page be incomplete.[100]

By going to great pains to avoid any textual 'overflow' – a word which recalls Joyce's formal excesses – Beckett appears to have been attempting to push back against the material constraints of the book with its preset margins, uncut pages and rigid spine. According to Deirdre Bair, there was a standing joke at Grove Press that there was both a 'house' style and a 'Beckett' style, 'and [the printers] scrupulously followed the latter no matter how it might deviate from the former'.[101] Working with the page proofs of *How It Is* was 'difficult' as, according to Beckett, 'the printer had a problem with his page endings'.[102] These difficulties were compounded when it came to translating the text, with the author going to great lengths to preserve its many 'oddities' of expression and typesetting in English.[103]

The inconsistency of Beckett's approach to the layout of the French, English and American editions of *How It Is* resulted in multiple, at times conflicting versions of the text, thwarting its appearance as a single coherent entity. These *ver*-sions resemble worms 'cut in two', regenerating themselves from various editorial mutilations – the author's own included. Before the text had been published in English, Beckett took the unusual step of offering three translated extracts from *How It Is* to periodicals, all of which contain variants.[104] The frequent blurring of the distinction between draft, extract, translation and edition suggests that Beckett was keen to experiment with the possibilities of textual scissiparity, obstructing the possibility of a single version of the text, while also introducing variations so slight that the texts resemble almost identical offspring of one another. Seemingly, if the author felt that in the years after *The Unnamable*, 'I was saying the same thing over and over again', he was able to elevate this perceived failing into an integral feature of his late style, reworking the material of his existing corpus in a manner akin to the earthworm's overturning of the earth: composition as composting.[105] Beckett's aesthetic of incompletion appears to have paid off, with readers often remarking that the text appears arrested in the caterpillar phase of composition. Hugh Kenner, for instance, argues that the text resembles 'a draft of itself', while Frederik Smith proposes that it dramatises the compositional process 'at a more primal stage'.[106]

Further insight into the larval aspirations of *How It Is* can be found in the speaker's reference to being 'mad or worse transformed a la Haeckel . . . the shadow he casts', as well as his tendency to 'recapitulate the sack the tins the mud the dark the silence the solitude' (*HI* 34, 4). Beckett owned and annotated a copy of Ernst Haeckel's *The Riddle of the Universe* (1901), which includes references to his controversial recapitulation theory. Haeckel famously claimed that an embryo goes through successive adult stages of its evolutionary ancestors during the course of its development – a human embryo, for instance, undergoes a gilled, fishlike stage. In a chapter entitled 'The Embryology of the Soul', Haeckel also likens the developmental phases of the human soul to the life cycle of an insect:

> We have a similar long sleep in the chrysalis stage of those insects which undergo a complete metamorphosis – butterflies, bees, flies, beetles, and so forth. This sleep of the pupa, during which the most important formations of organs and tissues take place, is the more interesting from the fact that the preceding condition of the free larva (caterpillar, grub, or maggot) included a highly developed psychic activity, and that this is, significantly, lower than the stage which is seen afterwards (when the chrysalis sleep is over) in the perfect, winged, sexually mature insect. Man's psychic activity . . . runs the same evolution – upward progress, full maturity, and downward degeneration – as every other vital activity in his organization.[107]

Haeckel's account of the larval stage as one of 'highly developed psychic activity', but also significantly 'lower than the stage . . . afterwards', resonates with Beckett's interest in the 'worm-state' as that which, though rudimentary, displays a surprising amount of vitality. Ackerley and Gontarski speculate that this passage may lurk behind Murphy's 'larval and dark' zone, while Michael Beausang proposes that *Watt* 'feature[s] a satirical exploitation of Ernest Haeckel's disproved formula "ontogeny recapitulates phylogeny"'.[108] Circling back to this text, as he did with Darwin's *Origin of Species*, at various stages of his writing career, Beckett appears to have discovered fresh inspiration for his efforts to resist the logic of 'upward progress' and 'downward degeneration', recognising that there may be some value in returning to 'the preceding condition'.[109]

By the time Beckett wrote *How It Is*, Haeckel's theory of recapitulation had been widely discounted in scientific circles, and yet as Nick Hopwood

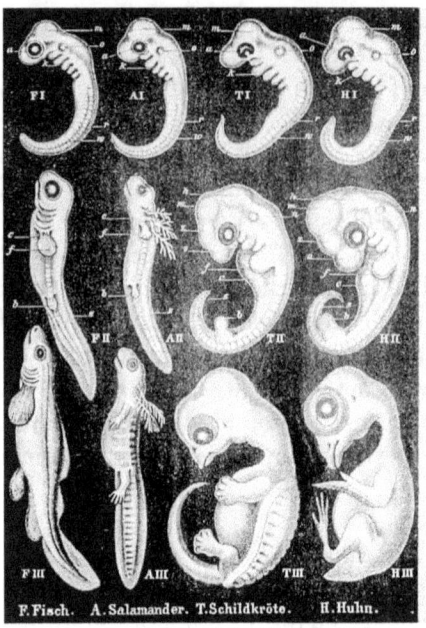 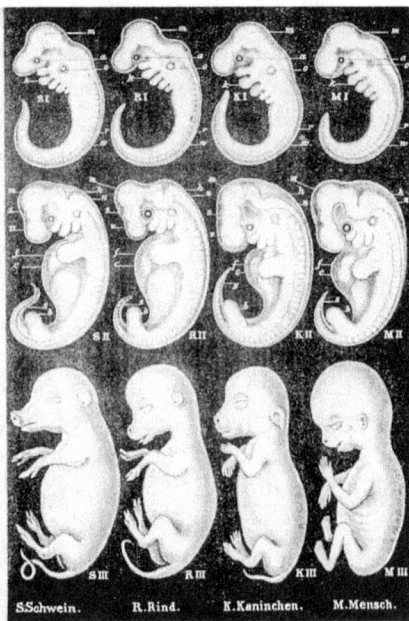

Figure 4.4 Embryos of fish, salamander, turtle, chick, pig, cow, rabbit and human, at 'very early', 'somewhat later' and 'still later' stages. Ernst Haeckel, *Anthropogenie*, 1874

notes, Haeckel's iconic illustrations of human and animal embryos persisted in the popular imagination long after they had been proved to be false.[110] Julian Murphet surmises that Haeckel's presentation of the human 'perched precariously over an inhuman abyss, found reaffirmation in the aftermath of Auschwitz'.[111] In Beckett's depiction of what Alain Badiou, in a reading of *How It Is*, describes as 'the larvae of essential humanity', it is possible to discern the shadowy presence of Haeckel's ghostly embryos suspended in amniotic fluid.[112]

The above image is a fraudulent depiction of the fetus as it recapitulates its evolutionary ancestry from invertebrate to fish to mammal. Yet it also presents a compelling vision of the human subject as developing *in utero* from a 'worm-state'. Haeckel shared Darwin's belief in common descent, a concept described in the closing lines of the *Origin of Species*: 'from so simple a beginning endless forms most beautiful and most wonderful have been, and are being, evolved'.[113] Beckett's writing also appears preoccupied with the notion of a single originary form. In *How It Is*, the speaker refers to himself as 'Belacqua fallen on his side' (*HI* 18), conjuring an image of himself as the larval predecessor of the protagonist of Beckett's first novel, *Dream of Fair to Middling Women* (1932), as well as his short story collection *More Pricks Than Kicks* (1934). Beckett's foregrounding of the common ancestry of his characters is also suggested by his frequent use of M-names, Murphy, Molloy, Malone, Moran, Mahood – as well as Bim, Bom, Pim, Prim, Krim, Kram, Pam and Worm, in which the M has moved from head to tail. These overt likenesses convey a fantasy of continuity in rupture, in which, like the wormlike mud-dwellers of *How It Is*, the Beckettian subject is 'one and all', individual and multitude, human and worm.

In *Difference and Repetition*, Gilles Deleuze observes how, in all of the author's novels:

> Beckett has traced the inventory of peculiarities pursued with fatigue and passion by larval subjects: Molloy's series of stones, Murphy's biscuits, Malone's possessions – it is always a question of drawing a small difference, a weak generality, from the repetition of elements or the organisation of cases. It is undoubtedly one of the more profound intentions of the 'new novel' to rediscover, below the level of active syntheses, the domain of passive syntheses which constitute us, the domain of modifications, tropisms and little peculiarities.[114]

Deleuze's account of the small differences and weak generalities that constitute these 'larval subjects' harks back to Sarraute's account of modernism's 'little larval actions' that linger on the threshold of consciousness. Beckett's post-war writing, in particular, presents the subject as a multitude of minor selves, distinguishable only by subtle variations and 'little peculiarities'. Crucially, however, in this divided state the subject is capable of surprising feats of survival:

> Embryology already displays the truth that there are systematic vital movements, torsions and drifts, that only the embryo can sustain: an adult would be torn apart by them. There are movements for which one can only be a patient, but the patient in turn can only be a larva ... they alone are capable of sustaining the lines, the slippages and the rotations.[115]

Beckett recorded a similar sentiment in his early notes for *How It Is*, transcribing the following line from Victor Hugo's 1869 novel, *L'Homme qui rit* [*The Man Who Laughs*]: 'Être un ver, quelle force!' [To be a worm, what strength!].[116] To be a defenceless larva is to endure in ways denied to the fully developed self. In this embryonic state, the subject is able to preserve itself against even the most harmful forces, sustaining the lines of expression that are unique to this incipient mode of being.

To exist in this way is to remain open to suffering, and indeed there are important parallels to be discerned between Beckett's helpless larvae subject to 'torsions and drifts' and Woolf's quivering bug, Lewis's insect-mimics, Lawrence's formicating subjects, or H.D.'s suspended caterpillars. Although his subjects have no shell to hide behind, Beckett's writing demonstrates a shared emphasis on creative forms of survival inspired by entomological life forms. More so than his fellow writers, the author struggles to reconcile his vision of an 'eternally larval' art with the material constraints of language, but it is important not to overlook the author's 'inkling' that something new might yet emerge from this process of struggling and striving and so often failing. In *Three Dialogues*, Beckett writes that the contemporary artist 'seems literally skewered on the ferocious dilemma of expression. Yet he continues to wriggle' (*PTD* 101). With recourse to worms of various kinds, Beckett began to find a way of wriggling out of this dilemma, with his post-war writing asking what it might mean for the human subject and its forms of expression to persist in a state of squirming division, resembling twitching remnants that can't go on but somehow do.

Notes

1. According to Adam Piette, Beckett quoted this line in his 'Pim' manuscript, which contains early notes and ideas for *How It Is*, 'Torture, Text, Human Rights', 154.
2. Beckett, *Letters*, Vol. 2, 102.
3. Adorno, 'Trying to Understand *Endgame*', 128, 122.
4. *Letters*, Vol. 2, 18.
5. 'inkling, *n*.', OED.
6. Ackerley and Gontarski, *The Grove Companion*, 309.
7. Moorjani, 'The Dancing Bees', 165; Carney, 'The Buzzing of B', 230; Connor, 'Making Flies Mean Something', 48. According to Van Hulle and Nixon, Beckett owned a 1902 publication of Darwin's *Origin of Species*, which is based on the second edition of the text. His surviving library also contains the *Penguin Dictionary of Natural History* (1967), the two-volume Larousse edition of *La Vie des animaux* [*The Lives of Animals*] (1952), Konrad Z. Lorenz's *King Solomon's Ring: New Light on Animal Ways* (1965) as well as Jean Rostand's 1967 study *Inquiétudes d'un biologiste* [*Concerns of a Biologist*], *Samuel Beckett's Library*, 206.
8. Darwin, *Origin of Species*, 377.
9. *Letters*, Vol. 2, 162, 271.
10. Jameson, *Fables of Aggression*, 14.
11. Keller, *Beckett and the Primacy of Love*, 56.
12. Bixby, 'Beckett at the GPO', 88.
13. Woolf, *Mrs Dalloway*, 4.
14. Freud, *Beyond the Pleasure Principle*, 299.
15. Adorno, *Aesthetic Theory*, 34.
16. Weisberg, *Chronicles of Disorder*, 30; MacKay, *Modernism and World War II*, 18.
17. Quoted in Ellmann, 'The Linati and Gorman-Gilbert Schemas', 186.
18. Quoted in Knowlson, *Damned to Fame*, 102 n. 61.
19. Ellmann, *The Nets of Modernism*, 151.
20. Quoted in *Damned to Fame*, 352.

21. Miller, *Late Modernism*, 18.
22. *Late Modernism*, 13; Benjamin, *Origin of German Tragic Drama*, 176.
23. Beckett, *Disjecta*, 19.
24. *Grove Companion*, 309; Alighieri, *Purgatorio*, 165.
25. Caselli, *Beckett's Dantes*, 81–8.
26. Diderot, *D'Alembert's Dream*, 233.
27. *Origin of Species*, 156.
28. 'embarrassed, *adj.*', OED.
29. Beckett, *Echo's Bones*, 42; *Watt*, 194.
30. Newman identifies a further allusion to Darwin's caterpillar in *The Unnamable* when the narrator is describing his treatment at the hands of his tormentors: 'it is only when they see me stranded that they take up again the thread of my misfortunes, judging me insufficiently vitalized to bring them to successful conclusion alone. But instead of making the junction, I have often noticed this, I mean instead of resuming me at the point where I was left off, they pick me up at a much later stage, perhaps thereby hoping to induce in me the illusion that I had got through the interval all on my own', *TN* 324; 'Beginning Again', 174.
31. Beckett, *Letters*, Vol. 1, 111; *Letters*, Vol. 3, 389.
32. Shepherd-Barr, 'Beckett's Old Muckball', 250; Chiong, 'Nauman's Beckett Walk', 63; Beausang, '*Watt*: Logic, Insanity, Aphasia', 504.
33. Newman, 'Beginning Again', 168.
34. Cohn, *A Beckett Canon*, 80.
35. *Murphy*, 44; Porter Abbott, *Form and Effect*, 39.
36. Bolin, *Beckett and the Modern Novel*, 48.
37. Rabaté, *The Ghosts of Modernity*, 166.
38. Quoted in Ackerley and Gontarski, *Grove Companion*, 309.
39. The resemblance of Beckett's protagonist to a vermicular entity was recognised by Joyce, who penned a playful limerick in response to the text about a 'maevusmarked maggot called Murphy' who 'worms off for a breeze down the surfy', quoted in Ellmann, *James Joyce*, 701.
40. The word peristalsis denotes the wormlike movement of the digestive system as food passes through it. The resemblance is such that the *OED* lists the adjective 'peristaltic' as a synonym of 'vermicular', 'peristaltic, *adj.*', OED.
41. 'vermigrade, *adj.*', 'worm, *v.*', OED.
42. *Letters*, Vol. 1, 518.
43. *Letters*, Vol. 1, 518.
44. Sarraute, 'Conversation and Subconversation', 91–2.
45. 'Conversation and Subconversation', 92, 90.
46. Quoted in Knowlson, *Damned to Fame*, 358; Gontarski, 'Creative Involution', 611.
47. Kenner, *Samuel Beckett*, 128; Kristeva, *Black Sun*, 258.
48. Beckett, *Malone meurt*, 90.
49. Salisbury, *Laughing Matters*, 32.
50. Schopenhauer, *The World as Will and Representation*, 1–92. I am grateful to Steven Connor for pointing this out to me.

51. Bergson, *Creative Evolution*, 104.
52. *Creative Evolution*, 104.
53. *Samuel Beckett's Library*, 203.
54. Nordau, *Degeneration*, 248–9; Tajiri, *Beckett and the Prosthetic Body*, 98–9.
55. Quoted in Uhlmann, *Beckett and the Philosophical Image*, 29; original emphasis.
56. *Creative Evolution*, 134, 165.
57. Fabre, 'The Modern Theory of Instinct', 15, 21.
58. *Creative Evolution*, 168.
59. *Creative Evolution*, 130.
60. *Creative Evolution*, 127–8.
61. Connor, 'Beckett's Punctuation', 278.
62. For more on the pathology of spasms, tics and convulsions in Beckett's writing see Salisbury, *Laughing Matters*, 77–112.
63. 'brain' 1911: 401. Beckett consulted and later owned a copy of the 1911 edition of the *Encyclopedia Britannica*, and Van Hulle and Nixon state that the 'folded entry on the "Brain" could conceivably have interested him', *Samuel Beckett's Library*, 193.
64. Salisbury and Code reach a similar conclusion from a different starting point in their essay on automatic and involuntary language in Beckett, 'Jackson's Parrot', 205–22.
65. Quoted in Shenker, *The Critical Heritage*, 148.
66. Blanchot, 'The Unnamable', 119.
67. *Letters*, Vol. 1, 514.
68. 'larva, *n*.', OED.
69. 'thrust, *v*.', OED.
70. Rose, 'Revisiting *The Unnamable*', 222.
71. James Knowlson recounts a conversation between Gottfried Buttner and Beckett in 1967 in which the author related Freud's account of man's 'congenital yearning for the mineral condition' in *Beyond the Pleasure Principle* to his childhood love of stones, *Damned to Fame*, 29, 177.
72. *Beyond the Pleasure Principle*, 313.
73. Baker, 'Beckett Beyond the Pleasure Principle', 128.
74. *Beyond the Pleasure Principle*, 312.
75. Connor, 'Preface', *The Unnamable*, xviii; Robinson, *The Long Sonata of the Dead*, 191.
76. Beckett, *Disjecta*, 171–2.
77. *Letters*, Vol. 2, 162, 232.
78. *Letters*, Vol. 2, 241.
79. *Letters*, Vol. 2, 434.
80. Beckett, *En attendant Godot*, 53.
81. *Letters*, Vol. 2, 241, 274.
82. *Letters*, Vol. 2, 457.
83. Critchley, *Very Little . . . Almost Nothing*, 198; original emphasis.
84. *Letters*, Vol. 2, 86.
85. To which Mercier responds: 'Certainly not, what an idea', *Mercier and Camier*, 83.

86. Kamuf, 'Your Worm', 161.
87. Smith, *Beckett and Ethics*, 8.
88. Darwin, *The Formation of Vegetable Mould*, 54, 102.
89. Phillips, 'Darwin Turns the Worm', 63.
90. *The Formation of Vegetable Mould*, 5.
91. Howard, 'Introduction', *Friend Earthworm*, 168.
92. Examples include E. B. Balfour, *The Living Soil: Evidence of the Importance to Human Health of Soil Vitality* (1943); F. H. Billington, *Compost* (1942); T. J. Barrett, *Harnessing the Earthworm* (1949).
93. Kenner, *Samuel Beckett*, 242; Porter Abbott, 'Beginning Again', 120.
94. Caselli, *Beckett's Dantes*, 157.
95. Perry, *Coleridge and the Uses of Division*, 3.
96. Magessa O'Reilly, 'English Introduction', ix–xxxvi.
97. *Letters*, Vol. 3, 337, 260.
98. 'English Introduction', xx.
99. Caselli, *Beckett's Dantes*, 158.
100. 'English Introduction', x.
101. Bair, *Samuel Beckett*, 474.
102. Mistakes were inevitably made during this process, with Kenner attributing 'three full stops' in the original version of the text to the 'printer's inadvertencies', *Samuel Beckett*, 242. Beckett would also notice his own errors along the way, *Letters*, Vol. 3, 378.
103. *Letters*, Vol. 3, 389, 577.
104. 'English Introduction', xv n. 7.
105. Quoted in Shenker, *The Critical Heritage*, 148.
106. Kenner, *Samuel Beckett*, 242; Smith, 'Fiction as Composing Process', 108.
107. Haeckel, *The Riddle of the Universe*, 146–7.
108. *Grove Companion*, 309; Beausang, '*Watt*: Logic, Insanity, Aphasia', 503.
109. In his 'Addenda' to *Watt*, Beckett transcribes the lines: 'the foetal soul is full-grown (Cangiamila's *Sacred Embryology* and Pope Benedict XIV's *De Synodo Diocesana*, Bk. 7, Chap. 4, Sec. 6)', *Watt*, 248.
110. Hopwood, *Haeckel's Embryos*, 1–7.
111. Murphet, 'France, Europe, the World', 129.
112. Badiou, *Conditions*, 255.
113. *Origin of Species*, 360.
114. Deleuze, *Difference and Repetition*, 79.
115. *Difference and Repetition*, 118, 219.
116. Quoted in Piette, 'Torture, Text, Human Rights', 154.

CONCLUSION: 'THINGS THAT WON'T QUITE FORMULATE'

On New Year's Day 1917, Robert Frost wrote to his friend Louis Untermeyer:

> What I like about Bergson and Fabre is that they have bothered our evolutionism so much with the cases of instincts they have brought up. You get more credit for thinking if you restate formulae or cite cases that fall easily under formulae, but all the fun is outside: saying things that suggest things that won't quite formulate.[1]

Frost's poem 'The White-Tailed Hornet' (1936), which is subtitled 'or, The Revision of Theories', appears to do precisely this. Observing the behaviour of a nearby hornet as it pursues a fly, the speaker prepares to marvel at the creature's powers of instinct:

> Verse could be written on the certainty
> With which it penetrates my best defense
> . . . To stab me in the sneeze-nerve of a nostril.[2]

Frost is alluding to Fabre's account of the paralysing precision of the hairy sand wasp which, as we saw in the preceding chapter, was cited by Bergson to illustrate his theory of instinct as 'nowhere so developed as in the insect world'.[3]

Initially, the behaviour of the hornet seems to confirm this view. But something goes wrong:

> Here he is at his best, but even here –
> I watched him where he swooped, he pounced, he struck;
> But what he found he had was just a nailhead.

By mistaking a nailhead for a fly, the hornet exhibits a curiously imprecise mode of behaviour that 'won't quite formulate' to Bergson and Fabre's theories, prompting the speaker to ask: 'Won't this whole instinct matter bear revision?'[4]

Frost's fascination with insect behaviour was long-standing: from early poems such as 'A Prayer in Spring' (1915) to later verses – 'A Considerable Speck' (1939), 'Pod of the Milkweed' (1954) – the author details his observations of ants, mites, wasps, butterflies and moths.[5] In 'The White-Tailed Hornet', however, the sense of admiration that runs through many of Frost's insect poems is replaced by a tone of deflation. No longer capable of arresting the human onlooker in a state of awe, the creature misses its mark; rather than hitting on the poet's 'sneeze-nerve', what it strikes is 'just a nailhead'. The hornet's failure to pin down its prey is also part of the fun of the poem: as Robert Faggen notes, Frost takes pleasure in 'unsettling reified metaphors and frozen concepts'.[6] The poem turns on the epistemological gap between human and insectile modes of understanding, striking at what it cannot resolve and making this tension part of its frenzied energy as it circles, hornet-like, around its point. Although he quickly dismisses it, Frost's speaker briefly settles on the notion that by 'comparing | Nailhead with fly and fly with huckleberry', the hornet is engaged in its own kind of 'poetry'.[7]

Frost's sense of the value in 'saying things that suggest things that won't quite formulate' helps to illuminate an important aspect of the modernist writing examined by this study. Inspired by the adaptive behaviours of insects, Lewis's restive mimicry, Lawrence's swarming formations, H.D.'s cocoon states and Beckett's regressive squirms are fuelled by a resistance to set formulas of thought and expression, their own included. We see this in the rapidly mutating surface of Lewis's writing, which derives much of its dynamism from its fear of falling into a state of aesthetic uniformity – an anxiety which, paradoxically, results in various imitative strategies that seek to transform resemblance into menace. It is also discernible in Lawrence's efforts to exploit the ungovernable energies of collective life, presenting a vision of literary form that has 'escaped from the pin which was pushed through it' and now resembles a 'cloud of bees flying and veering round'.[8] At stake in this language of swarming is a relinquishment of authorial control, an investment in words as living entities capable of generating a host of new associations. An aversion to fixed expressions is also apparent in H.D.'s 'half formulated' narratives, which seek to maintain self and text alike in a pupal stage of development in order to prevent them from hardening into an 'absolute form' (*P* 107, 165). It may be seen too in Beckett's exploration of the possibility of an 'eternally larval' form of expression that remains in a state of origination, resembling something embryonic – still yet to be formulated.

Frost's remarks are therefore consistent with the role played by insects in modernist writing in helping to unsettle established ways of thinking. Throughout the preceding chapters, the presence of insects often appears bound up with unorthodox and seemingly illogical notions, in which what appears destructive turns out to have a creative function, and what might seem debilitating is reconceived in terms of its enabling potential. The possibility of achieving transformation through decay, of holding oneself together by being broken apart, of the enhanced perspective afforded by a reduced existence – these are just a few of the ideas that are touched on by the writers of this study. More so than other life forms, insects seem to allow for these surprising inversions, in which customary ways of perceiving the world are suddenly turned inside out. One reason why these entities appear to have enabled this kind of transformative thinking (other than the design quirk of wearing their insides on the outside) is that the findings of entomologists such as Fabre had prompted many to radically reassess their capabilities. Far from being mindless drones, insects had stunned early twentieth-century audiences with their powers of sophistication. This new understanding of the insect world can help to account for modernist writers' investment in the notion that what might appear negligible, meaningless or even detrimental may turn out to hold unforeseen value. Such turns can be unsettling, forcing readers to confront ideas that appear somewhat perverse – can there really be such a thing as enabling trauma or productive irritation? Is it actually possible to distinguish oneself through mimicry, or to produce something new from more of the same? The writing under consideration offers no easy answers to these questions, but in saying things that suggest things that won't quite formulate, it forces us to query our own instincts.

Framing my conclusion around the notion of things not formulating might seem somewhat counterintuitive: surely it is here more than anywhere that parts should be brought together and arguments firmly pinned down. Given that much of the writing under consideration appears resistant to final outcomes, though, Frost's observation serves as an important reminder of the danger of expressing things too rigidly and thereby eliding the nuances and complexities that arise from modernism's entomological evocations. The insect body helped writers to give shape to experiences in an age of unprecedented horrors, housing thoughts and impressions that might otherwise have escaped articulation. And yet as we have seen, the exoskeleton remains a highly versatile construct in modernist writing, adapting to suit the needs of its individual occupant and responding rapidly to the shifting social, cultural and political landscape of the inter-war period. Perhaps most compelling about the modernist exoskeleton is the way that, like the white-tailed hornet, it doesn't quite behave in the way that you might expect; what initially seems fixed and stable reveals itself to be fluid and changeable, while what we might think of as a hard and impermeable barrier turns out to be a highly sensitive organ. More remarkably still, this structure is often most effective as a form of defence when it begins to break down, giving rise to instances of eruption, exposure, incoherence – states of radical self-division that serve a protective and even restorative function.

All shells ossify over time. Like Murphy's worn-out suit with its 'inflexible autonomy of hang', what was once a newly moulted concept is destined to become something of a rigid formula (*M* 45). The exoskeletal defences of modernist writing arose in accordance with a particular set of psychological pressures, in which the subject was assailed from all sides by the combined forces of urban modernity, industrial warfare, mass culture and totalitarian ideology. Although writers would continue to face similar adversities, they would also develop new ways of responding to them. As we saw in the preceding chapter, the dissolution of the exoskeleton as a psychic and formal construct is coterminous with the end of the period commonly associated with high modernism. To recall an earlier image from Walter Benjamin's *Origin of German Tragic Drama* (1928): 'the simile ceases to exist, and the cosmos it contained shrivels up'. And yet it is important not to forget the 'dry rebuses which remain' and the insights that they contain.[9] While contemplating the way that certain narrative genres are able to survive the moment of their production, Fredric Jameson suggests that 'form, secreted like a shell or exoskeleton, continues to emit its ideological message long after the extinction of its host'.[10] As we draw to the close of this study, I want to turn to a selection of experimental prose texts from the 1950s and 1960s, exploring the ways in which modernism's entomological aesthetics continued to shape the formally innovative methods of mid-twentieth-century writers.

THE OUTER LIMITS

The Passion According to G.H. (1964) by Clarice Lispector and 'Order of Insects' (1968) by William H. Gass both centre on transformative roach encounters. 'I had now abandoned myself', states the first-person narrator of Lispector's novel, having given herself over to a dying cockroach that oozes out its life in front of her.[11] After tasting the roach's innards, the speaker, identified only as G.H., begins to relinquish her former life as well as her human identity. Similarly, in Gass's short story, an anonymous housewife passes over into a new order of being after becoming fixated by the dead roaches that litter her carpet: 'I lay shell-like in our bed, turned inside out, driving my mind away.'[12] Rather than displaying the kind of disruptive liveliness seen in modernist writing, the insects that appear in these texts are either dead or dying – reduced to broken carapaces and scattered limbs. In both narratives, these deconstructed forms correspond to the rupturing of reality, the breakdown of language as a signifying structure and the shedding of the self as a coherent entity. 'Finally, finally, my husk had really broken, and I was without limit', exclaims Lispector's protagonist: 'By not being, I was. To the edge of what I wasn't, I was. What I am not, I am.'[13] These paradoxical enumerations suggest a sloughing of binary oppositions, with the text exposing their hollowness and inefficacy ('what I wasn't, I was') while also gesturing towards a mode of existence that lies beyond these structural limitations.

In 'Order of Insects', the coming apart of '[l]egs and other parts I couldn't then identify' empowers the speaker to redefine her relations to things and to reassemble what has 'come undone'. This process is reflected in the ellipses of 'woman . . . bugs' and 'a roach . . . and you a woman', with the punctuation of the text resembling joints of connection (legs and other parts) between these oppositions, while also evoking the epistemological gap opened up by these exoskeletal encounters.[14] Alain Robbe-Grillet's novel *Jealousy* (1957) is similarly punctuated by torn apart insects, the presence of which corresponds to a breach or fissure in the surface of reality. Set on a colonial banana plantation, the events of the narrative are seen through the eyes of a man who suspects that his wife – known only as 'A . . .' – may be having an affair with a neighbouring plantation owner called Franck. The text repeatedly circles back to Franck's squashing of a centipede in the presence of A . . ., 'a common *Scutigera* of average size', which leaves an indelible mark on the wall comprised of 'sections of legs and the partial form of a body convulsed into a question mark'. In accordance with its insected form, the centipede incident resurfaces in fragments over the course of the text, growing to dominate the narrator's field of vision until what was initially an average-sized creature 'covers the area of an ordinary dinner plate'. As a structuring device, the centipede functions as a centripetal force around which the husband's jealousy orbits: like the swarm of insects he observes circling the kerosene lamp with 'their . . . flattened ellipses in horizontal planes or at slight angles', the creature resembles the central question mark around which the many gaps and omissions of the text cluster.[15]

The Woman in the Dunes (1964), by the writer and amateur entomologist Kōbō Abe, also associates insects with a radical reorientation of perspective. The novel details the plight of schoolteacher and insect collector Niki Jumpei, who, after travelling to a remote fishing village in search of a rare sand beetle, finds himself imprisoned by the locals in a deep pit in the sand dunes. The text establishes an equivalence between insects and sand as 'intermingling intermediate forms' that disrupt the protagonist's rigid binaries of wet/dry, sold/liquid, living/dead, undermining his attempts to classify and in turn impose a degree of control over his amorphous environment. Just as Lispector's protagonist is able to overcome the structural limitations that define her existence following her insect encounter, Jumpei quickly recognises something liberating in the abandoning of stable categories:

> Certainly sand was not suitable for life. Yet, was a stationary condition absolutely indispensable for existence? Didn't unpleasant competition arise precisely because one tried to cling to a fixed position? If one were to give up a fixed position and abandon oneself to the movement of the sands, competition would soon stop. Actually, in the deserts flowers bloomed and insects and other animals lived their lives. . . . While he mused on the effect of the flowing sands, he was seized from time to time by hallucinations in which he himself began to move with the flow.[16]

Abe was influenced by the work of Kafka and Beckett, and here too there is an emphasis on a human subject who, having been reduced to the level of a helpless bug, recognises the potential for this diminished state to lead to an expanded sense of being. By abandoning his 'fixed position' in relation to the shifting sandscape, Jumpei's perspective on the world is transformed: rather than continuing to define himself against his non-human surroundings, he begins to work with them, quite literally harnessing their 'flow' by constructing a device capable of drawing purified water out of the sand. Over the course of the text, Abe indicates that the subject's survival hinges on his 'insectlike' adaptability to his surroundings with their 'shapeless, destructive power'.[17]

With modernist writing these texts share an emphasis on the ability of insects to unsettle the boundaries of the self, opening up the human subject to ways of perceiving the world that are at once unsettling and revelatory. The housewife in 'Order of Insects', for instance, 'could not shake [her] point of view, infected as it was' that the true 'order, wholeness, and divinity' of life is contained in the ruptured bugs beneath her feet and not in her 'tidy and punctual' domestic life.[18] There is also a shared understanding of insects as things that won't formulate, with the images of squashed abdomens, broken shells and 'sections of legs' corresponding to the inarticulate sensations that lie in the gaps and fissures of language. In contrast to modernist writing, however, the abandoned shells strewn across these mid-century narratives represent a more radical break with the concept of individual identity. Robbe-Grillet's *Jealousy* eschews the subjectivity of the 'I' entirely, framing events from the perspective of a human observer who has less of a physical presence in the text than a centipede. In an essay on the *nouveau roman* written during the same period, Robbe-Grillet reflects on this shift in outlook:

> Our world today is less sure of itself and more modest, perhaps because it has abandoned the idea of the omnipotence of the individual . . . The exclusive cult of the 'human' has given way to a vaster less anthropocentric perspective.[19]

This perspective is apparent in all of these mid-century insect narratives, which gesture towards an experience of the world that lies beyond the limits of human subjectivity. In remarks that echo Joyce's oft-quoted pronouncement on the 'conception and technique' of *Ulysses*, Rosi Braidotti argues that the cockroach epiphany in Lispector's *Passion* 'connects her to the pre-human, but also projects her inexorably towards a post-human interconnectedness'.[20] Over the course of the text, the speaker gradually peels away the outer layers of herself, beginning with her social and gendered identity and culminating in her decision to hand herself over 'to whatever was no longer I, whatever is already inhuman'.[21]

The process of self-abandonment that takes place over the course of these insect texts is consistent with the experience of reading them. Bertrand Gervais writes that Gass's story 'seduces us, even obsesses us slightly and calls for an investment of ourselves that is no stranger to the loss of self experienced by the narrator'.[22] Further insight into this process of readerly self-relinquishment can be found in Maurice Blanchot's experimental narrative *Thomas the Obscure* (1950), which characterises the act of interpretation in entomological terms:

> He was reading with unsurpassable meticulousness and attention. In relation to every symbol, he was in the position of the male praying mantis about to be devoured by the female. They looked at each other. The words, coming forth from the book which was taking on the power of life and death, exercised a gentle and peaceful attraction over the glance which played over them ... Thomas slipped toward these corridors, approaching them defencelessly until the moment he was perceived by the very quick of the word ... Rather than withdraw from a text whose defences were so strong, he pitted all his strength in the will to seize it, obstinately refusing to withdraw his glance and still thinking himself a profound reader, even when the words were already taking hold of him and beginning to read him.[23]

Blanchot's mantis analogy relates an experience of reading that involves succumbing to the pleasures of the text and being taken over by its seductive possibilities. It also suggests that to enter into this state of passive concentration is to be deprived of one's human identity in a way that is liberating but also somewhat disturbing. In contrast to Thomas's readerly defencelessness, modernism might be said to cultivate a defensive response, encouraging the reader to resist the seductive appeal of language. Lawrence's strident assertion to his readers in *Fantasia of the Unconscious* that 'I am I, but also you are you' is indicative of the way that modernist writing impels readers to reassert their selfhood in response to the threat of words 'coming forth from the book' like a swarm of bees – to shed their defences, but also to reform them anew.[24]

While reading Blanchot's account of Thomas's obstinate refusal to 'withdraw his glance' from the words that 'were already taking hold of him', we might recall Freud's image of the receptive cortical layer as a set of 'feelers which are all the time making tentative advances towards the world and then drawing back from it'.[25] The writing of Lewis, Lawrence, H.D. and Beckett tends to shift back and forth between positions of engagement and withdrawal, exposure and defence, encouraging subject and reader alike to remain open to non-human life while also guarding them against a total transformation into otherness. Beckett's post-war writing comes closest to renouncing 'the idea . . . of the individual', yet even the larval subject of *How It Is*, who announces at the beginning of the text 'here all self to be abandoned', continues to cling to some notion of human identity, describing himself as 'hanging on by the fingernails onto one's species' (*HI* 72, 20). Consistent throughout the preceding chapters has been an emphasis on the ways in which insects are able to renew the outline of the human subject by threatening its dissolution and loss. Although the self is frequently imperilled in the work of Lewis, Lawrence, H.D. and Beckett – left clinging, like Woolf's tremulous insect, to some fragile support in order not to be swept away by the gusts of war, industrial modernity and mass society – it is also reinforced by these entomological incursions.

In its struggle to hold on to some notion of human identity, modernist writing may appear limited by some standards – self-involved, still invested in the 'omnipotence of the individual', too eager to maintain the old species hierarchies. Posthumanist theory has endeavoured to think beyond these restrictive frameworks, stripping away the old binaries of self/other, human/animal, subject/object. It has done important work in highlighting the interconnectedness of human and non-human lives, helping readers to recognise that our fate as a species is bound up in myriad ways with the organisms with which we share the planet.[26] If modernism's continued investment in the idea of the human appears somewhat narrow-minded when held up to these ways of thinking, then it is important to remember that this outlook was the product of a particular set of historical concerns. Roger Fry voiced an anxiety that was shared by many in inter-war Britain when he remarked that modern citizens have 'lost their power to be individuals. They have become social insects like bees and ants. They are just lost to humanity.'[27] During an age in which many felt that they had been divested of their humanness and deprived of their individuality, it is understandable that modernist writers would want to conserve these categories.

In his essay 'Berlin Childhood' (1938), Walter Benjamin recollects the pursuit of a butterfly during his youth:

> Between us, now, the old law of the hunt took hold: the more I strove to conform, in all the fibers [*sic*] of my being, to the animal – the more butterfly-like I became in my heart and soul – the more this butterfly

itself, in everything it did took on the colour of human volition; and in the end, it was as if its capture was the price I had to pay to regain my human existence.²⁸

The passage evokes the struggle, discernible throughout the foregoing chapters, to regain some notion of humanness by conforming, however briefly, to the laws of the insect world. Paul Sheehan touches on a key aspect of this dynamic when he remarks that 'what is contingently human' in modernist narratives 'comes to life as the human merges with, and emerges from, its inhuman others'.²⁹ For the modernist writers of this study, to understand what it meant to be human involved capturing in their writing what it felt like to become something radically other. Thus, modernism's insect encounters may be understood not as an attempt to reassert a traditional, humanist understanding of selfhood, but to establish a new kind of human existence. The self that emerges from this engagement with entomological otherness is more aware of its surroundings, more receptive to other ways of being, more conscious of its frailty. It is a self that observes certain limits, fearing that without them it might resemble, to recall the words of Lewis, 'mirror-images of alien realities'. And yet, for all of the constraints that modernism's exoskeletal structures seem to impose, these outer limits represent not a closing down but rather an opening out of self to world.

Notes

1. Quoted in Faggen, *Robert Frost*, 95.
2. Frost, 'The White-Tailed Hornet', 277–8.
3. Bergson, *Creative Evolution*, 141. Frost may also be alluding to Fabre's account of the yellow-winged Sphex, a type of wasp which paralyses its cricket prey by stinging it in three separate nerve-centres, *The Hunting Wasps*, 61–79. Bergson also refers to this account in *Creative Evolution*, 172.
4. 'The White-Tailed Hornet', 278.
5. Cohen, 'Robert Frost's Arthropods', 70–2.
6. Faggen, *Robert Frost*, 95.
7. 'The White-Tailed Hornet', 278.
8. Lawrence, *Fantasia of the Unconscious*, 72.
9. Benjamin, *Origin of German Tragic Drama*, 176.
10. Jameson, *The Political Unconscious*, 151.
11. Lispector, *The Passion According to G.H.*, 88.
12. Gass, 'Order of Insects', 168.
13. *Passion According to G.H.*, 172.
14. 'Order of Insects', 163, 169, 164, 167.
15. Robbe-Grillet, *Jealousy*, 31, 29, 85, 77.
16. Abe, *The Woman in the Dunes*, 13, 15.
17. *Woman in the Dunes*, 236, 31.

18. 'Order of Insects', 169–71.
19. Robbe-Grillet, *Towards a New Novel*, 61.
20. Braidotti, *Metamorphoses*, 167. Braidotti's remarks contain an echo of Joyce's assertion that in writing the 'Penelope' episode of *Ulysses*, 'I tried to depict the earth that is prehuman and presumably posthuman', *Letters*, Vol. 1, 180.
21. *Passion According to G.H.*, 173.
22. Gervais, Reading as a Close Encounter, 184.
23. Blanchot, *Thomas the Obscure*, 25–6.
24. *Fantasia of the Unconscious*, 72.
25. *Beyond the Pleasure Principle*, 299.
26. See Alaimo, *Bodily Natures*; Haraway, *Staying with the Trouble*.
27. Quoted in Woolf, *Roger Fry*, 272.
28. Benjamin, 'Berlin Childhood', 351.
29. Sheehan, 'Humanness Unbound', 192.

BIBLIOGRAPHY

Abe, Kōbō, *The Woman in the Dunes*, trans. E. Dale Saunders (London: Penguin, 2006).
Ackerley, C. J. and S. E. Gontarski, *The Grove Companion to Samuel Beckett* (New York: Grove Press, 2004).
Adorno, Theodor, *Aesthetic Theory*, trans. Robert Hullot-Kentor (London and New York: Continuum, 1997).
Adorno, Theodor, *Minima Moralia: Reflections from Damaged Life*, trans. E. F. N. Jephcott (London and New York: Verso, 2005).
Adorno, Theodor, 'Trying to Understand *Endgame*', trans. Michael T. Jones, *New German Critique*, 26 (1982), 119–50.
Alaimo, Stacy, *Bodily Natures: Science, Environment, and the Material Self* (Bloomington, IN: Indiana University Press, 2010).
Alighieri, Dante, *The Divine Comedy of Dante Alighieri, Vol. 2: The Purgatorio*, trans. Robert M. Durling (New York: Oxford University Press, 2003).
Alt, Christina, *Virginia Woolf and the Study of Nature* (Cambridge: Cambridge University Press, 2006).
'antenna, *n.*', *OED Online*, Oxford University Press, <http://www.oed.com/view/Entry/8277?redirectedFrom=antennae#eid> (last accessed 29 October 2017).
Anzieu, Didier, *The Skin Ego*, trans. Chris Turner (New Haven, CT: Yale University Press, 1989).
Aristotle, *Parts of Animals*, in Jonathan Barnes (ed.), *The Complete Works of Aristotle* (Princeton, NJ: Princeton University Press, 1984), 994–1086.

Aristotle, *The Works of Aristotle, Vol. 5: Historia Animalium*, trans. D'Arcy Wentworth Thompson (Oxford: Clarendon Press, 1910).
Armstrong, Tim, 'The Human Animal: Biological Tropes in Interwar Poetry', in John Holmes (ed.), *Science in Modern Poetry: New Directions* (Liverpool: Liverpool University Press, 2012), 101–15.
Armstrong, Tim, 'The Self and the Senses', in *Modernism: A Cultural History* (Cambridge and Malden, MA: Polity, 2005), 90–114.
Bachelard, Gaston, *The Poetics of Space*, trans. Marie Jolas (New York: Penguin, 2014).
Badiou, Alain, *Conditions*, trans. Steven Corcoran (London and New York: Continuum, 2008).
Baehr, Peter, 'The "Iron Cage" and the "Shell as Hard as Steel": Parsons, Weber, and the Stahlhartes Gehäuse Metaphor in the *Protestant Ethic and the Spirit of Capitalism*', *History and Theory*, 40: 2 (May 2001), 153–69.
Bair, Deirdre, *Samuel Beckett: A Biography* (New York: Simon & Schuster, 1990).
Baker, Phil, 'Beckett Beyond the Pleasure Principle', in *Beckett and the Mythology of Psychoanalysis* (London: Macmillan, 1997), 128–44.
Balfour, E. B., *The Living Soil: Evidence of the Importance to Human Health of Soil Vitality: With Special Reference to Post-War Planning* (London: Faber, 1943).
Barker, Pat, *Regeneration* (New York: Plume, 1993).
Barnes, Djuna, 'Rite of Spring', Djuna Barnes Papers, Special Collections, University of Maryland Libraries.
Barrett, T. J., *Harnessing the Earthworm* (London: Faber, 1949).
Barthes, Roland, *The Rustle of Language*, trans. Richard Howard (Berkeley and Los Angeles: University of California Press, 1984).
Barthes, Roland, *Writing Degree Zero*, trans. Annette Lavers and Colin Smith (London: Jonathan Cape, 1967).
Baudelaire, Charles, *Charles Baudelaire: Complete Poems*, trans. Walter Martin (London: Carcanet, 1997).
Baudelaire, Charles, 'The Painter of Modern Life', in *Selected Writings on Art and Literature*, trans. P. E. Charvet (London: Penguin, 2006), 390–435.
Beausang, Michael, '*Watt*: Logic, Insanity, Aphasia', *Style*, 3: 3 (Fall 1996), 495–513.
Beckett, Samuel, *Disjecta: Miscellaneous Writings and a Dramatic Fragment*, ed. Ruby Cohn (London: John Calder, 1983).
Beckett, Samuel, *Echo's Bones* (London: Faber, 2014).
Beckett, Samuel, *En attendant Godot*, ed. Colin Duckworth (London: George G. Harrap, 1966).
Beckett, Samuel, *How It Is* (London: Faber, 2009).
Beckett, Samuel, *Malone meurt* (Paris: Éditions de Minuit, 1951).

Beckett, Samuel, *Mercier and Camier* (London: Faber & Faber, 2010).
Beckett, Samuel, *Murphy* (London: Picador, 1973).
Beckett, Samuel, *Proust and Three Dialogues* (London: John Calder, 1965).
Beckett, Samuel, *Samuel Beckett: The Complete Dramatic Works* (London: Faber, 1990).
Beckett, Samuel, *Samuel Beckett: The Complete Short Prose, 1929–1989*, ed. S. E. Gontarski (New York: Grove Press, 1995).
Beckett, Samuel, *The Letters of Samuel Beckett: Volume 1, 1929–1940*, ed. Martha Dow Fehsenfeld, Lois More Overbeck, Dan Gunn and George Craig (Cambridge: Cambridge University Press, 2009).
Beckett, Samuel, *The Letters of Samuel Beckett: Volume 2: 1941–1956*, ed. George Craig, Martha Dow Fehsenfeld, Dan Gunn and Lois More Overbeck (Cambridge: Cambridge University Press, 2011).
Beckett, Samuel, *The Letters of Samuel Beckett: Volume 3, 1956–1967*, ed. Martha Dow Fehsenfeld, Lois More Overbeck, Dan Gunn and George Craig (Cambridge: Cambridge University Press, 2014).
Beckett, Samuel, *Three Novels: Molloy, Malone Dies, The Unnamable* (New York: Grove Press, 2009).
Beckett, Samuel, *Watt* (London: Faber, 2009).
Bell, Michael, *D. H. Lawrence: Language and Being* (Cambridge: Cambridge University Press, 1992).
Bell, Quentin, *Virginia Woolf: A Biography*, Vol. 2 (London: Hogarth Press, 1972).
Benjamin, Walter, 'Berlin Childhood around 1900', in *Walter Benjamin: Selected Writings, 1935–1938*, Vol. 3, trans. Edmund Jephcott (London and Cambridge, MA: Belknap Press, 2002), 344–414.
Benjamin, Walter, 'On Some Motifs in Baudelaire', in *Walter Benjamin: Selected Writings, 1938–1940*, Vol. 4, trans. Edmund Jephcott (London and Cambridge, MA: Belknap Press, 2006), 313–55.
Benjamin, Walter, *One-way Street and Other Writings*, trans. J. A. Underwood (London: Penguin, 2009).
Benjamin, Walter, *The Origin of German Tragic Drama*, trans. John Osborne (London and New York: Verso, 2003).
Bennett, Jane, *Vibrant Matter: A Political Ecology of Things* (Durham, NC: Duke University Press, 2010).
Benthien, Claudia, *Skin: On the Cultural Border Between Self and World*, trans. Thomas Dunlap (New York: Columbia University Press, 2002).
Bergson, Henri, *Creative Evolution*, trans. Arthur Mitchell (New York: Henry Holt, 1911).
Bhabha, Homi K., 'Of Mimicry and Man: The Ambivalence of Colonial Discourse', in *The Location of Culture* (New York: Routledge, 2010), 121–31.
Billington, F. H., *Compost* (London: Faber, 1942).

Bixby, Patrick W., 'Beckett at the GPO: *Murphy, Ireland,* and the Unhomely', in Seán Kennedy (ed.), *Beckett and Ireland* (New York: Cambridge University Press, 2010), 78–95.
Blanchot, Maurice, 'The Unnamable', trans. Richard Howard, in Lawrence Graver and Roger Federman (eds), *Samuel Beckett: The Critical Heritage* (London and Boston: Routledge & Kegan Paul, 1979), 116–21.
Blanchot, Maurice, *Thomas the Obscure*, trans. Robert Lamberton (New York: Station Hill Press, 1988).
Blau DuPlessis, Rachel, *The Pink Guitar: Writing as Feminist Practice* (New York: Routledge, 1990).
Bolin, John, *Beckett and the Modern Novel* (Cambridge: Cambridge University Press, 2012).
Bonheim, Helmut, 'Review of *A Wake Bestiary*', *James Joyce Quarterly*, 38: 1–2 (2000/1), 235–6.
Botar, Oliver and Isabel Wünsche, *Biocentrism and Modernism* (Abingdon and New York: Ashgate, 2011).
Braidotti, Rosi, *Metamorphoses: Towards a Materialist Theory of Becoming* (Cambridge and Malden, MA: Polity, 2006).
'brain (A.S. braegen)', *Encyclopedia Britannica*, Vol. 4 (New York: Cambridge University Press, 1911), 401.
Brightwell, Cecilia Lucy, *Palissy: The Huguenot Potter* (Boston: Ira Bradley, 1902).
Brion, Marcel, 'The Idea of Time in the Work of James Joyce', in *Our Exagmination Round his Factification for Incamination of Work In Progress* (New York: New Directions, 1972), 25–34.
Brown, Eric C., 'Reading the Insect', in Eric C. Brown (ed.), *Insect Poetics* (Minneapolis, MN: Minnesota University Press, 2006), ix–xxiii.
Buck-Morss, Susan, 'Aesthetics and Anaesthetics: Walter Benjamin's Artwork Essay Reconsidered', *October*, 62 (Autumn 1992), 3–41.
'bug, $n.^{1}$', *OED Online*, Oxford University Press, <http://www.oed.com/view/Entry/24351?rskey=AjesbD&result=1&isAdvanced=false#eid> (last accessed 15 November 2018).
'bug, $n.^{2}$', *OED Online*, Oxford University Press, <http://www.oed.com/view/Entry/24352?rskey=c8RB72&result=2&isAdvanced=false#eid> (last accessed 16 November 2018).
'bug, $v.^{1}$', *OED Online*, Oxford University Press, <http://www.oed.com/view/Entry/24354?rskey=WYs2Ji&result=4&isAdvanced=false#eid> (last accessed 16 November 2018).
Burnett, Gary, 'A Poetics Out of War: H.D.'s Responses to the First World War', *Agenda*, 25: 3–4 (1987/8), 54–63.
Burstein, Jessica, *Cold Modernism: Literature, Fashion, Art* (University Park, PA: Penn State University Press, 2012).

Burstein, Jessica, 'Waspish Segments: Lewis, Prosthesis, Fascism', *Modernism/modernity*, 4: 2 (April 1997), 139–64.
Burwell, Rose Marie, 'A Checklist of Lawrence's Reading', in *A D. H. Lawrence Handbook*, ed. Keith Sagar (New York and Manchester: Manchester University Press, 1982), 59–126.
Caillois, Roger, 'Mimicry and Legendary Psychanesthesia', trans. John Shepley, *October*, 31 (Winter 1984), 16–32.
Campbell, Patrick, *Siegfried Sassoon: A Study of the War Poetry* (Jefferson, NC: McFarland, 2007).
Čapek, Karel and Josef Čapek, *The Insect Play*, in *Čapek Four Plays: R.U.R., The Insect Play, The Makropulous Case, The White Plague*, trans. Peter Majer and Cathy Porter (New York and London: Bloomsbury, 1999), 93–164.
Carey, John, *The Intellectuals and the Masses: Pride and Prejudice Amongst the Literary Intelligentsia, 1880–1939* (London: Faber, 1992).
Carney, James, 'The Buzzing of B: The Subject as Insect in Beckett's *Molloy*', in James Carney, Leonard Madden, Michael O'Sullivan and Karl White (eds), *Beckett Re-Membered: After the Centenary* (Newcastle: Cambridge Scholars, 2012), 228–41.
Carter, Huntly, *The New Spirit in the Cinema* (London: Howard Shaylor, 1930).
Caruth, Cathy, *Unclaimed Experience: Trauma, Narrative, and History* (Baltimore, MD and London: Johns Hopkins University Press, 1996).
Caselli, Daniela, *Beckett's Dantes: Intertextuality in the Fiction and Criticism* (Manchester and New York: Manchester University Press, 2005).
Chance, Edgar (dir.), *Skilled Insect Artisans*, in *Secrets of Nature: Pioneering Science and Wildlife Films* (London: British Film Institute, 2010). DVD.
Chevalley, Abel, 'Abel Chevalley on Lawrence, from *Le Romain Anglais de Notre Temps*', trans. Ben Ray Redman, in R. P. Draper (ed.), *D. H. Lawrence: The Critical Heritage* (London: Routledge & Kegan Paul, 1979), 155–6.
Chiong, Kathryn, 'Nauman's Beckett Walk', *October*, 86 (Autumn 1998), 63–81.
Clarke, Colin, *River of Dissolution: D. H. Lawrence and English Romanticism* (London: Routledge & Kegan Paul, 1969).
Coats, Jason M., 'H.D.' and the Hermetic Impulse', *South Atlantic Review*, 77: 1/2 (2012), 79–98.
Cohen, Allen Carson, 'Robert Frost's Arthropods', *American Entomologist*, 45: 2 (April 1999), 70–2.
Cohen, Deborah, *The War Come Home: Disabled Veterans in Britain and Germany, 1914–1939* (Berkeley, CA: University of California Press, 2001).
Cohn, Ruby, *A Beckett Canon* (Ann Arbor, MI: Michigan University Press, 2001).
Collecott, Diana, *H.D. and Sapphic Modernism 1910–1950* (Cambridge: Cambridge University Press, 1999).
Connolly, Cyril, 'The Wild Body', *New Statesman*, 24 December 1927, 358–9.

Connor, Steven, 'As Entomate as Intimate Could Pinchably Be', *Modernist Transactions*, University of Birmingham, 13 June 2000, <http://steven-connor.com/insects/> (last accessed 22 March 2016).

Connor, Steven, 'Making Flies Mean Something', in *Beckett, Modernism, and the Material Imagination* (Cambridge: Cambridge University Press, 2014), 48–61.

Connor, Steven, 'Preface', in *The Unnamable* (London: Faber, 2010), vii–xxvi.

Connor, Steven, *The Book of Skin* (New York: Cornell University Press, 2004).

Connor, Steven, '"Was That a Point?": Beckett's Punctuation', in S. E. Gontarski (ed.), *The Edinburgh Companion to Samuel Beckett and the Arts* (Edinburgh: Edinburgh University Press, 2014), 269–81.

Conrad, Joseph, *Heart of Darkness* (London: Penguin Classics, 2007).

Conrad, Joseph, *Lord Jim*, ed. Jacques Berthoud (Oxford and New York: Oxford University Press, 2002).

Corbett, David Peters, '"Grief with a Yard-Wide Grin": War and Wyndham Lewis's Tyros', in *Wyndham Lewis and the Art of Modern War*, ed. David Peters Corbett (Cambridge: Cambridge University Press, 1998), 99–123.

Crawford, Robert, *The Savage and the City in the Work of T. S. Eliot* (New York: Oxford University Press, 1991).

Critchley, Simon, *Very Little ... Almost Nothing: Death, Philosophy, Literature* (London: Routledge, 2004).

Crossland, Rachel, *Modernist Physics: Waves, Particles, and Relativities in the Writings of Virginia Woolf and D. H. Lawrence* (Oxford: Oxford University Press, 2018).

Darwin, Charles, *On the Origin of Species* (Oxford and New York: Oxford University Press, 2008).

Darwin, Charles, *The Formation of Vegetable Mould through the Actions of Worms* (Gloucester: Echo Library, 2007).

Darwin, Charles, *The Origin of Species by Means of Natural Selection; or the Preservation of Favoured Races in the Struggle for Life* (London: John Murray, 1859).

'dazzle, v.', *OED Online*, Oxford University Press, <http://www.oed.com/view/Entry/47588?rskey=AyYsW8&result=2&isAdvanced=false#eid> (last accessed 22 March 2016).

Deleuze, Gilles, *Difference and Repetition*, trans. Paul Patton (New York: Columbia University Press, 1994).

Dickinson, Emily, *The Complete Poems of Emily Dickinson*, ed. T. H. Johnson (Boston: Little, Brown, 1960).

Diderot, Denis, *Rameaus's Nephew and D'Alembert's Dream*, trans. Leonard Tancock (London: Penguin, 1966).

Dillon, Sarah, 'Palimpsesting: Reading and Writing Lives in H.D.'s *Palimpsest*', *Critical Survey, Special Issue: Modernist Women Writers Using History*, ed. Ann Heilmann and Mark Llewellyn, 19: 1 (2007), 29–39.

Donne, John, *John Donne: The Major Works*, ed. John Carey (Oxford: Oxford University Press, 1990).

Douglas, Mary, *Purity and Danger: An Analysis of the Concepts of Pollution and Taboo* (London and New York: Routledge, 2001).

Driver, Tom, 'Interview with Beckett', in Lawrence Graver and Roger Federman (eds), *Samuel Beckett: The Critical Heritage* (London and Boston: Routledge & Kegan Paul, 1979), 217–23.

Dwan, David, 'The Problem of Romanticism in Wyndham Lewis', *Essays in Criticism*, 65: 2 (April 2015), 163–86.

Edwards, Paul, 'Afterword', in Wyndham Lewis, *Time and Western Man*, ed. Paul Edwards (Santa Rosa, CA: Black Sparrow Press, 1993), 455–508.

Edwards, Paul, 'Wyndham Lewis and the Uses of Shellshock: Meat and Postmodernism', in *Wyndham Lewis and the Cultures of Modernity*, ed. Andrzej Gąsiorek, Alice Reeve-Tucker and Nathan Waddell (Farnham: Ashgate, 2011), 221–40.

Eliot, T. S., *The Complete Poems and Plays of T. S. Eliot* (London: Faber, 2004).

Eliot, T. S., *The Varieties of Metaphysical Poetry: The Clark Lectures and the Turnbull Lectures* (New York: Harcourt, Brace, 1993).

Ellis, David, *D. H. Lawrence: Dying Game 1922–1930* (Cambridge: Cambridge University Press, 1997).

Ellmann, Maud, *The Nets of Modernism: Henry James, Virginia Woolf, James Joyce, and Sigmund Freud* (Cambridge: Cambridge University Press, 2010).

Ellmann, Richard, 'Appendix: The Linati and Gorman-Gilbert Schemas Compared', in *Ulysses on the Liffey* (Oxford: Oxford University Press, 1972), 186–9.

Ellmann, Richard, *James Joyce* (New York, Oxford and Toronto: Oxford University Press, 1982).

Elton, Arthur, *National Film Archive Catalogue, Part II: Silent Non-Fiction Films, 1895–1934* (London: BFI, 1960).

Evans, Arthur, *The Earlier Religion of Greece in the Light of Cretan Discoveries* (London and Ann Arbor, MI: Macmillan, 1978).

'exposure, *n.*', *OED Online*, Oxford University Press, <http://www.oed.com/view/Entry/66730?redirectedFrom=exposure#eid> (last accessed 12 June 2017).

Fabre, Jean-Henri, *The Hunting Wasps*, trans. Alexander Teixeira de Mattos (New York: Dodd, Mead, 1919).

Fabre, Jean-Henri, 'The Leaf-Cutters', trans. Alexander Teixeira de Mattos, *The English Review* (March 1915), 405–19.

Fabre, Jean-Henri, *The Life of the Caterpillar*, trans. Alexander Teixeira de Mattos (New York: Dodd, Mead, 1916).
Fabre, Jean-Henri, *The Mason-Bees*, trans. Alexander Teixeira de Mattos (New York: Garden City, 1925).
Fabre, Jean-Henri, 'The Modern Theory of Instinct', trans. Alexander Teixeira de Mattos, *The English Review* (December 1912), 9–21.
Fabre, Jean-Henri, *The Sacred Beetle and Others*, trans. Alexander Teixeira De Mattos (New York: Dodd & Mead, 1918).
Fabre, Jean-Henri, 'The Scavengers', trans. Alexander Teixeira de Mattos, *The English Review* (September 1917), 238–45.
Fabre, Jean-Henri, 'The Weaving Spider: The Banded Epeira', trans. Alexander Teixeira de Mattos, *The English Review* (November 1912), 519–31.
Fabre, Jean-Henri, *The Wonders of Instinct: Chapters in the Psychology of Insects*, trans. Alexander Teixeira de Mattos and Bernard Miall (London: T. Fisher & Unwin, 1918).
Faggen, Robert, *Robert Frost and the Challenge of Darwin* (Ann Arbor, MI: University of Michigan Press, 2001).
Fairchild, David and Marian Fairchild, *Book of Monsters* (Washington, DC: National Geographic Society, 1914).
'fascia, *n.*', *OED Online*, Oxford University Press, <http://www.oed.com/view/Entry/68341?redirectedFrom=fascia#eid> (last accessed 29 July 2017).
Felt, E. P., 'Bugs and Antennae', *Science*, 55: 1429 (May 1922), 528–30, <http://science.sciencemag.org/content/55/1429/528> (last accessed 6 March 2019).
Fernihough, Anne, *D. H. Lawrence: Aesthetics and Ideology* (Oxford: Clarendon Press, 1993).
Fernihough, Anne, 'Introduction', in *The Cambridge Companion to D. H. Lawrence* (Cambridge: Cambridge University Press, 2001), 1–12.
'Fly Nurses a Miniature Doll', *The Daily Mirror*, 13 November 1908, <http://collection.sciencemuseum.org.uk/objects/co8428002/fly-nurses-a-miniature-doll-poster-advertising-poster-film-poster> (last accessed 29 October 2017).
Fogg, Anna, Saffron Parker and Ian O'Sullivan, 'The Film Society 1925–1939, A Guide to the Collections', pp. 5–7, <https://www.bfi.org.uk/sites/bfi.org.uk/files/downloads/bfi-the-film-society-1925-1939-a-guide-to-collections.pdf> (last accessed 10 December 2018).
Forbes, Peter, *Dazzled and Deceived: Mimicry and Camouflage* (London and New Haven, CT: Yale University Press, 2011).
Foster, Hal, *Prosthetic Gods* (Cambridge, MA and London: Massachusetts Institute of Technology Press, 2004).
Freud, Sigmund, *Beyond the Pleasure Principle*, in *On Metapsychology: The Theory of Psychoanalysis*, trans. James Strachey (Harmondsworth: Penguin, 1987), 269–338.

Freud, Sigmund, 'Instincts and Their Vicissitudes', in *On Metapsychology: The Theory of Psychoanalysis*, trans. James Strachey (Harmondsworth: Penguin, 1987), 113–38.

Freud, Sigmund, 'Project for a Scientific Psychology', in *Standard Edition of the Complete Psychological Works of Sigmund Freud*, Vol. 1, trans. James Strachey (London: Hogarth Press, 1975), 283–397.

Friedman, Susan Stanford, *Penelope's Web: Gender, Modernity, H.D.'s Fiction* (New York: Cambridge University Press, 1990).

Frost, Robert, 'The White-Tailed Hornet', in *Robert Frost: The Collected Poems* (London: Vintage, 2013), 277–9.

Galloway, Alexander R. and Eugene Thacker, *The Exploit: A Theory of Networks* (London and Minneapolis, MN: University of Minnesota Press, 2007).

Gass, William H., 'Order of Insects', in *In the Heart of the Heart of the Country* (New York: New York Review of Books, 2015), 163–71.

Gaycken, Oliver, *Devices of Curiosity: Early Cinema and Popular Science* (Oxford: Oxford University Press, 2015).

Gervais, Bertrand, 'Reading as a Close Encounter of the Third Kind: An Experiment with Gass's "Order of Insects"', in Eric C. Brown (ed.), *Insect Poetics* (Minneapolis, MN: Minnesota University Press, 2006), 179–99.

Gontarski, S. E., 'Creative Involution: Beckett, Bergson, Deleuze', *Deleuze Studies*, 6: 4 (2012), 601–13.

Graham, W. S., *Collected Poems: 1942–1977* (London: Faber, 1979).

Gregory, Alyse, 'Review of *Kangaroo*', in R. P. Draper (ed.), *D. H. Lawrence: The Critical Heritage* (London: Routledge & Kegan Paul, 1979), 217–23.

Haeckel, Ernst, *The Riddle of the Universe* (New York and London: Harper Brothers, 1905).

Haraway, Donna, *Staying with the Trouble: Making Kin in the Cthulucene* (Durham, NC: Duke University Press, 2016).

Hardy, Barbara, *The Appropriate Form: An Essay on the Novel* (London: Athlone Press, 1964).

Harrison, Andrew, *D. H. Lawrence and Italian Futurism: A Study of Influence* (Amsterdam and New York: Rodopi, 2003).

H.D., 'Art and Ardor in World War One: Selected Letters from H.D. to John Cournos', ed. Donna Krolik Hollenberg, *Iowa Review*, 16: 3 (Autumn 1986), 126–55.

H.D., *Asphodel* (Durham, NC and London: Duke University Press, 1992).

H.D., *Bid Me to Live: A Madrigal*, ed. Caroline Zilboorg (Gainesville, FL: Florida University Press, 2015).

H.D., *End to Torment: A Memoir of Ezra Pound* (New York: New Directions, 1979).

H.D., 'H.D. by Delia Alton', *Iowa Review*, 16: 3 (Autumn 1986), 180–221.

H.D., *Hedylus* (Connecticut: Black Swan Books, 1980).

H.D., *Helen in Egypt* (New York: New Directions, 1961).
H.D., *Her* (London: Virago, 1984).
H.D., *Kora and Ka, with Mira-Mare* (New York: New Directions, 1996).
H.D., *Magic Mirror, Compassionate Friendship, Thorn Thicket: A Tribute to Erich Heydt* (Victoria: ELS Editions, 2012).
H.D., 'Marianne Moore', *The Egoist*, 3: 8 (August 1916), 118–19.
H.D., *Nights* (New York: New Directions, 1986).
H.D., *Notes on Thought and Vision and The Wise Sappho* (San Francisco: City Lights, 1982).
H.D., *Palimpsest* (Carbondale and Edwardsville, IL: Southern Illinois University Press, 1968).
H.D., *Pilate's Wife*, ed. Joan A. Burke (New York: New Directions, 2000).
H.D., 'The Cinema and the Classics II: Restraint', in *Close Up, 1927–1933: Cinema and Modernism*, ed. James Donald, Arthur Friedberg and Laura Marcus (Princeton, NJ: Princeton University Press, 1998), 110–14.
H.D., 'The Cinema and the Classics III: The Mask and the Movietone', *Close Up, 1927–1933: Cinema and Modernism*, ed. James Donald, Arthur Friedberg and Laura Marcus (Princeton, NJ: Princeton University Press, 1998), 114–20.
H.D., *The Gift: The Complete Text*, ed. Jane Augustine (Gainesville, FL: Florida University Press, 1998).
H.D., *The Sword Went Out to Sea*, ed. Cynthia Hogue (Gainesville, FL: Florida University Press, 2007).
H.D., *The Walls Do Not Fall*, in *Trilogy* (New York: New Directions, 1973), 1–60.
H.D., *Tribute to Freud* (New York: New Directions, 2012).
H.D., *Within the Walls and What Do I Love?*, ed. Annette Debo (Gainesville, FL: Florida University Press, 2016).
H.D. and Richard Aldington, *Richard Aldington and H.D.: Their Lives in Letters, 1918–1961*, ed. Caroline Zilboorg (Manchester: Manchester University Press, 2003).
H.D., Bryher et al., *Analyzing Freud: Letters of H.D., Bryher, and Their Circle*, ed. Susan Stanford Friedman (New York: New Directions, 2002).
Henke, Suzette, 'H.D.: Psychoanalytic Self-Imaging', in *Shattered Subjects: Trauma and Testimony in Women's Life-Writing* (Basingstoke: Macmillan, 2000), 25–54.
Henry, Holly, *Virginia Woolf and the Discourse of Science* (Cambridge: Cambridge University Press, 2003).
Hollingsworth, Cristopher, *Poetics of the Hive: The Insect Metaphor in Literature* (Iowa City, IA: University of Iowa Press, 2001).
Homer, *The Iliad of Homer*, trans. Richard Lattimore (Chicago: University of Chicago Press, 1961).

Hopwood, Nick, *Haeckel's Embryos: Image, Evolution, Fraud* (Chicago: University of Chicago Press, 2015).
Hovanec, Caroline, *Animal Subjects: Literature, Zoology, and British Modernism* (New York and Cambridge: Cambridge University Press, 2018).
Hovanec, Caroline, *Zoological Modernism: Literature, Science, and Animals in Early Twentieth-Century Britain*, unpublished doctoral thesis, Vanderbilt University, 2013, <https://etd.library.vanderbilt.edu/available/etd-07022013-113128/unrestricted/HovanecDissertation.pdf> (last accessed 15 March 2019).
Howard, Albert, 'Introduction', in Melanie Billings (ed.), *Friend Earthworm* (Chicago: Review Press, 2009), 156–68.
Howard, L. O., 'Entomology and the War', *Scientific Monthly*, 8: 2 (February 1919), 109–17.
Howe, Irving, *Politics and the Novel* (New York: Horizon, 1957).
Hugo, Victor, *L'Homme qui rit*, in *Oeuvres Complètes*, Vol. 8 (Paris: Éditions Rencontre, 1967).
Hulme, T. E., 'Modern Art and Its Philosophy', in *Speculations: Essays on Humanism and the Philosophy of Art*, ed. Herbert Read (London: Routledge & Kegan Paul, 1924), 73–131.
Hulme, T. E., 'Romanticism and Classicism', in Patrick McGuinness (ed.), *T. E. Hulme: Selected Writings* (New York: Routledge, 2003), 68–83.
Humma, John B., *Metaphor and Meaning in D. H. Lawrence's Later Novels* (Columbia, MO: University of Missouri Press, 1990).
Humphreys, Richard, *Wyndham Lewis* (London: Tate, 2004).
Huyssen, Andreas, *After the Great Divide: Modernism, Mass Culture, Postmodernism* (Bloomington and Indianapolis, IN: Indiana University Press, 1986).
Huyssen, Andreas, *Present Pasts: Urban Palimpsests and the Politics of Memory* (Stanford, CA: Stanford University Press, 2003).
'imaginal, *adj.*[1]', *OED Online*, Oxford University Press, <http://www.oed.com/view/Entry/91635?rskey=EmAAFa&result=1&isAdvanced=false#eid> (last accessed 5 January 2019).
'imaginal, *adj.*[2]', *OED Online*, Oxford University Press, <http://www.oed.com/view/Entry/91636?rskey=EmAAFa&result=2&isAdvanced=false#eid> (last accessed 5 January 2019).
Imms, A. D., *Insect Natural History* (London: Collins, 1947).
'inkling, *n.*', *OED Online*, Oxford University Press, <http://www.oed.com/view/Entry/96141?rskey=VZbS47&result=2&isAdvanced=false#eid> (last accessed 26 September 2017).
'involution, *n.*', *OED Online*, Oxford University Press, <http://www.oed.com/view/Entry/99200?redirectedFrom=involution#eid> (last accessed 26 August 2017).

'irritation, *n*.', *OED Online*, Oxford University Press, <http://www.oed.com/view/Entry/99865?redirectedFrom=irritation#eid> (last accessed 21 November 2018).

Isyanova, Gulya, 'The Consumer Sphinx: From French Trench to Parisian Market', in *Contested Objects: Material Memories of the Great War*, ed. Nicholas J. Saunders and Paul Cornish (New York and Abingdon: Routledge, 2009), 130–43.

Jameson, Fredric, *Fables of Aggression: Wyndham Lewis, the Modernist as Fascist* (New York: Verso, 2008).

Jameson, Fredric, *The Political Unconscious: Narrative as a Socially Symbolic Act* (Ithaca, NY: Cornell University Press, 1981).

Jones, Richard, 'The Parasite Within', in *Mosquito* (London: Reaktion, 2010), 73–103.

Joyce, James, *A Portrait of the Artist as a Young Man: Text, Criticism, and Notes*, ed. Chester G. Anderson (New York: Viking Press, 1964).

Joyce, James, 'Continuation of A Work in Progress', *transition* 12 (March 1928), 7–27.

Joyce, James, *Finnegans Wake*, ed. Robbert-Jan Henkes, Erik Bindervoet and Finn Fordham (Oxford: Oxford University Press, 2012).

Joyce, James, *The Letters of James Joyce*, Vol. 1, ed. Stuart Gilbert (New York: Viking Press, 1966).

Kafka, Franz, *Metamorphosis*, in *Metamorphosis and Other Stories*, trans. Michael Hofmann (London: Penguin, 2007), 87–146.

Kamuf, Peggy, 'Your Worm', in Lynn Turner (ed.), *The Animal Question in Deconstruction*, ed. Lynn Turner (Edinburgh: Edinburgh University Press, 2013), 158–75.

Keller, John, *Samuel Beckett and the Primacy of Love* (Manchester: Manchester University Press, 2002).

Kenner, Hugh, *A Sinking Island: The Modern English Writers* (New York: Knopf, 1988).

Kenner, Hugh, *Samuel Beckett: A Critical Study* (London: Calder & Boyars, 1962).

Kenner, Hugh, *The Pound Era* (Berkeley and Los Angeles: California University Press, 1971).

Kenner, Hugh, *Wyndham Lewis* (London: Methuen, 1954).

Kermode, Frank, *D. H. Lawrence* (London: Fontana, 1973).

Kime Scott, Bonnie, 'Diversions of Darwin and Natural History', in *In the Hollow of the Wave: Virginia Woolf and the Modernist Uses of Nature* (Charlottesville, VA: Virginia University Press, 2012), 42–70.

King, Simon, *Insect Nations: Visions of the Ant World from Kropotkin to Bergson* (Ashford: Inkermen Press, 2006).

Klein, Scott, *The Fictions of James Joyce and Wyndham Lewis: Monsters of Nature and Design* (Cambridge: Cambridge University Press, 1994).

Kloepfer, Deborah Kelly, 'Fishing the Murex Up: Sense and Resonance in H.D.'s *Palimpsest*', in Susan Stanford Friedman and Rachel Blau DuPlessis (eds), *Signets: Reading H.D.* (Madison, WI: Wisconsin University Press, 1986), 183–232.

Knowlson, James, *Damned to Fame: The Life of Samuel Beckett* (London: Bloomsbury, 1997).

Kristeva, Julia, *Black Sun: Depression and Melancholia*, trans. Leon S. Roudiez (New York: Columbia University Press, 1989).

Lacan, Jacques, 'The Line and the Light', in Jacques-Alain Miller (ed.), *The Four Fundamental Concepts of Psychoanalysis*, trans. Alan Sheridan (London: Vintage, 1998), 91–119.

Land, Norman, 'Giotto's Fly, Cimabue's Gesture, and a *Madonna and Child* by Carlo Crivelli', *Source: Notes in the History of Art*, 15: 4 (Summer 1996), 11–15.

Langston, Nancy, 'New Chemical Bodies', in Andrew C. Isenberg (ed.), *The Oxford Handbook of Environmental History* (Oxford and New York: Oxford University Press, 2014), 259–81.

La Vopa, Anthony, 'The Philosopher and the *Schwärmer*: On the Career of a German Epithet from Luther to Kant', *Huntingdon Library Quarterly*, 60: 1/2 (1997), 85–115.

LaCapra, Dominick, *Writing History, Writing Trauma* (Baltimore, MD: Johns Hopkins University Press, 2014).

Laplanche, Jean and Jean-Bertrand Pontalis, *The Language of Psychoanalysis* (London: Karnac Books, 1973).

'larva, *n.*', *OED Online*, Oxford University Press, <http://www.oed.com/view/Entry/105914?redirectedFrom=larva#eid> (last accessed 24 September 2017).

Latham, Sean and Gayle Rogers, *Modernism: Evolution of an Idea* (London and New York: Bloomsbury, 2015).

Lawrence, D. H., *Aaron's Rod*, ed. Mara Kalnins (Cambridge: Cambridge University Press, 1988).

Lawrence, D. H., *D. H. Lawrence: The Poems*, Vol. 1, ed. Christopher Pollintz (Cambridge: Cambridge University Press, 2013).

Lawrence, D. H., 'Epilogue', in *Movements in European History*, ed. Philip Crumpton (Cambridge: Cambridge University Press, 2002), 253–64.

Lawrence, D. H., *Introductions and Reviews*, ed. N. H. Reeve and John Worthen (Cambridge: Cambridge University Press, 2005).

Lawrence, D. H., *Kangaroo*, ed. Bruce Steele (Cambridge: Cambridge University Press, 1994).

Lawrence, D. H., *Lady Chatterley's Lover and 'A Propos of Lady Chatterley's Lover'*, ed. Michael Squires (Cambridge: Cambridge University Press, 2002).

Lawrence, D. H., *Late Essays and Articles*, ed. James T. Boulton (Cambridge: Cambridge University Press, 2004).
Lawrence, D. H., *Mr Noon*, ed. Lindeth Vasey (Cambridge: Cambridge University Press, 1984).
Lawrence, D. H., *Psychoanalysis of the Unconscious and Fantasia of the Unconscious*, ed. Bruce Steele (Cambridge: Cambridge University Press, 2004).
Lawrence, D. H., *Reflections on the Death of a Porcupine and Other Essays*, ed. Michael Herbert (Cambridge: Cambridge University Press, 1988).
Lawrence, D. H., *Sons and Lovers*, ed. Helen Baron and Carl Baron (Cambridge: Cambridge University Press, 1992).
Lawrence, D. H., *Study of Thomas Hardy and Other Essays*, ed. Bruce Steele (Cambridge: Cambridge University Press, 1985).
Lawrence, D. H., *The First and Second Lady Chatterley's Lover*, ed. Dieter Mehl and Christa Jansohn (Cambridge: Cambridge University Press, 1999).
Lawrence, D. H., *The Fox, The Captain's Doll, The Ladybird*, ed. Dieter Mehl (Cambridge: Cambridge University Press, 1992).
Lawrence, D. H., *The Letters of D. H. Lawrence*, Vol. 1, ed. James T. Boulton (Cambridge: Cambridge University Press, 1979).
Lawrence, D. H., *The Letters of D. H. Lawrence*, Vol. 2, ed. James T. Boulton and George J. Zytaruk (Cambridge: Cambridge University Press, 1981).
Lawrence, D. H., *The Letters of D. H. Lawrence*, Vol. 3, ed. James T. Boulton and Andrew Robertson (Cambridge: Cambridge University Press, 1984).
Lawrence, D. H., *The Letters of D. H. Lawrence*, Vol. 4, ed. James T. Boulton, Warren Roberts and Elizabeth Mansfield (Cambridge: Cambridge University Press, 1987).
Lawrence, D. H., *The Letters of D. H. Lawrence*. Vol. 5, ed. James T. Boulton and Lindeth Vasey (Cambridge: Cambridge University Press, 2003).
Lawrence, D. H., *The Letters of D. H. Lawrence*, Vol. 6, ed. James T. Boulton, Margaret H. Boulton and Gerald M. Lacey (Cambridge: Cambridge University Press, 2002).
Lawrence, D. H., *The Plumed Serpent*, ed. L. D. Clark (Cambridge: Cambridge University Press, 2002).
Lawrence, D. H., *The Rainbow*, ed. Mark Kinkead-Weekes (Cambridge: Cambridge University Press, 1989).
Lawrence, D. H., *The Trespasser*, ed. Elizabeth Mansfield (Cambridge: Cambridge University Press, 1981).
Lawrence, D. H., *Women in Love*, ed. David Farmer, Lindeth Vasey and John Worthen (Cambridge: Cambridge University Press, 1987).
Lawrence, D. H. and M. L. Skinner, *The Boy in the Bush*, ed. Paul Eggert (Cambridge: Cambridge University Press, 1990).

Legros, G. V., *Fabre: Poet of Science* (New York: Century, 1913).
Leighton, Angela, 'Form's Matter: A Retrospective', in *On Form: Poetry, Aestheticism, and the Legacy of a Word* (Oxford and New York: Oxford University Press, 2007), 1–29.
Lens, 'The New Entomology', *New Statesman*, 13 February 1915, 459–60.
Lessing, Doris, 'Testament of Love', *The Guardian*, 15 July 2006, <https://www.theguardian.com/books/2006/jul/15/classics.dhlawrence> (last accessed 10 March 2019).
Lévi-Strauss, Claude, *Introduction to the Work of Marcel Mauss*, trans. Felicity Barker (London: Routledge & Kegan Paul, 1987).
Lewis, Pericles, *The Cambridge Introduction to Modernism* (New York: Cambridge University Press, 2007).
Lewis, Wyndham, 'A Soldier of Humour', in *The Complete Wild Body*, ed. Bernard Lafourcade (Santa Barbara, CA: Black Sparrow Press, 1982), 17–48.
Lewis, Wyndham, 'Bestre', *The Tyro: A Review of The Arts of Painting Sculpture and Design*, 2 (1922), 53–63.
Lewis, Wyndham, *Blasting and Bombardiering* (London: Eyre & Spottiswoode, 1937).
Lewis, Wyndham, 'Cantleman's Spring-Mate', *The Little Review*, 4: 6 (October 1917), 8–14.
Lewis, Wyndham, 'Editorial', *BLAST: Review of the Great English Vortex*, 2 (July 1915), 5–6.
Lewis, Wyndham, 'Essay (entomology) for Semester VI', *Joint*, unpublished MS, Box 16, Folder 12, Wyndham Lewis Collection 1877–1975, Cornell University Library.
Lewis, Wyndham, 'Essay on the Objective of Plastic Art in Our Time', *The Tyro: A Review of The Arts of Painting Sculpture and Design*, 2 (1922), 21–37.
Lewis, Wyndham, *Hitler* (London: Chatto & Windus, 1931).
Lewis, Wyndham, 'Inferior Religions', *The Little Review*, 4: 5 (September 1917), 3–8.
Lewis, Wyndham, *Men Without Art* (New York: Russell & Russell, 1964).
Lewis, Wyndham, 'Note on Tyros', in *The Tyro: A Review of The Arts of Painting Sculpture and Design*, 1 (1921), 2.
Lewis, Wyndham, *One-Way Song* (London: Methuen, 1960).
Lewis, Wyndham, *Paleface: The Philosophy of the 'Melting-Pot'* (London: Chatto & Windus, 1929).
Lewis, Wyndham, *Rude Assignment: A Narrative of My Career Up-To-Date* (London: Hutchinson, 1950).
Lewis, Wyndham, *Self Condemned* (Toronto: Dundurn Press, 2010).

Lewis, Wyndham, 'Some Innkeepers and Bestre', in *The Complete Wild Body*, ed. Bernard Lafourcade (Santa Barbara, CA: Black Sparrow Press, 1984), 221–36.

Lewis, Wyndham, *Snooty Baronet*, ed. Bernard Lafourcade (Santa Rosa, CA: Black Sparrow Press, 1983).

Lewis, Wyndham, *Tarr: The 1918 Version*, ed. Paul O'Keeffe (Santa Rosa, CA: Black Sparrow Press, 1996).

Lewis, Wyndham, *The Art of Being Ruled* (London: Chatto & Windus, 1926).

Lewis, Wyndham, *The Caliph's Design: Architects! Where Is Your Vortex?*, ed. Paul Edwards (Santa Barbara, CA: Black Sparrow Press, 1986).

Lewis, Wyndham, *The Enemy: A Review of Art and Literature*, No. 1 (Santa Barbara, CA: Black Sparrow Press, 1994).

Lewis, Wyndham, 'The French Poodle', *The Egoist*, 3 (March 1916), 39–41.

Lewis, Wyndham, *The Human Age: Book I: The Childermass* (London: Methuen, 1955).

Lewis, Wyndham, *The Ideal Giant, The Code of a Herdsman, Cantelman's Spring-Mate* (London: The Little Review, 1917).

Lewis, Wyndham, *The Letters of Wyndham Lewis*, ed. W. K. Rose (London: Methuen, 1963).

Lewis, Wyndham, *The Revenge for Love* (London: Penguin, 1972).

Lewis, Wyndham, *The Roaring Queen* (London: Secker & Warburg, 1973).

Lewis, Wyndham, 'The War Baby, in C. J. Fox and Robert T. Chapman (eds), *Unlucky for Pringle, Unpublished and Other Stories* (London: Vision Press, 1973), 85–108.

Lewis, Wyndham, *Time and Western Man*, ed. Paul Edwards (Santa Rosa, CA: Black Sparrow Press, 1993).

Lewis, Wyndham, *Wyndham Lewis on Art*, ed. Walter Michel and C. J. Fox (London: Thames & Hudson, 1969).

Lewis, Wyndham, 'Wyndham Lewis on James Joyce', in Robert Deming (ed.), *James Joyce: The Critical Heritage*, Vol. 2 (London and New York: Routledge, 1970).

Lewis, Wyndham, Ezra Pound et al., 'Manifesto', in *BLAST: Review of the Great English Vortex*, 1 (July 1914), 30–43.

Lispector, Clarice, *The Passion According to G. H.*, trans. Ronald W. Sousa (Minneapolis, MN: University of Minnesota Press, 1988).

'loom, $n.^1$', *OED Online*, Oxford University Press, <http://www.oed.com/view/Entry/110148?rskey=qmG2Se&result=2&isAdvanced=false#eid> (last accessed 27 August 2017).

'loom, $v.^2$', *OED Online*, Oxford University Press, <http://www.oed.com/view/Entry/110153?rskey=hGr6Dc&result=7&isAdvanced=false#eid> (last accessed 27 August 2017).

Lowell, Amy, 'Preface', in *Some Imagist Poets* (Boston: Houghton Mifflin, 1915), v–viii.
McCabe, Susan, 'H.D.'s Borderline Bodies', in *Cinematic Modernism: Modernist Poetry and Film* (Cambridge: Cambridge University Press, 2005), 133–83.
McCarthy, Jeffrey, *Green Modernism: Nature and the English Novel, 1900–1930* (New York: Palgrave, 2015).
McHugh, Roland, *Annotations to Finnegans Wake* (Baltimore, MD: Johns Hopkins University Press, 2016).
MacKay, Marina, *Modernism and World War II* (Cambridge: Cambridge University Press, 2007).
McLuhan, Marshall, *Understanding Media: The Extensions of Man*, ed. Terrence Gordon (Corte Madera, CA: Gingko Press, 2003).
Maeterlinck, Maurice, *The Life of the Ant*, trans. Bernard Miall (London and Toronto: Cassell, 1930).
Magessa O'Reilly, Édouard, 'English Introduction', in *Comment c'est, How It Is And/Et L'Image: A Critical Genetic Edition* (London and New York: Routledge, 2001), ix–xxxvi.
Marcus, Laura, *The Tenth Muse: Writing About Cinema in the Modernist Period* (Oxford: Oxford University Press, 2007).
Marren, Peter and Richard Mabey, *Bugs Britannica* (London: Chatto & Windus, 2010).
Meyers, Jeffrey, *The Enemy: A Biography of Wyndham Lewis* (London: Routledge & Kegan Paul, 1980).
Miller, Lawrence, *Samuel Beckett: The Expressive Dilemma* (Basingstoke: Macmillan, 1992).
Miller, Tyrus, *Late Modernism: Politics, Fiction, and the Arts between the World Wars* (Berkeley, CA: California University Press, 1999).
Millett, Kate, 'D. H. Lawrence', in *Sexual Politics* (Urbana and Chicago: University of Illinois Press, 2000), 237–93.
Mirrlees, Hope, 'Preface', in *Madeleine: One of Love's Jansenists*, <http://hopemirrlees.com/texts/madeleine.html> (last accessed 3 April 2017).
Monroe, Harriet, 'Book Review: Two Anthologies – "Some Imagist Poets: 1916" and "Georgian Poetry: 1913–1915"', *Poetry: A Magazine of Verse*, 8: 5 (August 1916), 255–9.
Moore, Marianne, *The Complete Prose of Marianne Moore*, ed. Patricia C. Willis (New York: Viking, 1986).
Moore, Marianne, *The Poems of Marianne Moore*, ed. Grace Schulman (New York: Penguin, 2005).
Moorjani, Angela, 'The Dancing Bees in Samuel Beckett's *Molloy*: The Rapture of Unknowing', in Mary Bryden (ed.), *Beckett and Animals* (Cambridge: Cambridge University Press, 2012), 165–76.

Morris, Adalaide, 'Science and the Mythopoeic Mind: The Case of H.D.', in Katherine N. Hayles (ed.), *Chaos and Order: Complex Dynamics in Science and Literature* (Chicago and London: University of Chicago Press, 1991), 195–218.
Moynahan, Julian, *The Deed of Life: The Novels and Tales of D. H. Lawrence* (Princeton, NJ: Princeton University Press, 1963).
Murphet, Julian, 'France, Europe, the World: 1945–89', in Anthony Uhlmann (ed.), *Samuel Beckett in Context* (Cambridge: Cambridge University Press, 2013), 126–38.
Murphy, Hugh and Martin Bellamy, 'The Dazzling Zoologist: John Graham Kerr and the Early Development of Ship Camouflage', in *The Northern Mariner/Le marin du nord*, 19 (April 2009), 171–92.
Murray, Rachel, 'Beelines: Joyce's Apian Aesthetics', *Humanities*, 6: 2 (2017), 1–14.
Musil, Robert, *Die Schwärmer*, in *Prosa, Dramen, Späte Briefe*, ed. Adolf Frisé (Reinbek: Rowohlt, 1957), 303–401.
Nabokov, Vladimir, *Ada or Ardor: A Family Chronicle* (Harmondsworth: Penguin, 1970).
Nabokov, Vladimir, *Speak Memory* (London: Penguin, 2000).
Neville, G. H., *The Betrayal: A Memoir of D. H. Lawrence*, ed. Carl Baron (Cambridge: Cambridge University Press, 1981).
Newman, Daniel Aureliano, 'Beginning Again: Darwin's Caterpillar from George Eliot to Beckett', in *Modernist Life Histories: Biological Theory and the Experimental Bildungsroman* (Edinburgh: Edinburgh University Press, 2018), 163–87.
Ngai, Sianne, 'Irritation', in *Ugly Feelings* (Cambridge, MA: Harvard University Press, 2005), 174–208.
Nicholls, Peter, 'Apes and Familiars: Modernism, Mimesis and the Work of Wyndham Lewis', *Textual Practice*, 6: 3 (Winter 1992), 421–38.
Nicholls, Peter, 'Hard and Soft Modernism: Politics as "Theory"', in *A Handbook of Modernist Studies*, ed. Jean-Michel Rabaté (Boston: Wiley-Blackwell, 2013), 15–34.
Nicholls, Peter, *Modernisms: A Literary Guide* (Basingstoke: Palgrave, 2009).
Nordau, Max, *Degeneration* (London: Heinemann, 1895).
Norris, Margot, *Beasts of the Modern Imagination: Darwin, Nietzsche, Kafka, Ernst, and Lawrence* (Baltimore, MD: Johns Hopkins University Press, 1985).
'observe, *v*.', *OED Online*, Oxford University Press, <http://www.oed.com/view/Entry/129893?rskey=utG19c&result=2&isAdvanced=false#eid> (last accessed 12 June 2017).
O'Keeffe, Paul, *Some Sort of Genius: A Life of Wyndham Lewis* (London: Jonathan Cape, 2000).

Parikka, Jussi, *Insect Media: An Archaeology of Animals and Technology* (Minneapolis, MN: University of Minnesota Press, 2010).
'peristaltic, *adj.*', *OED Online*, Oxford University Press, <http://www.oed.com/view/Entry/141075?redirectedFrom=peristaltic#eid> (last accessed 23 September 2017).
Perry, Seamus, *Coleridge and the Uses of Division* (Oxford: Oxford University Press, 1999).
Phillips, Adam, 'Darwin Turns the Worm', in *Darwin's Worms* (London: Faber, 1999), 33–64.
Piette, Adam, 'Torture, Text, Human Rights: Beckett's *Comment c'est/How It Is* and the Algerian War', in Allan Hepburn (ed.), *Around 1945: Literature, Citizenship, Rights* (Montreal: McGill-Queen's University Press, 2016), 151–74.
Pinkney, Tony, *D. H. Lawrence and Modernism* (Iowa City, IA: University of Iowa Press, 1990).
Porteous, Richard, '*Schwärmerei*: Walter Pater and the Case of the Disappearing "Swarm"', *Studies in Walter Pater and Aestheticism*, 1: 1 (2016), 23–40.
Porter Abbott, H., 'Beginning Again: The Post-Narrative Art of *Texts for Nothing* and *How It Is*', in John Pilling (ed.), *The Cambridge Companion to Samuel Beckett* (Cambridge: Cambridge University Press, 1994), 106–23.
Porter Abbott, H., *The Fiction of Samuel Beckett: Form and Effect* (Berkeley, CA: University of California Press, 1973).
Poulton, Edward, *The Colours of Animals* (London: Kegan Paul, 1890).
Pound, Ezra, *Ezra Pound and the Visual Arts*, ed. Harriet Zinnes (New York: New Directions, 1980).
Pound, Ezra, *Gaudier-Brzeska: A Memoir* (New York: New Directions, 1970).
Pound, Ezra, *The ABC of Reading* (London: Faber, 1991).
Pound, Ezra, *The Literary Essays of Ezra Pound* (New York: New Directions, 1968).
Pound, Ezra, 'Translator's Postscript', in Remy de Gourmont, *The Natural Philosophy of Love*, trans. Ezra Pound (New York: Boni & Liveright, 1922), 206–19.
Pressly, W. L., 'The Praying Mantis in Surrealist Art', *Art Bulletin*, 55: 4 (December 1973), 600–15.
Proust, Marcel, *Swann's Way*, trans. William C. Carter (London and New Haven, CT: Yale University Press, 2013).
'quick, *adj.*, *n.*[1], and *adv.*', *OED Online*, Oxford University Press, <http://www.oed.com/view/Entry/156418?rskey=w2JBp6&result=2&isAdvanced=false#eid> (last accessed 12 July 2017).

Rabaté, Jean-Michel, 'Beckett and the Ghosts of Departed Qualities', in *The Ghosts of Modernity* (Gainesville, FL: University of Florida Press, 1996), 148–70.
Rabaté, Jean-Michel, 'Theory's Slice of Life', in *James Joyce and the Politics of Egoism* (Cambridge: Cambridge University Press, 2001), 85–106.
Randall, Bryony, 'War-Days: H.D., Time, and the First World War', in *Modernism, Daily Time, and Everyday Life* (Cambridge: Cambridge University Press, 2009), 124–55.
Rivers, W. H. R., *Instinct and the Unconscious: A Contribution to a Biological Theory of the Psycho-Neuroses* (Cambridge: Cambridge University Press, 1920).
Robbe-Grillet, Alain, *Jealousy*, trans. Robert Howard (London: Alma Classics, 2008).
Robbe-Grillet, Alain, *Snapshots and Towards a New Novel*, trans. Barbara Wright (London: Calder & Boyars, 1965).
Robinson, Michael, *The Long Sonata of the Dead: A Study of Samuel Beckett* (New York: Grove Press, 1969).
Rodker, John, 'W. H. Hudson', *The Little Review*, 7: 1 (May–June 1920), 18–28.
Rohman, Carrie, *Stalking the Subject: Modernism and the Animal* (New York: Columbia University Press, 2008).
Rose, Arthur, '"So Little in Doubt?": Revisiting *The Unnamable*', in David Tucker, Mark Nixon and Dirk Van Hulle (eds), *Samuel Beckett Today/ Aujourd'hui: Revisiting Molloy, Malone Dies and The Unnamable* (New York and Amsterdam: Rodopi, 2014), 211–24.
Ross, Kristin, 'The Swarm', in *The Emergence of Social Space: Rimbaud and the Paris Commune* (Basingstoke: Macmillan, 1988), 100–22.
Royle, Nicholas, 'Veering with Lawrence', in *Veering: A Theory of Literature* (Edinburgh: Edinburgh University Press, 2011), 177–209.
Russell, Edmund, *War and Insects: Fighting Humans and Insects with Chemicals from World War I to Silent Spring* (Cambridge: Cambridge University Press, 2001).
Ryan, Derek, 'Following Snakes and Moths: Modernist Ethics and Posthumanism', *Twentieth-Century Literature*, 61: 3 (September 2015), 287–304.
Rylance, Rick, 'Lawrence's Politics', in *Rethinking Lawrence*, ed. Keith Brown (Buckingham: Open University Press, 1990), 163–80.
Sagar, Keith, *D. H. Lawrence: Poet* (Tirril: Humanities-EBooks, 2007).
Sagar, Keith, *The Art of D. H. Lawrence* (Cambridge: Cambridge University Press, 1966).
Saint-Amour, Paul, *Tense Future: Modernism, Total War, Encyclopedic Form* (New York: Oxford University Press, 2015).

Salisbury, Laura, *Samuel Beckett: Laughing Matters, Comic Timing* (Edinburgh: Edinburgh University Press, 2012).
Salisbury, Laura and Chris Code, 'Jackson's Parrot: Samuel Beckett, Aphasic Speech Automatisms, and Psychosomatic Language', *Journal of Medical Humanities*, 37: 2 (June 2016), 205–22.
Sarraute, Nathalie, 'Conversation and Subconversation', in *The Age of Suspicion: Essays on the Novel*, trans. Marie Jolas (New York: Braziller, 1963), 75–118.
Saunders, Max, *Ford Madox Ford: A Dual Life*, Vol. 2 (Oxford: Oxford University Press, 1996).
Schopenhauer, Arthur, *The World as Will and Representation*, Vol. 1, trans. E. F. J. Payne (New York: Dover, 1966).
Senn, Fritz, 'Insects Appalling', in *Twelve & A Tilly: Essays on the Occasion of the 25th Anniversary of Finnegans Wake*, ed. Jack P. Dalton and Clive Hart (London: Faber, 1966), 36–40.
Setz, Cathryn, *Primordial Modernism: Animals, Ideas, transition (1927–1938)* (Edinburgh: Edinburgh University Press, 2019).
Sheehan, Paul, 'Humanness Unbound', in *Modernism, Narrative, and Humanism* (Cambridge: Cambridge University Press, 2010), 180–92.
Sheehan, Paul, *Modernism and the Aesthetics of Violence* (Cambridge: Cambridge University Press, 2013).
'shell, *v.*', *OED Online*, Oxford University Press, <http://www.oed.com/view/Entry/177874?rskey=lu0YBA&result=2&isAdvanced=false#eid> (last accessed 30 July 2017).
Shelley, Mary, *Frankenstein, or The Modern Prometheus* (London: Penguin, 2003).
Shenker, Israel, 'An Interview with Beckett' in Lawrence Graver and Roger Federman (eds), *Samuel Beckett: The Critical Heritage* (London and Boston: Routledge & Kegan Paul, 1979), 146–9.
Shepherd-Barr, Kirsten, 'Beckett's Old Muckball', in *Theatre and Evolution from Ibsen to Beckett* (New York: Columbia University Press, 2015), 237–72.
Sherman, Stuart P., 'Lawrence Cultivates His Beard', in R. P. Draper (ed.), *D. H. Lawrence: The Critical Heritage* (London: Routledge & Kegan Paul, 1979), 250–7.
Simmel, Georg, 'The Metropolis and Mental Life', in Sophie Bridge and Gary Watson (eds), *The Blackwell City Reader* (Oxford and Malden, MA: Wiley Blackwell, 2002), 11–19.
Siraganian, Lisa, *Modernism's Other Work: The Art Object's Political Life* (New York: Oxford University Press, 2012).
Sleigh, Charlotte, *Six Legs Better: A Cultural History of Myrmecology* (Baltimore, MD: Johns Hopkins University Press, 2007).

Smith, Frederik, 'Fiction as Composing Process in *How It Is*', in Morris Beja, S. E. Gontarski and Pierre Astier (eds), *Samuel Beckett: Humanistic Perspectives* (Columbus, OH: Ohio State University Press, 1983), 107–28.
Smith, F. Percy (dir.), *The Acrobatic Fly*, <https://www.youtube.com/watch?v=8hlocZhNc0M> (last accessed 27 March 2019).
Smith, Rowland, '*Snooty Baronet*: Satire and Censorship', in *Wyndham Lewis: A Revaluation*, ed. Jeffrey Meyers (London: Athlone Press, 1980), 181–95.
Smith, Russell, 'Introduction: Beckett's Ethical Undoing', in Russell Smith (ed.), *Beckett and Ethics* (London and New York: Continuum, 2008), 1–20.
Sontag, Susan, 'Notes on "Camp"', in *Against Interpretation* (London: Vintage, 1994), 275–92.
'spin, *n.*[1]', *OED Online*, Oxford University Press, <http://www.oed.com/view/Entry/186658?rskey=Z5RKDF&result=1&isAdvanced=false#eid> (last accessed 17 January 2019).
Spoo, Robert, 'H.D. Prosed: The Future of an Imagist Poet', in Hugh Witemeyer (ed.), *The Future of Modernism* (Ann Arbor, MI: Michigan University Press, 1997), 201–21.
Spoo, Robert, 'H.D.'s Dating of Asphodel: A Reassessment', *H.D. Newsletter*, 4: 2 (Winter 1991), <http://www.imagists.org/hd/hdrs42.html> (last accessed 17 November 2017).
Squires, Michael, *The Creation of Lady Chatterley's Lover* (Baltimore, MD and London: Johns Hopkins University Press, 1983).
Sultzbach, Kelly, *Ecocriticism in the Modernist Imagination: Forster, Woolf, Auden* (Cambridge: Cambridge University Press, 2016).
'swarm, *n.*', *OED Online*, Oxford University Press, <http://www.oed.com/view/Entry/195492?rskey=9fADB5&result=1&isAdvanced=false#eid> (last accessed 19 November 2018).
Swift, Jonathan, *Jonathan Swift: The Major Works*, ed. Angus Ross and David Woolley (Oxford: Oxford University Press, 2003).
Tajiri, Yoshiki, *Samuel Beckett and the Prosthetic Body: The Organs and the Senses in Modernism* (Basingstoke: Palgrave, 2007).
Thayer, Abbott H., *Concealing Colouration in the Animal Kingdom* (New York: Macmillan, 1909).
Theweleit, Klaus, *Male Fantasies: Male Bodies, Psychoanalyzing the White Terror*, Vol. 2, ed. Wlad Godzich and Jochen Schulte-Sasse (Minneapolis, MN: University of Minnesota Press, 1989).
Thomson, J. Arthur, *Outlines of Zoology* (Edinburgh, Glasgow and London: Hodder & Stoughton, 1914).
'thrust, *v.*', *OED Online*, Oxford University Press, <http://www.oed.com/view/Entry/201458?rskey=XeAl3a&result=3&isAdvanced=false#eid> (last accessed 24 September 2017).

'transport, *v.*', *OED Online*, Oxford University Press, <http://www.oed.com/view/Entry/205017?rskey=woXbSa&result=2&isAdvanced=false#eid> (last accessed 19 November 2018).

Trotter, David, *Paranoid Modernism: Literary Experiment, Psychosis, and the Professionalization of English Society* (Oxford: Oxford University Press, 2001).

Trotter, Wilfred, *Instincts of the Herd in War and Peace* (London: T. Fisher & Unwin, 1921).

Uhlmann, Anthony, *Samuel Beckett and the Philosophical Image* (Cambridge: Cambridge University Press, 2009).

Van Hulle, Dirk and Mark Nixon, *Samuel Beckett's Library* (New York: Cambridge University Press, 2013).

Vivas, Eliseo, *D. H. Lawrence: The Failure and the Triumph of Art* (London: George Allen & Unwin, 1961).

Warner, Marina, *Fantastic Metamorphoses, Other Worlds: Ways of Telling the Self* (Oxford: Oxford University Press, 2004).

Waugh, Arthur, 'The New Poetry', in Timothy Rogers (ed.), *Georgian Poetry 1911–1922: The Critical Heritage* (London and New York: Routledge, 1977), 139–59.

Weisberg, David, *Chronicles of Disorder: Samuel Beckett and the Cultural Politics of the Modern Novel* (Albany, NY: State University of New York Press, 2000).

West, Rebecca, *Black Lamb and Grey Falcon: The Record of a Journey through Yugoslavia in 1937*, Vol. 1 (London: Macmillan, 1946).

West, Rebecca, *The Strange Necessity: Essays and Reviews* (London and Toronto: Jonathan Cape, 1931).

White, Eric, 'Technicities of Deception: Dazzle Camouflage, Avant-Gardes, and Sensory Augmentation in the First World War', *Modernist Cultures*, 12: 1 (March 2017), 36–58.

Wigglesworth, Brian, *Insect Physiology* (London: Methuen, 1946).

Wilkinson, Norman, *A Brush with Life* (London: Seeley Service, 1969).

Williams, William Carlos, *The Autobiography of William Carlos Williams* (New York: New Directions, 1967).

Wilson, Janet, Gerri Kimber and Susan Reid, *Katherine Mansfield and Literary Modernism* (London: Bloomsbury, 2011).

Wolle, Francis, *Desmids of the United States and List of American Pediastrums* (Bethlehem: Moravian Publication Office, 1884).

Wolle, Francis, *Fresh-Water Algae of the United States* (Bethlehem: Comenius Press, 1887).

Woolf, Virginia, *Mrs Dalloway* (Oxford and New York: Oxford University Press, 2009).

Woolf, Virginia, *Roger Fry* (New York: Harcourt, Brace, 1940).

Woolf, Virginia, 'The Cinema', in *Virginia Woolf: Selected Essays*, ed. David Bradshaw (Oxford: Oxford University Press, 2008), 172–6.
Woolf, Virginia, *The Death of the Moth and Other Essays* (Harmondsworth: Penguin, 1961).
Woolf, Virginia, *The Diary of Virginia Woolf: 1915–1919*, Vol. 1, ed. Anne Olivier Bell (London: Penguin, 1981).
Woolf, Virginia, *The Diary of Virginia Woolf: 1920–1924*, Vol. 2, ed. Anne Olivier Bell (London: Penguin, 1981).
Woolf, Virginia, *The Diary of Virginia Woolf: 1925–1930*, Vol. 3, ed. Anne Olivier Bell (London: Penguin, 1982).
Woolf, Virginia, *The Diary of Virginia Woolf: 1931–1935*, Vol. 4, ed. Anne Olivier Bell (London: Penguin, 1982).
Woolf, Virginia, *The Years* (London: Vintage Classics, 2004).
Woolf, Virginia, *Virginia Woolf's Reading Notebooks*, ed. Brenda R. Silver (Princeton, NJ: Princeton University Press, 1983).
Woolf, Virginia, 'Walter Sickert: A Conversation', in *Collected Essays*, Vol. 2 (London: Hogarth Press, 1966), 233–44.
'worm, *v.*', *OED Online*, Oxford University Press, <http://www.oed.com/view/Entry/230284?rskey=nYZGYE&result=3&isAdvanced=false#eid> (last accessed 23 September 2017).
Worthen, John, *D. H. Lawrence and the Idea of the Novel* (London: Macmillan, 1979).

INDEX

Abe, Kōbō, 20, 170–1
Ackerley and Gontarski, 131, 136, 159
Acrobatic Fly, The, 10
adaptation
    as aesthetic strategy, 13–14, 17, 27, 55, 167–8, 171
    failed adaptation, 41
    in insects, 13, 26–7, 35, 40, 53
    psychic adaptation, 15, 112–13
Adorno, Theodor, 101, 130, 134
Aesop, 44; *see also* fable
Aiken, Conrad, 108
Aldington, Richard, 97, 98, 102, 110
Alectryon, 47–9
algae, 102
allegory, 46, 77
Ancient Egypt, 70–2
animal studies, 17
ant, 3, 10, 11, 12, 14, 25, 44, 63, 69, 76, 80, 81–3, 89, 93n31, 99, 101, 103, 173
antennae, 10–11, 16, 112; *see also* feelers

anthropocentrism, 18, 75, 171
anthropomorphism, 10, 101, 137
Anzieu, Didier, 84
aphid, 131
Archimedes, 7
Aristotle, 11, 96
Armstrong, Tim, 8, 15, 21n29
Asquith, Cynthia, 67
autotomy *see* self-mimesis

Bachelard, Gaston, 99
Badiou, Alain, 160
Bair, Deirdre, 158
Baker, Phil, 148
Balancing Bluebottle, The, 9
Barker, Pat, 95–6
Barnes, Djuna, 95, 125
Barthes, Roland, 89, 110
Baudelaire, Charles, 63, 112–13
Beausang, Michael, 138, 159
Beckett, Samuel, 9, 13, 20, 110, 125, 167–8, 171
    'The Capital of the Ruins', 130

Dream of Fair to Middling Women, 160
'Echo's Bones', 137
En attendant Godot, 151
Endgame, 130, 147
Fizzles 5, 156
'From an Abandoned Work', 149, 153–4, 156
Happy Days, 93n31, 147
How It Is, 20, 131, 139, 146, 155–61, 173
and Joyce, 134–5, 152, 158, 163n39
and the larval stage, 125, 130–1, 132, 135–9, 141, 144, 148–9, 152, 159, 161
The Lost Ones, 156
Malone Dies, 141, 149, 151, 152, 161
Malone meurt, 141
Mercier and Camier, 153, 164–5n85
Molloy, 131, 135, 141, 142, 161
More Pricks Than Kicks, 161
Murphy, 131, 132–6, 138–40, 141, 145, 147, 148, 149, 159, 161, 163n39, 169
Play, 147
Proust, 141, 143
Texts for Nothing, 149, 151, 155
That Time, 136
Three Dialogues, 129–30, 148, 162
The Unnamable, 12, 80, 131, 135, 141, 143–9, 151, 152, 158, 163n30
Waiting for Godot, 129, 151
Watt, 137, 159, 165n109
see also worm
bee, 26, 34, 45–6, 58n11, 69, 74, 75, 76, 80, 82, 100, 131, 167, 172, 173
dancing bees, 131
leaf-cutting bee, 7
see also Maeterlinck, Maurice
beetle, 12, 25–7, 36, 48, 63, 67–8, 69, 74, 92n9, 99, 106, 170

Burying Beetle, 26
Capricorn, 26
Colorado beetle, 149
dung beetle, 5, 9, 22n37, 24, 70–2, 74, 88
Dysticus, 104
scarab beetle, 28, 68, 70–2, 74
Bell, Michael, 76
Bell, Vanessa, 8, 21n29
Benjamin, Walter, 79, 113, 134–5, 169, 173–4
Benson, Stella, 50, 52, 56
Benthien, Claudia, 58n1, 88
Bergson, Henri, 20, 39, 41, 44, 47, 166–7
Creative Evolution, 8, 131, 142–145, 146, 174n3
Bhabha, Homi K., 42
biology, 7–8, 25, 33, 40, 48, 53, 65, 96, 101, 102, 103, 131, 162n7; see also evolution
bird, 1–2, 3, 28, 35, 102, 119, 126n18, 142
nightingale, 29
owl, 35, 40
Bixby, Patrick, 133
Blanchot, Maurice, 147, 152, 172–3
BLAST, 15, 25
Bolin, John, 138
Botar and Wünsche, 17
Braidotti, Rosi, 18, 172, 175n21
brain, 146, 164n63; see also mind
Brion, Marcel, 80
Brownian motion, 80
Browning, Robert, 107
Bryher, 117, 126n12
bug, 44, 61, 63, 69–70, 81, 93n34, 170
bedbug, 17, 73
buggery, 88
Buñuel, Luis, 21n29
Burrows, Rachel, 143
Burstein, Jessica, 14, 27, 53

butterfly, 95–6, 102, 109, 111, 117–18, 120–1, 125, 131, 136, 139, 150, 173–4
  Caligo butterfly, 35, 40
  comma butterfly, 100, 104
  fritillary, 102
  swallowtail, 102, 139
Brown, Eric C., 11
Buck-Morss, Susan, 15

Cabinet of Dr Caligari, The, 103–4
Caillois, Roger, 21n29, 35, 42, 47
camouflage, 5, 29
  as aesthetic strategy, 18, 34, 38, 47, 49, 56
  dazzle camouflage, 31–3, 38
  in insects, 18, 32, 35, 42
  see also mimicry
Čapek, Karel and Josef, 1
capitalism, 2, 15, 19, 55, 78, 133
caprella, 42–3
Carney, James, 131
Carter, Huntly, 100
Caruth, Cathy, 105
Caselli, Daniela, 136, 157
caterpillar, 34, 66, 100–1, 114–15, 117, 119, 121, 126n19, 131, 141, 143, 131, 159
  dissolving, 9, 19, 95–6, 109, 115
  embarrassed, 20, 137–8, 142, 146, 163n30
  hawk moth caterpillar, 35
centipede, 170, 171
cephalopod, 42
Chatto & Windus, 50
Chiong, Kathryn, 137–8
chrysalis *see* cocoon
Churchill, Winston, 32
Clarke, Colin, 72
Close Up, 98
Coats, Jason M., 120–1
cockroach, 169–70, 172
cocoon, 95–6, 100–2, 114–15, 117, 126n19, 159
  as aesthetic construct, 19, 92, 97–100, 104–11, 113, 116, 120–1, 125, 136, 167
  as Minoan symbol, 117–18
  as sensory apparatus, 20, 112, 122, 124
Cohn, Ruby, 138
communism, 56, 76
Connolly, Cyril, 27
Connor, Steven, 12, 14, 46, 83, 131, 146
Conrad, Joseph, 3, 12
Corbett, David Peters, 33
Cournos, John, 97
crab, 35
Crawford, Robert, 5
Critchley, Simon, 152
Crivelli, Carlo, 106
Crossland, Rachel, 82
Cubism, 33

Daily Herald, 52
Daily Mail, 9
Daily Mirror, 9
Dalí, Salvador, 21n29
Dante, 136
Darwin, Charles, 20, 40, 131, 154, 160
  on Fabre, 7
  The Formation of Vegetable Mould, 154–5
  Origin of Species, 65, 131, 137, 142, 159–60, 162n7
Darwinism, 5, 141, 142
Debussy, Claude, 111
de Gourmont, Remy, 8
De Groene Amsterdammer, 6
Deleuze, Gilles, 161
Dickinson, Emily, 95
Diderot, Denis, 136
Diggers, 81, 93n60
Dillon, Sarah, 107–8
Donne, John, 61
Doolittle, Charles, 102

Douglas, Mary, 12
DuPlessis, Rachel Blau, 124
Duthuit, Georges, 129–130, 131, 148, 149, 152
Dwan, David, 49

ecdysis, 65
Edison, Thomas, 61, 70, 91
Edwards, Paul, 31
egg, 34, 93n31, 96, 131, 143, 147
Egoist, The, 27
Einstein, Albert, 74–5
élan vital, 142, 144; *see also* Bergson, Henri
Eliot, George, 138
Eliot, T. S., 2, 7, 11, 39
  'The Love Song of J. Alfred Prufrock', 12, 119
  The Waste Land, 63, 85
Ellmann, Maud, 80, 134
Ellmann, Richard, 134
embryology, 159–61, 165n109
Empson, William, 8, 21n29
Encyclopedia Britannica, 146, 164n63
Enemy, The, 39, 44, 59n37
English Review, The, 9, 26, 58n9, 71
entomology, 21n26, 45, 66, 98, 101–2, 168, 170
  economic entomology, 6
  etymology, 139, 146
  influence on scientific thought, 8, 35, 82, 96
  popular entomology, 3, 7–9, 10–11, 14
  see also insect
ethology, 7, 131
Evans, Arthur, 117–18, 120
evolution, 65, 70–1, 131, 136–7, 148–9, 159–60, 162n7, 166
  common descent, 160
  devolution, 5, 20, 41, 70–2, 95–6, 138–9, 141–2, 144, 146, 148, 153, 159–60
  and language, 138, 145–6

and narrative, 20, 138, 144–6, 149
recapitulation theory, 159
see also Bergson, Henri; Darwin, Charles; Haeckel, Ernst
exoskeleton, 4, 7, 13, 40
  breakdown of, 29, 33, 80, 133–4, 135, 147, 169–70
  as container, 14, 115–16, 124, 135, 138, 147, 148, 169
  as formal construct, 3, 13–15, 16, 18–19, 65, 88, 98, 132–5, 138, 147, 168–9, 174
  insensitivity of, 15, 53, 62–3, 65, 67, 81–2, 84, 86, 112
  as protective shield, 15, 27, 37, 105, 110, 113, 147
  sensitivity of, 4, 14–16, 84, 112, 121
  shedding of, 64–5, 66, 68, 72, 86–7, 88, 90–1, 124, 135, 172
  see also shell
exposure, 19, 29, 37–8, 42, 52, 58, 76, 87, 111–13, 169
  double exposure, 115
  self-exposure, 18, 30, 37–8, 53, 57, 63–4, 79–82, 84–5, 91 119
  publicity, 52–3, 56

fable, 18, 44–6
Fabre, Jean-Henri, 7–10, 34, 36–7, 40, 52–3, 58n9, 66, 70–2, 88, 96, 143, 166–7, 174n3
  influence of, 8, 21n29, 22n37, 26, 35, 168
  The Life of the Caterpillar, 66
  popularity of, 8–9
  The Sacred Beetle and Others, 24
  'The Scavengers', 9
  The Wonders of Instinct, 25–6
  see also instinct
Faggen, Robert, 167
Fairchild, David and Marian, 9
fascism, 47–9, 76, 81–2, 84, 86, 101, 114–15, 118, 121

feelers, 16–17, 111–12, 117, 122–3, 127n50, 173; *see also* antennae
Felt, E. P., 10–11
Fernihough, Anne, 64
film, 10, 101–2, 104, 115, 116, 126n19, 127n31
 and insects, 9–10, 99–100, 103–4, 114–15
 silent cinema, 99, 103–4, 105, 114–15, 116, 123, 127n29, 136
First World War, 5–8, 10, 15–16, 19, 24–5, 28–31, 40, 54, 67–8, 83–4, 86, 95–8 104–14, 121, 123–5
 chemical weapons, 6–7
 and entomology, 8–9, 71
 and insect imagery, 5–7, 9, 12, 14, 22n37, 63, 67, 71–2, 77–8
 shell-art, 31
 see also shell shock; camouflage
flâneur, 112–13, 133
floating signifier, 116, 118
fly, 5, 9–10, 74, 77–8, 81, 106, 130, 131, 135, 146, 167
 gadfly, 73, 87
 green-fly, 76
 mayfly, 149
Forbes, Peter, 33
Ford, Ford Madox, 5, 71
Forel, Auguste, 7, 26, 58n11
form, 12–14, 31, 43, 63, 64, 66–7, 73–5, 80, 85–6, 91, 92n15, 100–1, 107–8, 112–14, 133, 136, 140–1, 144–5, 148–9, 168–70
formication, 19, 63, 68, 74, 81–3, 87, 89, 92n9, 93n31
fornication, 69, 86, 89, 93n31
Fortnightly Review, The, 9
Foster, Hal, 2, 27
Freud, Sigmund, 47, 154, 164n71
 Beyond the Pleasure Principle, 16, 31, 37, 48, 81, 84, 105, 112–13, 118, 133, 148, 173
 Group Psychology and the Analysis of the Ego, 1–2

 and H.D., 102, 104, 114–15, 116–18, 121
 'Instincts and their Vicissitudes', 37–8, 47
 'Project for a Scientific Psychology', 105
Friedman, Susan Stanford, 108, 122
Frisch, Karl von, 131
Frost, Robert, 20, 166–8, 174n3
Fry, Roger, 9, 10, 173

Galloway and Thacker, 75
Garnett, David, 64, 66
Gass, William H., 20, 169–71, 172
Gervais, Bertrand, 172
Goethe, 75
Gontarski, S. E., 141
Graham, W. S., 66
Grant, Duncan, 67
grasshopper, 8, 44
Gregory, Alyse, 85

Haeckel, Ernst, 65, 131, 159–60
Haldane, J. B. S., 8
Hardy, Barbara, 89
Harrison, Andrew, 66
H.D., 9, 10, 13, 17, 19–20, 67, 73, 92, 132, 134, 141, 167–8
 Asphodel, 19, 96, 102, 104, 109–12, 113, 115, 121, 122, 123, 126n5, 134
 Bid Me to Live, 19, 97, 109, 121–5
 and entomology, 99–100, 102–3
 and Freud, 102, 104, 114–15, 116–18, 121
 The Gift, 125
 Hedylus, 123
 Helen in Egypt, 122–3, 125
 Her, 100, 102, 111
 and Imagism, 15, 98, 99, 108, 126n12
 and Lawrence, 123–4
 'The Mask and the Movietone', 10, 19, 98–9, 100–1, 105, 115

Mira-Mare, 102
Nights, 111
'Notes on Thought and Vision', 105, 127n50
on the novel, 97, 108
Palimpsest, 19, 97, 104–8, 115, 118, 122, 168
and perfection, 98–9, 101, 103, 107–8, 111, 116, 126n12
and suspense, 114, 117–21
Tribute to Freud, 102–3, 104, 113, 114–17, 121, 122
The Walls Do Not Fall, 119–21, 122
see also cocoon
Henry, Holly, 2
Hitler, 1, 48–9; *see also* fascism
Hollingsworth, Cristopher, 4
Homer, 3
Hopwood, Nick, 159–60
hornet, 69, 99, 101
  white-tailed hornet, 166–7, 169
Hovanec, Caroline, 8, 18, 101–2
Howard, Albert, 154–5
Howard, L. O., 6
Huber, Pierre, 137
Hugo, Victor, 129, 161, 162n1
Hulme, T. E., 15, 27–8
Humma, John, 85
Humphreys, Richard, 33
Huxley, Julian, 8
Huxley, T. H., 65
Huyssen, Andreas, 97, 114

imaginal cells, 96–7; *see also* cocoon
Imagism, 15, 98, 99, 108, 126n12
imago, 48, 97, 98, 100, 110, 139
Imms, A. D., 101–2
insects
  and art, 2–3, 106
  collecting of, 7, 12, 66, 102, 170, 173–4
  disruptiveness of, 33, 61–2, 64, 69, 70–1, 89, 91–2, 96, 139, 146, 169

etymology, 11, 139, 147
formal indeterminacy of, 11–14, 20, 57–8, 80, 97–8, 101–3, 116, 125, 136, 147, 168, 169–71
and human identity, 3–4, 5, 9, 17–18, 53, 62–3, 109, 154, 167, 171–2, 173–4
and the individual, 1–3, 4, 18, 29–30, 62, 65, 67–8, 75, 89, 91, 96, 109, 171–2, 173
and language, 12, 19, 49, 69, 74, 80, 85, 87, 89–90, 116, 120, 140, 143, 154, 167, 169–71
and monstrosity, 3, 5, 9–10, 110
observation of, 7, 10, 28–9, 34, 61, 66, 142, 149–50, 167, 170
and technology, 9–11, 70, 99–101, 103–4, 111, 114–15
instinct, 8, 20, 25–6, 34, 37–8, 96, 137, 143–4, 148, 166–7
  herd instinct, 1, 82
  language of, 138, 143, 146
inter-war period, 38, 41, 63–4, 86, 107, 118, 132–3 168, 173
  General Strike, 41
  Great Depression, 41, 49
  ideology, 17, 19, 41, 63, 76, 83–6
  literary scene, 38–9, 43, 48, 55–6, 133–4
  lost generation, 105
  mass culture, 19, 41, 79–80
  mass existence, 2, 3, 63, 75–78, 80, 81–2, 83–4, 91
  see also fascism; socialism
Irish Bee-Keeper, 45
Irish Times, 130

Jameson, Fredric, 56, 132, 169
jellyfish, 28, 39, 127n50
Joyce, James, 49, 62, 65, 110, 140
  and Beckett, 134–5, 152, 158, 163n39
  and entomology, 44–5
  Finnegans Wake, 41, 44, 80

Joyce, James (*cont.*)
   and Lewis, 27, 39, 41, 44–7, 60n67, 141
   'The Ondt and the Gracehoper', 18, 44–6
   Ulysses, 44–5, 79, 133, 134, 172, 175n21

Kafka, Franz, 4–5, 171
Kaun, Axel, 140
Keller, John, 132–3
Kenner, Hugh, 7, 11, 56, 141, 155, 159, 165n102
Kermode, Frank, 88, 93n57
Kerr, John Graham, 32
Keynes, Maynard, 67
King, Simon, 63
Klee, Paul, 152
Klein, Scott, 46
Kloepfer, Deborah Kelly, 108
Kristeva, Julia, 141

Lacan, Jacques, 42
LaCapra, Dominic, 110
ladybird, 68–9, 70, 74
Land, Norman, 106
larva, 20, 69, 100, 103, 104, 109, 114–15, 130, 137, 147, 159, 161
   see also Beckett, Samuel; caterpillar; worm
Laplanche and Pontalis, 48
Latham and Rogers, 11
Lawrence, D. H., 13, 17, 19, 27, 52, 58, 113, 134, 162, 167
   Aaron's Rod, 19, 76–8
   The Boy in the Bush, 89
   and contamination, 62, 64, 67–8, 70, 74, 77, 81, 83–4, 85–6, 88, 90
   and entomology, 8, 9, 65–6, 70, 72, 82
   Fantasia of the Unconscious, 74–5, 84, 167, 172
   'Gloire de Dijon', 124
   and H.D., 123–4
   and irritation, 61, 84–6
   The Ladybird, 22n37, 64, 68–74, 85
   Lady Chatterley's Lover, 19, 64, 82, 86–91
   and Lewis, 60n91
   Kangaroo, 19, 64, 77–86, 90, 119
   'The Mosquito', 61–2, 64, 70, 73, 87, 89
   Mr Noon, 63
   on the novel, 17, 66, 73, 86
   The Plumed Serpent, 63, 85, 86
   'Preface' to *New Poems*, 79, 80
   The Rainbow, 64–5, 67, 72, 77, 91
   and sex, 86–91
   'Song of a Man Who is Not Loved', 73
   Sons and Lovers, 15, 64
   The Trespasser, 63
   Women in Love, 63, 65, 67, 69, 71, 77, 88, 92n9
   see also swarm
Legros, G. V., 7
Leighton, Angela, 13
Lessing, Doris, 91
Lévi-Strauss, Claude, 116, 118
Lewis, Pericles, 3
Lewis, Wyndham, 5, 9, 15, 17, 18–19, 65, 73, 83, 113, 132, 134, 141, 143, 162, 167
   The Apes of God, 39, 45, 49, 50, 55–6
   'Bestre', 33–8, 42, 45, 47, 52, 54, 55
   Blasting and Bombardiering, 5, 28, 30, 38, 40, 43
   The Caliph's Design, 7, 24–5, 36, 45, 57
   'Cantleman's Spring-Mate', 28–31, 38, 119
   The Childermass, 39, 40–3, 46–9, 55, 59n47–8
   and entomology, 7, 8, 9, 25–6, 34, 40–1, 44–5, 48–9, 52–3, 58n11
   externalism, 18, 26–8, 51, 53
   'The French Poodle', 28

Hitler, 48, 50
'Inferior Religions', 26
and Joyce, 27, 39, 41, 44–7, 60n67, 141
and Lawrence, 60n91
Men Without Art, 18, 26, 27, 39, 46, 54
'Mr Wyndham Lewis as a Tyro', 33, 51
One-Way Song, 56
The Revenge for Love, 56–7
Rude Assignment, 46
'Self-Portrait', 50–1
Snooty Baronet, 27, 49–55, 57, 90
'A Soldier of Humour', 80
'Some Innkeepers and Bestre', 26
Tarr, 15–16, 27–8, 32–3, 42, 43, 44, 54
Thirty Personalities and a Self-Portrait, 50
Time and Western Man, 43, 59n48, 174
and Vorticism, 15, 31, 32–3, 39
see also mimicry
lice, 5–6, 44, 60n67, 62, 63, 78
Linnaeus, Carl, 147
Lispector, Clarice, 20, 169–70, 172
London Film Society, 10, 104, 127n31
Lubbock, John, 18, 26, 40
Lucretius, 76
Luther, Martin, 75

McCabe, Susan, 110
McCarthy, Jeffrey, 17
MacGreevy, Thomas, 142
McHugh, Roland, 45
MacKay, Marina, 134
McLuhan, Marshall, 41
madrigal, 122
Maeterlinck, Maurice, 7
  The Life of the Ant, 14
  The Life of the Bee, 26, 44–5, 58n11, 131
Magessa O'Reilly, Édouard, 157, 158

maggot, 131, 151, 152, 159, 163n39
malaria, 5, 62, 87
Mansfield, Katherine, 8, 21n29
mantis, 11
  Empusa, 26
  orchid mantis, 40
  praying mantis, 21n29, 172
Marcus, Laura, 116
Mehl, Dieter, 73
metamorphosis, 4, 5, 41, 67, 100, 101–2, 110, 114, 126n19
  interrupted, 95–6, 109–11, 137–8
  in reverse, 2, 125, 141, 142, 159
metropolis, 14–15, 63, 79, 112–13, 133
middle voice, 110, 111–12, 113
Miller, Tyrus, 49, 56, 134
mimesis, 40, 47, 59n43, 83, 101
  anti-mimesis, 39
mimicry, 17, 18, 41–3, 46–9, 54–6, 76, 83, 95, 168
  in insects, 18, 33, 35, 40, 42, 53
  and modernism, 39, 41, 43, 59n43
mind, 16, 19, 63, 69, 79, 99, 105, 114, 116, 125, 127n50, 132, 136, 139, 142, 151, 169; see also psyche
Mirrlees, Hope, 1, 14
modernism
  and aesthetic autonomy, 16–17, 23n72, 133–5
  and decay, 5, 9, 48, 70–2, 95–6, 133–4, 154, 168
  and epiphany, 64, 113, 125, 172
  and hardness, 14–15, 57, 90–1, 98, 99, 133, 147, 169
  and insects, 3, 11–13, 18, 20, 80, 119, 168–9, 171, 173–4
  late modernism, 134–5
  and linguistic excess, 13, 46–7, 79, 80, 84, 85, 98, 108, 112, 119, 134, 141, 146, 151, 158
  and the non-human, 17–18, 75, 80, 160, 171, 173–4
  see also form

modernity, 2–3, 4, 10, 12, 16, 19, 62–3, 72, 76, 82, 86, 110, 112–13, 132, 169, 173
modern subject, 2–3, 4–5, 8, 14–16, 31, 41, 62, 67, 78, 112–13, 119, 173; *see also* self
Moore, Marianne, 8, 98
Moorjani, Angela, 131
Morris, Adalaide, 103
Morse code, 111
mosquito, 5, 41, 61–2, 63, 65, 73, 86–7, 89, 111; *see also* malaria
moth, 21n29, 96, 99, 100–1, 102, 107, 109, 110, 111, 114–15, 126n19
  ailanthus silk moth, 100
  apple leaf miner moth, 137
  death-head moth, 102
  hawk moth, 35
  sphinx moth, 102
Moynahan, Julian, 72
mud, 5, 9, 22n37, 71–2, 74, 130, 139, 150–1, 153, 154, 155–7, 159; *see also* soil
Murphet, Julian, 160
Murry, John Middleton, 21n29, 73
Musil, Robert, 24

Nabokov, Vladimir, 30–1, 40
National Geographic, 9
National Socialism *see* fascism
Nature Book, The, 92n21
Nazi ideology *see* fascism
Neville, G. H., 66, 92n21
Newman, Daniel, 138, 163n30
New Statesman, 7
Ngai, Sianne, 85
Nicholls, Peter, 15, 27, 59n43
Nordau, Max, 14–15, 142
nouveau roman, 171
nuclear war, 121, 123

Owen, Wilfred, 95

palimpsest, 104, 118
Palissy, Bernard, 24, 27
Pall Mall Gazette, 70
Pater, Walter, 75
peristalsis, 140, 151, 163n40; *see also* worm
Perón, Maria, 150, 151
Perry, Seamus, 157
Phillips, Adam, 154
photography, 9, 101
Piette, Adam, 162n1
Pinkney, Tony, 79, 85
Plutarch, 39
Porteous, Richard, 75
Porter Abbott, H., 138, 155
postcolonial theory, 43
posthumanism, 18, 172, 173, 175n21
Poulton, Edward, 25
Pound, Ezra, 2, 8, 11, 15, 39, 65, 73, 111
Proust, Marcel, 8, 21n29, 43, 140–1, 143
psyche, 15–16, 31, 37, 41, 46, 48, 68, 78, 81–2, 90, 96, 98, 103, 105, 112, 115–16, 118, 122, 125, 132, 135, 148, 159; *see also* butterfly
psychoanalysis, 116–17
psychology, 3, 8, 25, 27, 35, 42, 47, 81–2, 84, 85, 95–6, 90, 105, 112, 139; *see also* Freud
pupa *see* cocoon

Rabaté, Jean-Michel, 62, 139
repetition, 5, 20, 71–2, 76, 87, 97–8, 105, 110, 124–5, 113, 138, 145, 148, 153, 155–6, 161, 170
reptile, 142
Rimbaud, Arthur, 78
Rivers, W. H. R., 8, 95–6
RMS *Lusitania*, 97
Robbe-Grillet, Alain, 20, 170–1
Robinson, Michael, 149
Rodker, John, 8, 21n29
Rose, Arthur, 148

Ross, Kristin, 78, 80, 134
Royle, Nicholas, 76
Rummel, Walter Morse, 110–11
Rylance, Rick, 67–8, 85

Sagar, Keith, 61–2
Saint-Amour, Paul, 118
Saint-Lô, 130, 151–2, 154
Salisbury, Laura, 142
Sarraute, Nathalie, 43, 50, 140–1, 161
Sassoon, Siegfried, 5, 95
Schopenhauer, 142
Schwärmerei, 75; *see also* swarm
Scientific Monthly, 6
scissiparity, 20, 146, 150, 153–4, 155–7, 158
scorpion, 67, 83
Second World War, 1, 20, 56, 114, 118–22, 123, 130, 132, 151, 154, 160
'Secrets of Nature', 10, 99–101, 115, 126n18–19
self, 2, 4, 5, 18, 20, 38, 43, 48, 57, 62, 63, 64–5, 68, 69, 75, 83, 88, 90–1, 92, 99, 105, 113, 124, 136, 139, 154, 161, 170–1, 174
   self-abandonment, 87, 172–3
   self-division, 12, 78, 109, 135, 153, 155–7, 169
   self-mimesis, 53, 56
   self-protection, 14, 15, 17, 31, 37, 57, 82, 89, 91, 96, 98, 110, 112, 117, 121, 167
Senn, Fritz, 44
Sheehan, Paul, 16, 29–30, 113, 174
shell, 18, 35, 40–1, 73, 90, 101, 106, 114, 115, 125, 132, 147, 151, 171
   as aesthetic construct, 1, 15, 27–8, 30–1, 33, 43, 46–7, 57, 64–5, 73, 80, 98, 101, 112, 121, 125, 132, 138, 140, 169
   as ammunition, 5, 29–31
   as architecture, 24–5, 30, 46
   murex, 24–5, 27, 107
   as psychic apparatus, 4, 15–16, 28, 30–1, 53–4, 56, 63, 121, 125, 133, 147, 151
   restrictiveness of, 15, 65, 67, 86, 88, 90, 98, 133–4, 139, 169
   whelk, 24–5
   see also exoskeleton
Shelley, Mary, 3
shell shock, 8, 15–16, 31, 38, 40, 43, 44, 54, 95–6, 110, 111; *see also* trauma
Shepherd-Barr, Kirsten, 137
Simmel, Georg, 14, 16
Siraganian, Lisa, 59n37
Skilled Insect Artisans, 10, 100, 101
skin, 19, 29–30, 39, 47, 61–2, 63, 65, 66, 68, 70, 73, 81, 83–5, 86, 88, 90, 104, 134
Skinner, Mollie, 89
Sleigh, Charlotte, 96
slug, 103
Smith, F. Percy, 9–10
Smith, Frederik, 159
Smith, Russell, 154
snail, 17, 92n15, 100
socialism, 76, 81, 83, 86
Socrates, 73
soil, 9, 72, 117, 151, 154–5, 165n92; *see also* mud
solipsism, 44, 105, 132, 139
Sontag, Susan, 106
Spencer, Herbert, 65, 142
spider, 5, 12, 41, 45–6, 67, 81, 83, 115, 119, 122–3, 128n73; *see also* web
sponge, 43
Spoo, Robert, 112, 126n5
Squires, Michael, 87
Stein, Gertrude, 39, 41
Sultzbach, Kelly, 17
Surrealism, 21, 35
swarm, 3, 12, 14, 19, 63, 67, 75–80, 81, 82–4, 85, 86, 91, 103, 113, 167, 170, 172

Swift, Jonathan, 45–6
Sydney Bulletin, The, 78–9
Symbolism, 78

tadpole, 103, 106, 149
taxonomy, 7, 12, 66, 101, 102, 147
termite, 146
Thayer, Abbott H., 32
Theweleit, Klaus, 81–2, 84
Thomson, J. Arthur, 18, 26, 40, 53
trauma, 19, 83, 95–8, 103, 104–9, 110, 111, 112–14, 117, 118, 120, 121–2
    enabling, 109, 113, 120, 124, 125
    and narrative, 105–6, 108, 112, 115–16, 123, 124–5
    see also shell shock
Trotter, David, 26, 37
Trotter, Wilfred, 8, 82
Tyro, The, 33, 37

Untermeyer, Louis, 166
Ussy-sur-Marne, 20, 149–51, 152, 153, 155

Van Hulle and Nixon, 131, 162n7, 164n63
Vorticism, 15, 31, 32, 33, 39
Voynich, Ethel, 73

Wadsworth, Edward, 31, 32
Warner, Marina, 4, 125
wasp, 3, 21n29, 25, 26, 45, 53, 174n3
    hairy sand wasp, 34, 143, 166
Waugh, Arthur, 91
Weaver, Harriet Shaw, 44
web, 41, 112, 115, 122–23, 125, 128n73
Weber, Max, 15
Weisberg, David, 134
Wells, H. G., 10
West, Rebecca, 8, 17, 21n29
Wheeler, W. M., 7
White, Eric, 32
Wilkinson, Norman, 31
Williams, William Carlos, 8
Wolle, Francis, 102, 126n26
Woolf, Virginia, 1–3, 4, 5, 7, 8, 9, 10, 16, 21n29, 27, 39, 65, 119, 128n73 133, 162
    'The Cinema', 103–4, 106, 127n29, 149
    and insect vision, 2–3
    on Lewis, 46
    'Thoughts on Peace in an Air Raid', 118–19
worm, 20, 28, 30, 41, 43, 114–15, 117, 119–20, 122, 123, 129, 131, 136, 139–40, 141, 144–9, 150–1, 153, 158, 161–2
    earthworm, 20, 29, 131, 150–5, 158
    etymology, 154
    flatworm, 150
    silkworm, 95, 100, 125
    slime-worm, 146, 156
    vermicular, 136, 146, 157, 163n40
    vermigrade, 140, 144
    Worm, 141, 142, 143–8, 152, 161
    worm-state, 20, 131, 150, 159, 160
    see also caterpillar; larva
Worthen, John, 85

EU representative:
Easy Access System Europe
Mustamäe tee 50, 10621 Tallinn, Estonia
Gpsr.requests@easproject.com

www.ingramcontent.com/pod-product-compliance
Lightning Source LLC
Chambersburg PA
CBHW070353240426
43671CB00013BA/2485